Leadership and Ethics

Bloomsbury Academic

An imprint of Bloomsbury Publishing Plc

50 Bedford Square	1385 Broadway
London	New York
WC1B 3DP	NY 10018
UK	USA

www.bloomsbury.com

BLOOMSBURY and the Diana logo are trademarks of Bloomsbury Publishing Plc

First published 2015
Paperback edition first published 2017

© Jacqueline Boaks, Michael Levine and contributors, 2015

Jacqueline Boaks and Michael Levine have asserted their rights under the Copyright, Designs and Patents Act, 1988, to be identified as Editors of this work.

British Library Cataloguing-in-Publication Data
A catalogue record for this book is available from the British Library.

ISBN: HB: 978-1-47257-066-6
PB: 978-1-35002-828-9
ePDF: 978-1-47257-068-0
ePub: 978-1-47257-067-3

Library of Congress Cataloging-in-Publication Data
A catalog record for this book is available from the Library of Congress.

Typeset by Fakenham Prepress Solutions, Fakenham, Norfolk NR21 8NN

Contents

Contributors

Tom Angier's research interests are in ethical theory, with a focus on two historical periods – ancient Greece (Plato and Aristotle), and 19th century continental Europe. His latest monograph is entitled "Techne in Aristotle's Ethics: Crafting the Moral Life" (2010). At present, he is editing a volume on "The History of Evil" (in the ancient period), which follows an edited volume on "Ethics: The Key Thinkers" (2012). He is currently planning papers on Plato and social equality, and Aristotle on work.

Jacqueline Boaks studied philosophy at The University of Western Australia before working in management roles in several large Perth organisations. She is completing her PhD in Philosophy looking at leadership in the areas of ethics, political philosophy and business literature. Her recent publications include "Who's Afraid of Leadership?" (2014) and "What Does Ethics Have to Do With Leadership?" with Michael Levine (2014).

Thom Brooks is Professor of Law and Government and Associate in Philosophy at Durham University. His books include Punishment (2012), Hegel's Political Philosophy (2007, 2d 2013) and Rawls's Political Liberalism (2015, co-edited with Martha C. Nussbaum). Brooks works broadly in ethics, law and public policy with special interests in political justice, sentencing policy and immigration law.

Damian Cox is Associate Professor of philosophy at Bond University. He writes on moral and political philosophy and philosophy of film. His books include *Thinking Through Film*, co-authored with Michael Levine (Wiley-Blackwell, 2012); *A Politics Most Unusual: violence, sovereignty and democracy in the war on terror*, co-authored with Michael Levine & Saul Newman (Palgrave Macmillan, 2009).

Joanne B. Ciulla is Professor and Coston Family Chair in Leadership and Ethics at the Jepson School of Leadership Studies at the University of Richmond in Virginia where she is one of the founders of the school. Ciulla has had academic appointments at La Salle University, The Harvard Business School, The Wharton

Preface

Jacqueline Boaks and Michael Levine

Morality and leadership are indivisible

Desmond Tutu[1]

Contemporary discussion about the nature of leadership and the need for 'good' strong leaders abounds. But what constitutes good leadership and what is a good leader? Are ethics and leadership even compatible? Are they related, and if so, how? Can Desmond Tutu's claim that 'morality and leadership are indivisible' be justified or is it merely wishful thinking?

This edited volume examines fundamental questions about the nature of leadership from a range of philosophical and theoretical perspectives, and by considering leadership, insofar as possible, separate from any formal office or role. It is not about specifically political, or business or university, or any other kind of leader or sphere of leadership per se. It is about all of these – and more. Unlike the philosophical literature on, for example, authority, *leadership* need not be so closely related to formal roles and positions and calls out for analysis independent of these. Leadership can and does occur in all areas of life. No doubt this is a reason it is so often talked and complained about, and why, theoretically and practically, it is worth getting clear about.

Accounts of leadership often lie at either end of a spectrum relating ethics to leadership. At one end are accounts that argue ethics are intrinsically linked to leadership. At the other are (Machiavellian) views that deny any such link – intrinsic or extrinsic. To account for the positive connotations it so often seems to have in our common and sometimes technical usage, leadership appears to require a positive normative component – some connection to ethics; otherwise 'leadership' amounts to no more than mere power or influence. However, it is not obvious that such attempts can meet the challenge raised by, and after, Machiavelli in *The Prince* (1532). Are accounts of leadership that posit a normative component coherent and justifiable?

All of the essays in the volume are concerned, though in various degrees, with leadership as it relates to ethics and questions of value. But what other philosophical issues underlie the disparate notions of leadership that are either simply assumed, or explicitly discussed by those – mostly non-specialists, but also academics, business 'leaders' and leadership gurus – who regard leadership as so politically, socially, economically and personally important? Why and how is leadership important?

There is no shortage of discussion about leadership in business ethics literature and of course 'leadership studies', though aside from a few special cases, like that of Machiavelli and Plato's philosopher-king, there is far less in philosophy generally. However, the idea for this volume arose from the view that much of that literature (too much of which is mere pronouncement) would benefit from the kinds of critical conceptual analysis that philosophy can sometimes bring. Critical engagement with existent literature as well as new theory from other disciplines and sources could lead to a deeper, better, even more useful understanding of the nature and significance of leadership. This seems to us especially so given the weight and cultural authority that such accounts often seem to have.

Furthermore, the available literature seemed to us to have coalesced around a few key themes and essays by a few important authors – mostly associated with business ethics literature (in many ways a dominant field with a highly receptive audience). This focus appeared to too narrowly circumscribe the field and narrow the issues. The literature on leadership was becoming, or had become, something of a world (specialized) unto itself; one in which, while some (too few) significant ideas were insightfully discussed, others were being either rehashed or altogether overlooked. Thus, the idea for this volume was to gather new ideas and perspectives about leadership as well as challenge some of these existing ideas and assumptions. We thought the way to do this, one way at any rate, was to seek authors who we expected would have an interest in leadership on the basis of their previous writing, but who specifically had not previously written on the topic.

Some of those we sought out surprised us. Some were of course too busy with other projects, or just not interested. Some did not answer us at all. Others however failed to see (or claimed they failed to see) any connection between past writing they had done and anything pertaining to issues of leadership. To paraphrase a puzzling response we received: 'I work on the notion of "power" not leadership.' We thought this remarkable, but also as perhaps reflecting something, though we are not sure what, about 'leadership' as well as some philosophy. Luckily, others understood just the kind of thing we were after and welcomed the opportunity to give thought to the notion of those aspects of leadership that were, in light of their past work, of interest to them and hopefully to others.

While the volume is intended to broaden the scope of discussion about leadership, there are some regrettable lacunas. We do not, for example, have any essay contributing a non-Western perspective where ideally we would have liked several. In this, and a few other cases, all we can say is that at various stages we tried but were unable to fill apparent gaps. There may be others that we are undoubtedly not even aware of.

While issues pertaining to leadership are generally associated with politics and business, for us, closer to home, issues arise in the context of universities as well. The managerialism now ingrained in higher education (just as so many areas of the private and public sectors) has raised specific questions about leadership in regard to the University and education generally. College presidents, deans and various administrators have unprecedented authority and power – at least some of which used to be shared with faculty. Their conception of leadership, their methods, the claim to be consultative, along with their idea of the nature and purpose of the University, has, to say the least, been challenged. We hoped that this volume could shed some light on that allegedly ongoing discussion. Some of the essays do touch on it.

This volume is meant to present new ideas about the nature of leadership and problems, theoretical and practical, associated with it. It is meant to clarify and even resolve certain problems while also raising new and additional difficulties in ways that could foment further and enlarged discussion. And strategically, it is meant to do so in ways somewhat removed from the existent literature.

As compared with much current literature on leadership in 'leadership studies' and business schools, the strength and difference envisioned for this volume was in its fresh perspectives and philosophical rigour. We tried for the most theoretically sophisticated collection of essays on leadership currently available, one that has the potential to affect the discourse on leadership. We sought to achieve this without sacrificing intelligibility, accessibility, utility or readership interest. As we see it, *Leadership and Ethics* should help fill a rather gaping 'niche' in the literature. To whatever extent the volume succeeds, the credit belongs to the contributors.

Note

1   'Archbishop Tutu refuses platform with Tony Blair over Iraq', available at
    http://www.bbc.co.uk/news/uk-politics-19400136

Foreword

Joanne B. Ciulla
University of Richmond

This book is a cause for celebration. Philosophic collections on leadership ethics are rare, and books this good, even rarer. It brings a breath of fresh air into the leadership literature. I congratulate editors Jacqueline Boaks and Michael Levine on pulling together what is, to my knowledge, the largest collection of original philosophic essays on leadership ethics. Since philosophers are not known for giving effusive praise of each other's work, the reader may wonder if I have already started celebrating. So, let me explain my enthusiasm by first offering a rather sobering account of research on ethics in leadership studies.

When I started working in leadership studies in 1991, I found little if any contemporary philosophical literature on leadership and ethics.[1] While social and political philosophers inevitably touch on leadership, few directly address it. Back then, leadership studies worked from what Joseph Rost called the 'industrial paradigm' of leadership as good management and, to some extent, I think it still does today.[2] Most of the literature came from academics with backgrounds in areas such as industrial or organizational psychology and management.

The only normative theory of leadership was James MacGregor Burns' theory of transforming leadership.[3] Burns was a political scientist and historian. He considered himself a conflict theorist who regarded leadership as a kind of dialogue with followers about values. In the course of this dialogue, leaders and followers morally improved each other. Burns measured the ultimate moral quality of leadership against what he called 'end values' of justice, equality and freedom. Burns' book *Leadership* inspired Bernard Bass to develop his theory of transformational leadership.[4] As a PhD in industrial psychology, Bass was interested in charisma and how leaders influenced and transformed followers. Bass and his colleagues developed a questionnaire on transformational leadership, and articles and studies using it proliferated in the literature.

In the early 1990s I criticized Bass' theory because he assumed that transformational leaders were good, when evil leaders also fit the description. I also commented that his handbook of leadership studies contained little relevant research on ethics in the section on ethics.[5] As someone new to the field, I was especially struck by the fact that social scientists in leadership studies criticized each other's research methods but not the normative assumptions or implications of their constructs. In response to my criticisms, Bass amended his theory in a paper where he asserted that only ethical leaders could be transformational leaders and unethical ones were pseudo-transformational leaders.[6] While this move would not satisfy most philosophers, it seemed to open the door for more work on ethics.[7]

The theory of authentic leadership then evolved out of transformational leadership and positive psychology.[8] Some articulations of this theory assume that authentic leaders – leaders who possess self-knowledge and other qualities – are ethical leaders. Since there is also a questionnaire associated authentic leadership and the idea of authenticity lends itself to interpretation, the literature on it also multiplied among researchers and in the popular press.[9]

In 2005, Michael Brown, Linda K. Treviño and David A. Harrison developed a construct that came to be known as 'ethical leadership'.[10] They used a questionnaire to determine if employees thought their leaders were ethical. I suspect most philosophers would find the ten questions in this questionnaire problematic. The test does not measure ethical leadership per se. It really measures respondents' perceptions of whether their leaders are ethical. Much of what is meant by 'ethical' is left to the respondent – e.g. one of the questions is: 'conducts his/her personal life in an ethical manner'.[11] This construct has taken off in the leadership literature. There are more articles based on it than on transformational and authentic leadership. While the Brown, Treviño and Harrison paper also increased the focus and literature on ethics and leadership, it inadvertently created confusion for scholars doing research in that area. Since 2005, most of the articles under the subject 'ethical leadership' are not about various aspects of ethics in leadership, they are about studies that use this specific construct and questionnaire or some variant of it. For a philosopher, or any researcher attempting to address the literature in leadership studies, this can be bewildering.

My intent in painting this brief and somewhat grim picture of work on ethics in leadership studies is not to disparage the work of these researchers but rather to illustrate why this collection is so important to leadership studies. I have also left out the fine work that has been done in this area by a handful of philosophers and more thoughtful leadership scholars because it has not had the same impact on mainstream leadership scholars.[12] The chapters in this book contribute to leadership ethics and leadership studies in two ways. First, they identify and discuss some of the distinctive normative issues in leadership. Second, they critically examine key conceptual issues that are vital to the study of ethics and leadership.

When it comes to perceptive discussions about the ethics of leadership, Plato and Aristotle are hard to beat. A number of authors in this book draw on the abundant literature on this topic in ancient philosophy. For instance, in *Republic* (Bk. I, 347b3), Plato argues that a just man would not want to rule and would only do so out of fear of punishment.[13] The punishment, according to Plato, is that someone worse than him will rule. Damian Cox and Peter Crook apply Plato's discussion of the reluctant leader to leaders today (Chapter 5). This insight poses a striking contrast to most of the leadership literature that seems to assume that being a leader is desirable, or at least not undesirable. I think it also explains why people do not trust politicians who work very hard to get elected.

One reason why some ancient Greek (and Roman) writers were interested in the ethics of leadership may partly stem from the invention of democracy. Democracy is the only system where, at least in theory, followers choose their leaders and can get rid of them without resorting to violence. Democracy entails a delicate moral and structural relationship between leaders and followers, which makes judgements about the ethics of both parties inevitable. Ethical questions concerning equality, autonomy, freedom and checks on power rarely come up in the management-based leadership literature because most organizations are not democratic. Nonetheless, such ethical considerations are just as relevant to leadership in business and other areas as they are in politics. Democratic values and assumptions permeate almost all of the chapters in this book and fill an enormous gap concerning the normative aspects of the leader/ follower relationship in the leadership literature.

The other valuable contribution of this book comes from the authors' careful analyses of what leadership means and their critical assessment of some of the leadership literature. Research in leadership studies tends to focus on leader effectiveness, yet at the same time scholars usually define leadership in normative terms. This is what led me to what is called the 'Hitler Problem'.[14] Good leaders lead effectively, yet many people would be reluctant to call someone like Hitler (who was arguably effective at many aspects of leadership) a good leader. There is a sense in which a good leader has to be both ethical and effective. These two aspects of leadership are so intertwined as to be almost inseparable. However, I have argued that what ethics and effectiveness mean,

Introduction: Leadership and Philosophy

Jacqueline Boaks and Michael Levine
University of Western Australia

Western philosophy's concern with leadership can be traced at least to Plato's *Republic* where the idea of the philosopher-king as the ideal ruler is defended on social, political, ethical and ultimately metaphysical grounds. (Eastern philosophy's concern is both earlier and possibly more central.) Subsequent philosophical discussion concerning leadership has, mostly, similarly focused on issues of justification: political and social questions regarding who is best suited to lead (rule) and why. What justification is there for assuming authority over another? The nature and justification of leadership raises fundamental questions concerning the relation between leadership and ethics. These have been addressed largely though not exclusively in political philosophy. They are often taken up in the context of the broader question of what form of government is best, and how and why such a form of government is to be morally, or in some other normative manner (politically, socially, personally and prudentially), justified. Just about every 'great' in Western philosophy has concerned themselves with these questions (e.g. Aristotle, Aquinas, Machiavelli, Hobbes, Spinoza, Locke, Hume, Kant, Hegel, Mill and Rawls), but so too have Eastern thinkers (e.g. Confucius and Lao Tzu, and those in the various Indian schools of philosophy).

Machiavellianism describes a cynical disregard for the basic requirement that political actions – particularly coercive political actions – be justified to those they affect (not just those nominally represented by political actors, but all those who fall under the umbrella of a state's coercive exercise of power). Understood in this way, Machiavellian princes – not only in states, but similarly in businesses and universities etc. – move easily between various forms of justification. At an extreme, the leaders can do no wrong merely because they are the leaders.

What has not for the most part been taken up directly in Western philosophy, or has been to a far lesser extent, are questions about the nature of leadership per se: that is, as apart from any specific, usually political, role or context. This may be part of the reason why there is something of a deficit of philosophical or other discipline based theory in much of the business ethics or 'leadership studies' (which is much the same) literature on leadership. So too in everyday discourse about leadership: about what makes one political leader 'good' and another 'bad'. Contemporary concerns and questions are rather different from those found in Plato and subsequent thinkers. Plato was not concerned with running a business. He never had a payroll to meet or stockholders to satisfy. Nor was he concerned with details of good governance insofar as they related to the day-to-day running of a state.

Why, it may well be asked, didn't these questions arise earlier? What is it about them, or us, that brought about their more or less recent appearance? And why do they seem pressing and omnipresent now? Is the relatively recent focus on 'leadership' per se simply a continuation of the old debate about authority or power with a new name or does it focus on a meaningfully different kind or construction of power? And whichever the case, why has this occurred and why now? The question 'why the concern with leadership now?' is a philosophical question about leadership. Addressing it may lend insight to notions of leadership itself. Concerns about leadership are neither accidentally shaped by current cultural milieus (neo-liberalism; 'globalization' in various guises; neo-conservatism), nor do they simply reflect them. They also help sustain and determine what the business world, politics, universities and so much more are like. World views and their corresponding ethos, though always in tension, also mutually support one another: the former by providing a picture of 'reality' as such, and the latter by emotionally (and ethically) sustaining it.[1] Current concern with leadership is a sign of the times, reflecting deep-seated worries and concerns.

What then are some of the central questions concerning leadership in the literature and what others may have been overlooked? What is a leader? What is a 'good' leader? 'Ethically good' seems hardly sufficient, but is it even necessary? More generally: Is 'leadership' a stable, univocal concept? (It clearly is not.) Does anything in fact answer to the terms 'leader' and 'leadership', and can any account of these terms withstand philosophical scrutiny? How are power and authority to be distinguished from leadership and legitimately employed by a leader? How is managerialism to be distinguished from leadership?[2]

Exercising power is not the same as exercising leadership. Nevertheless, while apart from further argument there is no good reason to regard morality as intrinsic to leadership – and many good reasons not to – this is not the case with power. Leadership does appear to intrinsically require the presence and exercise of power if for no other reason than that leadership requires an exercising influence, not necessarily always successfully, over others.

Can one be a good leader and fail? That is, is leadership conceptually or contingently linked to the notion of success? Suppose the Civil War was won by the South, Great Britain was defeated in World War II and the civil rights movement in the US failed? What then becomes of Lincoln, Churchill and King? If the allies had lost the war would Churchill still be regarded as a great leader – assuming he was? More to the point, regardless of how he happens to be regarded, suppose the allies lost the war; *should* Churchill (or Eisenhower) still be regarded as a great leader? Or suppose a business version of the same question. Can one be a successful leader in business if one's company goes under, or if it fails employees in significant ways? More to the point: Must not morally good leaders sometimes fail?

How are leaders to be distinguished from followers? Most of us, if not everyone, assume both the role of leader and follower in different walks of life at different times (even at different moments). Given that people have various roles and duties to fulfil it is likely that some of those roles cast them as a follower while undoubtedly others – parenting, teaching, working with others – put them in positions of leadership. The very same role, whether that of being a teacher or a CEO, suitably understood, may require leaders to be followers and vice versa, in such a way that being one and the other are essentially bound up with one another.

Consider the fact that those in positions of management will often see their primary role as that of a follower – one that does the bidding of those higher up and in charge. This may be used by managers and institutional power holders as mitigating certain responsibilities of good leadership. However, this is never sufficient in and of itself to absolve the responsibilities associated with leadership.

Each of these questions is fundamentally philosophical in nature, and in relative terms none of them have been the focus of much sustained philosophical investigation. Contemporary literature addressing these issues may at times seem in search of a theory (e.g. a specific normative ethical theory or thinker) that can rationally sustain the intuitions, assertions and arguments found in the deluge of publications on leadership. Empirical studies of various kinds and ethical theory have been the two dominant sources. However, management and business theory, economics, social, political and military theory, have been influential as well.

A proposed analysis

A typological analysis (one or more) of questions about leadership may prove useful. For example, the questions and issues outlined above can be categorized as follows:

1. Conceptually and descriptively: What is a leader? Is leadership a property of persons or merely a social function? Is leadership a particular kind of power and authority distinct from other kinds, or does it merely legitimate particular instances of power? Are the posited ethical aspects that make some instances of power 'leadership' objective properties, or do these function as a subjective endorsement of the power holder? How do cases of leadership relate to other forms of legitimate authority? Does leadership turn on consent and instrumentalism as found in the philosophical literature on legitimate authority, or are there also normative elements to leadership? Any adequate account of leadership must, at least in the first instance, be able to differentiate not only between leadership and good ethical character, but also between leadership and power, authority, influence, managerial ability and charisma.

2. Normatively: What is the connection between ethics and leadership? Surely morality and leadership are divisible? Does the emphasis on character and value prevalent in the leadership literature explain a credible connection between leadership and ethics? The centrality of 'value' in recent discussions of leadership can mislead one into thinking that values of a particular kind are sufficient for leadership. Clearly they are not. Focusing on character can lead to a similar error. Because good character is often a locus of descriptions of leaders, it might be assumed that such character is necessary and sufficient for leadership. Even if good character is necessary, it needs to be shown what the connection is and why it is necessary – particularly given that such a connection is explicitly denied in the Machiavellian literature on leadership. In any case, good character is clearly not sufficient for leadership.[3]

Through inattention or wishful thinking, accounts of leadership can become merely prescriptive and stipulate that ethics is a requisite and at least partly constitutive of leadership. This is partly due to a deep seated desire that it be the case that power and ethics should go together. We want to be taken care of as well as led by our leaders.

It is also apparent that applications of the term 'leadership' and ethics do not always coincide. While it may be true that some of us may at times desire our leaders to be moral, it is not the case much of the time. At least there is an ambivalence that needs to be taken seriously. Think of cases, for example, where one's material well-being is going to be even mildly, let alone substantially, affected. We want our fund managers and our prime ministers to 'show us the money'; and if doing so involves ethically questionable practices – a euphemism for practices either immoral but legal, or practices both immoral and illegal – then so be it. The balance of ethical versus skilful (whether strategic, transparent or dubious) behaviour that we want from those in power is not always clear nor is it what we always say we want it to be. At times it seems apparent that this is not merely because, given the choice between ethical and effective leaders, we would choose the latter. Often it is because we seem to have doubts about whether effectiveness is compatible with ethical behaviour in the realm of power and leadership.

In their introduction to the *Journal of Business Ethics*' recent special issue on leadership, ethics and identity, Eubanks, Brown and Ybema assert that 'Leadership is intrinsically bound up with ethics' (2012: 1). But the examples they offer the reader are in fact only examples of the fact that leadership behaviour (in the sense not only of actions, but also of relations to others and their decisions) has ethical implications – that is, it can be judged as more or less ethical. Thus, the focus is on whether leadership is ethically done rather than whether leadership itself is intrinsically ethical. We mention this example not because it is unique in this approach, but because just this oversight seems to us to be repeated across much of the literature.

Far from aiding or enhancing an understanding of leadership, approaches such as this with their supposition that ethics are intrinsic to 'good' leadership, as opposed to say ethical leadership, prevents one from investigating leadership: that is, leadership that is frequently unethical. It prevents it by stipulatively preventing any coherent conceptualization of it. On Ciulla's account, leadership that is unethical is not really leadership, or at least not any kind of leadership that should be of primary interest. This introduces a dilemma: we either think of, for example, David Cameron as both a leader and ethical, or we do not think of him as a leader. The dilemma is easily discarded if it is supposed, as many do, that while some of those whom we regard as leaders may exhibit moral character and make sound ethical decisions some of the time, particularly on matters of great importance, others routinely do not. Alternatively, the dilemma may point us in the right direction. Perhaps some of those we think of as leaders should not be regarded as such.

What is the connection between what we value and want, and the kind(s) of leadership we (allegedly) desire? Is leadership a (kind of) virtue? Do leaders have an obligation to lead? What is the connection between leadership and democracy? Is democracy hospitable to, or dependent upon, leadership? How does gender impact on issues of leadership?

Or the issues can be categorized in part as

3. Explanatory: What is the nature of the relationship between leaders and followers? How is leadership to be explained? Can puzzles such as why leaders seem at times to be relatively unconcerned with truth be explained? Or even more problematically, why do followers not seem to hold them accountable or mind being lied to? Should an account of leadership be expected to provide an explanatory framework capable of providing answers to questions like these? Does the fact that everyone assumes both roles (follower and leader) in various circumstances tell us anything about leadership(s)?

Typologies can be more or less fine-grained. This one is minimal, for simplicity, but also because it is unclear that a more fine-grained account would not obfuscate rather than clarify by separating issues that are intrinsically related in too many ways.

It is natural to think of this typology as hierarchical. That is, it might seem that even if one acknowledged the three-tier classificatory scheme as interrelated and permeable, it may still seem that one required a preliminary account of the conceptual issues in (1) ('What is a leader?') before one could discuss the questions in (2) and (3). This is likely, however, a mistake. The questions cannot be addressed sequentially, in a neat and discrete order. (1)–(3) are not merely related. They also mutually suggest or even entail aspects of just how questions in the other tiers need to be addressed. So, for example, apart from a theoretical framework sufficiently deep to address questions under (3) by giving an account of the relationships between leaders and followers, it may not be possible (at least in hindsight) to give a meaningful account of what leadership or a leader is without such theory. And despite what intuition may tell us, it may be even more problematic to give an account of the relation between leadership and ethics (2 above) without first giving an account of leadership per se and also the relationship between leaders and those whom they lead. In Boaks and Levine (2014) we argue that the question of the definition of leadership is both central to the question of its relationship to ethics, and also problematic. It cannot be ignored.

Here are some additional philosophical questions about leadership that involve all three categories of the typology – even if not all at once. What kind of leadership do we want? More specifically:

- Beyond the question of whether we want leaders to act ethically, do we want leaders to pursue the good? What 'good' and whose 'good' should a leader pursue? Is an apprehension of 'the good' part of the qualifications for leadership?
- Would we prefer a leader who acts in ways that advance one's (i.e. our) perceived interests at the expense of acting ethically (or pursing the good)?
- Must leaders treat followers ethically?
- Must they conduct themselves in an ethical manner in their private lives?
- Do we expect all or most of the above features of leadership to go together? Is it even possible that they do so? Are some of our preferences for certain leadership traits, and the traits themselves, more important than others? What impact does our existing, accepted ethical world view have on how we answer these questions?
- What should be said about Plato's claim that only those who are reluctant to lead are fit to lead?

Consider Plato's disturbing claim that the only persons fit to rule are those who must be compelled to rule through fear of being ruled by those less worthy.[4] Unlike others who fight for rule through ambition or a desire for riches or power over others, Plato's philosopher-kings are reluctant because they prefer their life of philosophy to any other life including rule.[5] They are, on Plato's view, 'truly rich' in reason and goodness.[6] In regard to contemporary politicians (and others) it is sometimes said that anyone who wants the job should not have it – why even in Plato's time he could note that 'it's commonly considered improper to accept authority except with reluctance or under pressure'.[7] And the reason wanting the job ipso facto may be thought to rule a person out is because such a position is regarded as incompatible with virtue and leadership in the broad Aristotelian sense as a master virtue.[8] Leaders frequently rely on such a tacit understanding of the requirements of the position of leadership to eschew meaningful culpability. Consider the fact that an aspect of being an ordinary university employee – let's say a professor, routinely (and as a result of university leadership and the 'system') requires one to fabricate, distort, deceive, use subterfuge and hyperbole, and otherwise go easy on the truth. The idea that those in more substantial positions of leadership (but also followers) must frequently put value and truth to the rear gains force. No person is an island.

And insofar as leadership, conceived of as a master virtue, requires a reasonably ethical environment in order to operate at all – let alone effectively – even if leadership were possible, its scope may be severely limited. The virtuous agent does the right thing in the right way – the implication here is one of skill as well as of intention. Suppose, however, that one lives in what is tantamount to a moral vacuum of sorts? What are the chances then of being able to exercise such virtues?

Both the typology in general, and the suggestion that the issues adddressed under (1)–(3) may be interrelated, are suggestive of why, where and how accounts of leadership or leadership ethics in the literature may go wrong or raise further questions. Any account of what it means to be a leader that is not embedded in an account of leadership that has the explanatory efficacy called for in (3), or that fails to address and substantiate its normative claims in (2), is apt to strike us in just the same ways that some of the accounts of leadership put forward in business ethics, or by leadership gurus and CEOs, do: as superficial, naive, empirically vacuous, scientistic, at times baselessly optimistic, and/or self-promoting and self-congratulatory.

Kouzes' (2010: xvii) set of conclusions based on survey responses, for example, are unconvincing and do not necessarily follow from the evidence he cites. For one thing, the framework assumes that those asked know which qualities in a leader they most admire and are answering truthfully. It might be that those who are asked are actually answering as they think they should rather than as they truly believe – citing qualities that they would like to most admire but in fact do not. Suppose those being asked are in the middle of some kind of leadership training course and thus primed to think of themselves as (presumably ethically good) leaders? Asking which leaders one most 'admires' and then taking these as the paradigmatic of leadership per se is not only tantamount to 'leading the witness', it also begs the question in assuming such characteristics are essential to leadership and to what we want in leaders.

Kouzes' account does place ethics, value and principle at the core of leadership, and thus superficially resembles a virtue theory account, but it does not tell us what leadership is or why value is essential – if it is. It is a report on what some people claim to think. It is however also what the intended audience for handbooks on leadership presumably wants to hear. After all, they mostly already are (or wish to be) in positions of management, presuming themselves to be 'leaders' and wanting to know how to be the kind of leader others admire.

If a typology is useful in suggesting strategies for addressing questions about how leadership may go wrong, it is bound to be suggestive of useful ways forward. It may seem obvious that a satisfactory explanation of what leadership is may – in fact, it will – have to explain something about the nature of leadership: that is, something about the source of the leader's 'power' for example – where power is not confused with straightforward authority as in being someone's boss. If it is obvious, it is also a point that is omitted, or barely acknowledged, in many accounts of leadership. Other accounts of leadership fail because although they do have explanatory hypotheses – what a leader is and the nature and source of their power – the ones employed are demonstrably false or shallow.

Dismissing a topological hierarchy does not mean that one need regard all the classificatory categories as equally significant in all contexts, or that one category cannot be regarded as fundamental in ways that the others may not be. Ultimately, if leadership is to be explained, and the questions raised in (1) and (2) adequately addressed, an explanatory framework (3) is needed. And it is just that category – an explanation of the dynamics of leadership – that is least discussed, when at all, in business ethics and other leadership literature – including notably the rather sparse philosophical accounts of leadership (and ethics).

One allegedly explanatory source frequently drawn upon by those who do wish to give an explanation of the nature of leadership, how it is able to work (i.e. 3), is Weber's (1922) account of the charismatic leader – given in the context of his discussion of authority. Such a leader is 'Set apart from ordinary men and is treated as endowed with … exceptional powers and qualities … [that] are not accessible to the ordinary person but are regarded as of divine origin or as exemplary, and on the basis of them the individual concerned is treated as a leader' (Weber 1947: 358–9).

Weber's account, however, is largely descriptive rather than explanatory in the sense that (3) in the topology is meant to capture. He tells us the qualities that the charismatic leader is believed to have, and so why one who believes such things may be expected to fall in line and follow such a person. (Presumably 'charismatic' applies primarily to political rather than business or other leaders, and even then to relatively few.) But he does not tell us why charismatic leaders are believed to have such special powers and qualities. What is the connection between leaders and followers that explains such apparently irrational beliefs?

In short, Weber is addressing (1) rather than (3). His account is better seen as descriptive and conceptual rather than as explanatory: as answering the question 'What is a (charismatic) leader?' The extent to which the notion of charismatic leadership can be applied to ordinary instances of leadership also needs to be explained. Few employees, even devoted ones, regard their CEOs as of 'divine origin', though many do regard them as in some ways 'exemplary' and as 'endowed with … exceptional powers and qualities'. Does Weber think otherwise? Furthermore, in connecting charismatic leadership with his account of authority, is Weber not muddying the waters? Isn't he connecting two things that had best be distinguished, that need to be distinguished, if we are to understand leadership as opposed to authority (or power)?

It might be argued that philosophy has no part to play in explaining leadership in the way that is called for by (3) in the above typology. Such explanations may be regarded as fundamentally psychological (or other) in nature but not philosophical. Perhaps this might explain some of the reluctance to tackle the topic of leadership that our experience shows philosophers have demonstrated. That is, perhaps philosophers have thought that leadership, or at least some of these important aspects of it, lies outside of what philosophy can properly deal with. They have nothing to do for example with conceptual analysis. The claim then is that explaining the nature of leadership in the ways that fall under (3) above is extra-philosophical. This claim in turn relies on the assumption that the categories (1–3) in the typology are not intrinsically connected, that they are completely distinguishable and that, in any case, they are less permeable than we have supposed them to be. It also rests on a conception of philosophy, or philosophy's task, as one largely, even if not exclusively, concerned with conceptual analysis.

For those who do not share this view there are important philosophical resources that have been relatively overlooked in addressing questions in all three categories of the typology – though especially (3). The kinds of explanations we have in mind may have surprising results – suggesting, for example, that the attractions of despotic (toxic) leadership may not be all too different (if different at all) than that of ethical, and in other ways, exemplary leadership. Wouldn't that, for example, tell us something about leadership that is both philosophically interesting and worth knowing?

There is another thing that this kind of explanation does. It draws a more definite line between leadership, or what it takes to be central cases of leadership, and other things referred to as leadership, such as forms of managerialism, authority and power relations.

Here then is one account of leadership (Freud 1921) that seeks to explain the nature of the relationship between leaders and followers (3 in the typology), but in so doing directly and indirectly addresses many of the questions in (1) and (2) as well. We need not be concerned here with whether or not, or to what extent, Freud's account, and the explanations he draws on, is right. We need only note that if elements of this or another account that is similarly broad are more or less right, then much of the writing on leadership has to be rethought. We put this forward as one example of a developed explanatory theory with important philosophical consequences, though it is an account with a history and chosen because we take it to have genuine explanatory power. It solves puzzles. It also serves as a useful example of what such an account might look like. It provides a template for how a richer account than those currently on offer will address the questions we have outlined above.

Why, for example, most notably in the political arena but certainly elsewhere as well, are people seemingly so little concerned with the mendacity of leaders? Leaders lie and we don't care. However, other explanatory accounts capable of addressing philosophical issues about leadership can be grounded elsewhere. Most, if we are right about the current state of leadership literature, are yet to be formulated. Philosophical psychology, philosophy of mind, well-developed accounts of emotion and psychologically astute moral philosophy can all be brought to bear on issues pertaining to leadership. Where the kinds of theories useful to these questions about leadership will not be formulated is in ethics or social and political philosophy by themselves: that is without a psychological underpinning.

Freud's view on leadership is of course grounded in psychoanalytic theory, and it has largely been overlooked in the leadership literature. From a philosophical perspective this is just a small part of the neglect on the part of contemporary analytic philosophy towards psychoanalysis. It is disregarded as philosophically irrelevant largely because it is assumed (though there are arguments as well) to be fundamentally mistaken.[9] As Wollheim says,

> Virtually all those who are not either ignorant of Freud or totally sceptical of his finding believe that he altered, radically altered, our conceptions of the mind. He effected a change in what we think we are like, and it was a big change. Astonishingly enough, it is philosophers who have been of all people the slowest to recognise this fact. They have been slowest to recognize that this fact has anything to do with them. (1993: 91)

If Wollheim (1993) and Pataki (2014) are right, then the kinds of questions raised here about leadership cannot be adequately understood apart from psychoanalytic theory (e.g. its account of human nature). Neither can swathes of social and political philosophy, philosophy of mind, ethics and more.

Let's focus on the puzzle about an apparent lack of concern with the truth. This is a different issue from the common problem of knowing one is being lied to and not being able to do anything about it. In *Psychologie des foules* (1895), Gustave Le Bon says 'groups have never thirsted after truth. They demand illusions, and cannot do without them. They constantly give what is unreal precedence over what is real; they are almost as strongly influenced by what is untrue as by what is true. They have an evident tendency not to distinguish between the two.'[10]

What Le Bon and Freud both say about groups' disregard for truth – and so reality – is troublingly applicable today. It proves to be a good, and perhaps even necessary, place to begin examining the sources of violence and terror in racial, religious, nationalistic and other prejudices. Given the extent of mendacity among leaders, the question as to why leaders lie and why many of those they lie to (supporters, 'followers') do not appear especially interested in holding them accountable is important in its own right. Here, however, we are interested in them only insofar as they tell us about the relationship between leaders and followers more generally in these paradigmatic cases. What needs to be explained is what underlies the abandonment of critical thought.[11] Therein especially lie many of the concerns we have about leadership, would-be leaders and their ability to influence us in ways and to ends we might be wary of. That is, the concern that the relationship between leaders and followers is not the kind that is proper to persons as critical reflective agents and might somehow lead us astray by undermining our ability to choose our own ideals, objectives and means in a way that reflects our status as ethical, autonomous agents. Philosophy's disinterest in this question may partly be due to a history of under-psychologizing political and other areas of philosophy. This in turn has arguably resulted in misplaced and unwarranted scientific and scientistic approaches by theorists seeking explanations for actions and events in terms of rational agents and/or historical, economic or political forces. Our claim is that other kinds of explanation, including fundamentally psychological ones, may at times be in order. They do not tell the whole story, but they are essential at the least to illuminate the kinds of questions that must be asked about leadership and what an adequate answer might look like.

Here a number of platitudes about the way groups influence beliefs must play some role in the emergence of political cultures of mendacity. Many judgements, actions and reactions are in some measure the product of our membership of groups: we only believe them (and act in a certain way) because of our place in the group. We are disposed to do what we have to do to remain comfortable within the group, including shunning criticism of the foundational ideas or ruling myths of the group. We often fear ostracism from the group and are sometimes prepared to lie and dissemble in order to avoid this. Foolish and implausible ideas – even downright delusional ideas – can sometimes be protected from serious criticism by becoming essential markers of group membership. Group membership can also essentially involve marking out others as non-members and this can be a source of prejudice and contempt: they are not one of us. And these phenomena of group psychological formation are not purely cognitive phenomena. They work through a sometimes disastrous economy of affect involving wish-fulfilling fantasy rooted in desire.

This may explain in a very general way how it is that allegiance to a leader and groups can have a distortional effect on a person's appreciation of reality, and can diminish their actual concern for the truth at the very moment that they dogmatically assert their possession of it. Yet the platitudes themselves are in need of explanation.

Our overall explanatory strategy does not depend upon the details of Freud's account, but is well illustrated by it. Freud describes an extreme form of group identification, one in which the psychological process of identifying with a group – and in particular with a leader or leading idea – automatically brings with it diminishment of capacities to connect with reality. Despite differences, Freud is largely in agreement with Le Bon's 'brilliantly executed picture of the group mind' (Freud 1921: 81). In addition to addressing some unanswered questions (e.g. the role of the leader), Freud's *Group Psychology* provides a theoretical framework for Le Bon's observations: why, for instance, group members 'have never thirsted after truth'.

Freud's explanation is based on his account of an individual's psychology in relation to others. 'In the individual's mental life someone else is invariably involved, as a model, as an object, as a helper, as an opponent; and so from the very first individual psychology, in this extended but entirely justifiable sense of the words, is at the same time social psychology as well' (ibid.: 69). Central to Freud's account and what enables us to understand the individual in relation to the group, is the role of libido: ' … libidinal ties [or "emotional ties"] are what characterize a group … [or] constitute the essence of the group mind' (ibid.: 91). Emotional ties hold a group together. It is what allows members to be influenced by others, and accounts for 'the need of being in harmony' (ibid.: 92) with others. These ties are made possible through a form of 'identification' – the way an individual ego identifies with an 'ideal type', usually a father figure, or in the case of the group, with the group's leader, who is a sort of substitute father figure: 'Identification endeavours to mould a person's own ego after the fashion of the one that has been taken as a model' (ibid.: 105–6).

Whatever other ties there may be, it is the 'illusion' of such a leader and their love, and the individual's unity with the leader – a 'substitute father' – that holds the group together. When a group's emotional ties languish, 'panic' in the sense of 'neurotic fear or anxiety' (ibid.: 97) results. The reaction is natural since what the individual must now face (psychically) alone he could previously face with the group as a whole. While a leader seems indispensable to a group, Freud suggests that an idea might take the place of leader (i.e. a 'leading idea'): 'The leader or the leading idea might also, so to speak, be negative; hatred against a particular person or intuition might operate in just the same unifying way, and might call up the same kind of emotional ties as positive attachment' (ibid.: 100).

There is an aspect to group psychology where the leader can also be regarded as part of the group, a follower, and so subject to the same dynamic. An account can also be given of how the group picks the leader it needs at the time, incorporates him and the leader responds to these needs at an unconscious level, as well as in all the usual political ways. This may result in part from projective identification: the leader is manipulated into playing out the worst impulses of the members of the group.

So how do the libidinal ties that unify groups result in a lack of concern with truth and reality? Idealization 'falsifies judgement'. We tend to overlook the faults of the objects we love and idealize. Freud says:

> [T]he object is being treated in the same way as our own ego, so that when we are in love a considerable amount of narcissistic libido overflows on to the object … in many forms of love-choice … the object serves as a substitute for some unattained ego ideal of our own. We love it on account of the perfections which we have striven to reach for our own ego, and which we should now like to procure in this roundabout way as a means of satisfying our narcissism. (ibid.: 112–13)

One's faculty for testing reality is rendered inoperable with the ego's, or ego-ideal's, replacement by the object. Freud says 'No wonder that the ego takes a perception for real if its reality is vouched for by the mental agency [the object that has replaced the ego] which ordinarily … [tests] the reality of things'. As in hypnosis or love 'the ego experiences in a dreamlike way whatever he [the hypnotist, lover, leader] may request or assert' (ibid.: 114).

Not only does Freud explicitly connect group psychology to prejudices, intolerance, stereotyping and the 'herd instinct', he also argues that these phenomena are widespread.

> We are reminded of how many of these phenomena of dependence [the individual upon the leader and equally other members of the group upon each

other] are part of the normal constitution of human society, of how little originality and personal courage are to be found in it, of how much every individual
is ruled by those attitudes of the group mind which exhibit themselves in such
forms as racial characteristics, class prejudices, public opinion, etc. (ibid.: 117)

There may be a tendency to think of groups as discrete entities focused around
a single leader or leading idea. But groups overlap and members may belong
to many with similarities that reinforce particular prejudices on behalf of ego
defence. Freud says,

> Each individual is a component part of numerous groups, he is bound by ties
> of identification in many directions, and he has built up his ego ideal upon the
> most various models. Each individual therefore has a share in numerous group
> minds – those of his race, of his class, of his creed, of his nationality, etc. …
> The individual gives up his ego ideal and substitutes for it the group ideal as
> embodied in the leader. … He [the leader] need often only possess the typical
> qualities of the individuals concerned in a particularly clearly marked and pure
> form. (ibid.: 129)

This is then one explanation of leadership. It explains not only the symbiotic
relation between leader and follower, but can be employed to address any
number of the questions raised in the typology. It also has various and disparate
implications for how the relationship between leadership and ethics might be
construed.

Our overall purpose in this chapter has been to provide a typology for
philosophical issues about leadership and to show how such reflecting on the
typology, and addressing the questions raised, can and likely would change the
face of leadership discourse and study. It would do this by redirecting its focus
in a way that promises to help us better understand leadership, especially as it
relates to ethics. While we ended with a psychoanalytic view about leadership
and groups, our purpose was not to defend it but to show how this or some
other deep psychological view seems necessary for the kind of theoretical
explanation of leadership capable of addressing issues across all three areas in
the typology.

The chapters

The chapters in this volume each go about addressing these questions in their
own way. They adopt a range of stances and explanations, as well as focusing on
a range of these questions, but each of them goes beyond the existing literature

as we have described it and address aspects of the topic in the more nuanced and comprehensive way that we think the topic merits.

The chapters do not reflect a neat division of topics – just as one would expect from the interrelatedness of the questions that we described above. However, we have grouped them into three broad categories.

The first of these categories focuses on the relationship between leadership and ethics – the question that, as we noted above, is so central to the topic of leadership, about which so much has been written, but which yet in our opinion remains to be satisfactorily addressed. Each of the three chapters in this section moves beyond the accounts current in the literature. The focus is on what grounds, if any, we have for asserting a relationship between leadership and ethics. In different ways, they seek to give a more robust answer to what we have described as the Machiavellian sceptic who simply rejects the idea of a relationship between leadership and ethics beyond the instrumental or the prudential.

The first of these, Tom Angier's chapter, takes as its topic ethics and leadership in the political sphere. To begin with, he documents the predominant ancient view, viz. that political leadership is aimed primarily at fostering the virtue of citizens. He then explores some good reasons for abandoning this view, both moral and pragmatic. Nevertheless he argues that contemporary political leaders can and must work to reinstate aspects of the ancient agenda, on pain of severe social consequences.

Anna Moltchanova's paper explores the notion of leadership from the perspective of social ontology, considering how leadership can be defined in the context of group agency and group actions. In particular, she explores how those performing the function of leadership shape the evaluative perspective of the group which motivates members to act as group members. Since the members' joint actions and shared beliefs about the goals, norms and rules of the group engender the group ethos, she considers two aspects of leadership: its ability to change the group's ethos and its relation to individual group members' autonomy.

She juxtaposes what it means to be a leader and what it means to be a ruler, ultimately arguing that defining leadership in its relation to group members' autonomy and moral values problematizes the leadership status of those at the helm of groups oppressing their members.

Completing this first section, Sarah Sorial's paper explores the relationship between authority and leadership. Persons in positions of authority do not necessarily demonstrate leadership, while some persons without the relevant kinds of authority do. Typically, persons come to have authority by virtue of (i) possessing a certain kind of recognized expertise concerning a particular issue; (ii) having some kind of legitimate institutional support or affiliation. By virtue of this, authoritative persons can enact norms and impose significant obligations on others to do what they say. Sorial argues that given the kinds of powers authoritative people possess, they have different kinds of responsibilities and so should be held to different standards of ethical and legal account-ability. One of the ethical responsibilities they have is to be able to exercise good leadership. In arguing for this claim, she examines what constitutes good leadership and why leadership is an inherently ethical concept.

The chapters in the second section take up some particular concerns about leadership. In the first of these, Jacqueline Boaks addresses the relationship between leadership and democracy. She argues that leadership and democracy are both answers to the question of what types of power are legitimate – democracy offering one answer to this question, and leadership offering another. She argues that it is easy to think (*prima facie*) that there is some natural affinity between leadership and democracy – that leadership's appeal to and reliance upon such criteria as the consent and support of followers makes it a natural fit with democracy. Further, the grounding of such leadership in the good of followers makes it a natural fit with democracy's focus on the equal consideration of the interests (and well-being) of persons. This chapter examines whether this *prima facie* affinity stands up to examination.

Next, Damian Cox and Peter Crook's paper addresses the question of the reluctant leader, and is an examination of the truth and significance of Plato's claim that only those who are reluctant to lead are fit to lead – a claim that, as we noted above, has become a commonplace view in our own time. A closely related claim is about qualities of leadership: qualities necessary to obtain leadership are – in many contexts – the very qualities that make a person unfit for leadership. The chapter examines two key questions. First, to what extent, and in what circumstances, does Plato's view hold up in contemporary contexts, especially political contexts? Second, what are the consequences of this for contemporary democratic practice?

Jessica Flanigan's paper examines a concept that has – as Joanne Ciulla notes in her foreword – become popular in the leadership literature, often being used as the cornerstone of ethical leadership (and at times seemingly taken as not only necessary but also all too near sufficient for ethical leadership): so-called 'authentic' leadership. Authentic leadership is a way of evaluating leadership by standards of honesty and faithfulness to a leader's principles. Implicit in authentic leadership theory is the assumption that it is wrong for a leader to misrepresent her values or commitments to subordinates. Yet authentic leadership as an ethical archetype is in tension with another ideal of leadership – moral ambition. A morally ambitious leader is one who applies higher moral standards to his own conduct than he applies to subordinates'. Flanigan's chapter examines what we should make of this conflict. Like many of the chapters in this book, her eventual conclusions run counter to much of the prevailing views in the literature and popular, pre-theoretical opinions on leadership.

Finally in this section, Fiona Jenkins' 'Leadership and Gender: Women's Mandate to Lead' takes up the topic of gender and leadership. Specifically Jenkins looks at how women's rise to leadership positions in organizations coincides with increasingly highly regulated modes of making appointments. Designed in part to generate equal opportunities, she argues that these policy and procedure based modes of selection and promotion are a source of ambivalent results for many women, and shape the forms of authority they are able to exercise, often with problematic implications for other women.

The third and final section of papers addresses applications and examples of leadership.

Thom Brooks' 'Leadership and Stakeholding' argues for the view that the most compelling view of leadership must incorporate the idea of stakeholding: that the leader and the led are together stakeholders in a common enterprise where mutual duties and responsibilities arise. Each has a stake in outcomes and so possesses a claim in how outcomes are decided. But how is this to be determined, especially where there is deep disagreement? Brooks argues that the idea of the stakeholder society offers an important new perspective on justice with wider relevance.

Allyn Fives' paper takes up the applied case of leadership with respect to parents and children, offering one way to shed light on what we should think regarding power, freedom and leadership. One requirement of good leadership, Fives asserts, is that it be non-dominating, and that one sphere where good leadership is required is in the relation between parents (or those in a parenting role) and children. Power is non-dominating to the extent that it does not undermine freedom. Examining parental domination of children is used to help resolve the disagreement between liberals and republicans over how to define domination.

As such, Fives' chapter is an example of just the kind of approach we outlined above – rather than addressing the conceptual and ethical questions separately and sequentially, looking at this applied case brings to light what we might think about the normative and conceptual questions.

Finally, Constantine Sandis and Nassim Taleb look at the case of leadership and asymmetry – arguing that problems arise in cases where leaders do not have what they refer to as 'skin in the game' and proposing a heuristic to resolve such lopsided risks between leaders and followers. They present ethical and prudential grounds for a symmetrical constraint on all forms of leadership.

Notes

1   Clifford Geertz, 'Religion as a Cultural System.' *The Interpretation of Cultures: Selected Essays by Clifford Geertz*. New York: Basic Books, 1973, chapter 4, 87–123. See 89–90. Geertz describes 'ethos' as 'the tone, character, and quality of their [a peoples'] life, its moral and aesthetic style-and mood.'

2   This last seems pressing and important to us. At best managerialism is an impoverished discourse; at its worst it risks cloaking often arbitrary and relatively unconstrained organizational power in the putative moral authority of 'leadership'.

3   See Boaks and Levine 2014 for a more complete account of how accounts of leadership in relation to ethics can go wrong.

4   Plato, *Republic*, translated by H. Lee, 2nd rev. edn. repr., with additional revisions. London, Penguin, 1987, 347.

5   Ibid., 521.

6   Ibid., 521.

7   Ibid. 347*b–c*.

8   We have argued (Boaks and Levine 2014) for a broadly Aristotelian account, one in which leadership can and should be conceived of as a master virtue that, correctly understood, serves human flourishing. (See Boaks, this volume.) This is both a way (not the only way) of grounding leadership in ethics and showing that there is an intrinsic connection between leadership and ethics—one that goes beyond mere wishful thinking or stipulation.

9   See Pataki 2014 for an impressive exception.

10 Quoted by Freud (1921) in *Group Psychology and the Analysis of the Ego, The Standard Edition of the Complete Psychological Works of Sigmund Freud*, vol. 18, p. 80. Henceforth, *Group Psychology* will be referred to in the text as [GP]. See the account of lying in politics in relation to Freud's *Group Psychology* in Cox et al. 2009, Ch. 3, 'Lying in the War on Terrorism.' Also see Arendt (1983); Cox and Levine (2010).

11 For a discussion of various interpretations of Machiavellianism as a justification for lying, see M. Ramsay (2000) 'Justifications for Lying in Politics', in Cliffe et al., *The Politics of Lying*, pp. 3–26. Again one sees excellent accounts of the political lies told and an account of the scope of the problem. But the reasons given for

the extraordinary lying are invariably rational. The reason for lying in politics is to knowingly (consciously) achieve some desired end. Whether this is viewed as moral or immoral or some kind of necessary political expediency that is supra-moral varies. See, for example, Ramsay's discussion of the causes of government deception (Cliffe et al. 2000: 44). On our account, the four kinds of reasons listed are superficial, or else just false.

Bibliography

Arendt, H. (1969), *Crises of the Republic*. New York: Harcourt Brace.

—(1983), *Men in Dark Times*. New York: Harcourt Brace.

Boaks, J. and Levine, M. (2014), 'What does ethics have to do with leadership?' *Journal of Business Ethics*, 124 (2): 225–42, available at http://link.springer.com/article/10.1007/s10551-013-1807-y

Burns, J. M. (1978), *Leadership*, New York: Harper & Row.

Ciulla, J. B. (2004), *Ethics, the Heart of Leadership* (2nd edn).Westport, CT: Praeger.

Cliffe, L., Ramsay, M. and Bartlett, D. (2000), *The Politics of Lying: Implications for Democracy*. Basingstoke and London: Macmillan.

Cox, D. and Levine, M. (2010), 'Damned Lying Politicians: Integrity and Truth in Politics', in T. Dare and B. Wendel (eds), *Personal Integrity and Professional Ethics*. Cambridge: Cambridge Scholars Press, pp. 44–67.

Cox, D., Levine. M. and Newman, S. (2009), *Politics Most Unusual: Violence, Sovereignty and Democracy in the 'War on Terror'*. London: Palgrave Macmillan.

Eubanks, D. L., Brown, A. D. and Ybema, S. (2012), 'Leadership, identity and ethics'. *Journal of Business Ethics*, 107 (1): 1–3.

Freud, S. (1921), *Group Psychology and the Analysis of the Ego, The Standard Edition of the Complete Psychological Works of Sigmund Freud*, vol. 18: 80.

—(1929, 1930), *The Standard Edition of the Complete Psychological Works of Sigmund Freud* (trans. and ed. J. Strachey), 24 vols. London: Hogarth.

Grint, K. (2010), *Leadership: A Very Short Introduction*. New York: Oxford University Press.

Hodgkinson, C. (1983), *The Philosophy of Leadership*. Charlotte, NC: Information Age Publishing (IAP).

Kellerman, B. (2004), *Bad Leadership: What it Is, How it Happens, Why it Matters*. Cambridge: Harvard Business School Press.

Kouzes, J. (2009), *The Jossey-Bass Reader on Nonprofit and Public Leadership*. San Francisco: Wiley, p. xvii.

Le Bon, G. (1895), *Psychologie des foules*, in S. Freud, *Group Psychology*, pp. 77–81.

Pataki, T. (2014), *Wish-fulfilment in Philosophy and Psychoanalysis: The Tyranny of Desire*. East Sussex and New York: Routledge.

Plato (1981), *Republic* (trans. G. M. A. Grube, rev. C. D. C. Reeve). Indianapolis, IN: Hackett Publishing Company.

Ramsay, M. (2000), 'Justifications for Lying in Politics', in Cliffe et al., *The Politics of Lying*, pp. 3–26.

Rustow, D. (1968), *Philosophers and Kings: Studies in Leadership*. Cambridge, MA: American Academy of Arts and Sciences.

Weber, M. (1922, 1947), 'The Nature of Charismatic Authority and its Routinization', in *The Theory of Social and Economic Organisations* (trans. A. M. Henderson and T. Parsons, ed. T. Parsons). New York: Free Press.

Wollheim, R. (1993), 'Desire, Belief, and Professor Grünbaum's Freud', in *The Mind and Its Depths*. Cambridge: Harvard University Press, pp. 91–111.

Part One

Just What is the Relationship Between Leadership and Ethics?

1

An Unjust Leader is No Leader

Tom Angier
University of St Andrews

Blessed is the man
Who walked not in the counsel of the wicked
Nor stood in the path of the sinful
Nor sat in the seat of scoffers

Ps. 1.1

I want money, fame, and integrity too

Eddie Izzard

Introduction

In this chapter I shall be exploring the relation of ethics and political leadership in the Western philosophical tradition. Restricting my purview to the West is simply a matter of my own education: there is, no doubt, much that marks Eastern traditions out as distinctive,[1] but discussion of them lies beyond my competence. (What I say concerning the aims and methods of political leadership will, nonetheless, be at a level of generality sufficient, I hope, to apply to most modes of politics.) Restricting myself to specifically political leadership is warranted, I think, because it is this form of leadership that has been most discussed in Western philosophy – most extensively by Plato and Aristotle. I'll begin, then, by looking at Keith Grint's well-known analysis of leadership and its supposed 'arts'.[2] This analysis is crucially illuminated, I'll argue, by Plato's and Aristotle's very different approach. I'll go on to unpack an argument from Plato's *Republic* concerning the aims or *ends* of political leadership, and then spend the rest of my time on what *means* can legitimately be taken to those ends: the so-called problem of 'dirty hands'. Overall, my argument will be that political leadership, properly understood, is importantly distinct in its goals from mere power-seeking. And while political leaders are at real risk of serious moral transgression in pursuit of those goals, I'll argue that this risk has been seriously exaggerated, and can be resisted in eminently 'realistic' ways.

Grint's analysis of leadership

There are two elements of Grint's analysis that I want to highlight: first, his emphasis on leaders necessarily being in relation to their particular constituencies,[3] and second, the idea that being a leader consists in, or is heavily dependent on, practising an 'ensemble of arts' (Grint 2000: 27). On the first point, Grint stresses that Carlyle's notion of leaders as great men, heroically achieving great things of which others are incapable, is at best only a half-truth. In reality, leaders who achieve great things, especially in the political realm, must rely on a host of people whose continuing allegiance is never guaranteed, and must thus be constantly buttressed and rendered secure. Moreover, leaders' 'own' achievements are strongly conditioned by the achievements of others, however much the latter are inspired, at least initially, by the leader himself. Even Weber's 'charismatic' leader (Grint 2010: 93–7), the twentieth century's 'great man'-type, is highly dependent on the co-operation, competence and regard of his subordinates for his own continuing prestige and success. (This is no less true of the tyrant, who may purport to rule with ineluctable and irresistible force, but in fact depends heavily on the consent and efficiency of his subordinates.) It follows that, as Grint puts it, real-world 'great men' rely just as much as Fordist managers on the 'trick of leadership': viz. developing 'followers who privately resolve the problems leaders have caused or cannot resolve' (Grint 2000: 420). Leaders of any stripe, that is, are never truly 'on top', but at best merely 'in front' (ibid.), and as soon as they lose the loyalty of their constituents, or find themselves saddled with bunglers (however loyal), their grip on power wanes. It follows, in turn, that charismatic leadership *eo ipso* is 'a deeply destabilising and itself unstable force' (Grint 2010: 95): its over-reliance on relatively superficial aspects of the personality, such as physical and rhetorical charm, will simply be inadequate when it comes to the day-to-day wielding of power, let alone the resolution of crises.[4]

The second element of Grint's analysis consists in the so-called 'arts' of leadership. Leadership may itself be an 'indeterminate skill' (Grint 2000: 419), but it devolves, nevertheless, into a set of four relatively determinate 'arts'. The first art, Grint informs us, is 'philosophical', and amounts to motivating or 'mobilizing' others, not only on the basis of personal charisma, but also on the basis of 'constructing' an identity to which one's constituency can aspire (ibid.: 409–11). Grint mentions Hitler's construction of German identity in terms of racial purity, and Martin Luther King's construction of American identity in terms of social unity as prime instances of this art. The second art is a 'fine' art, and centres on developing a 'strategic vision' or systematic goal that structures one's job as leader (ibid.: 411–13). For example, Grint writes, 'Ford wanted to revolutionize American transport, Nelson wanted to secure British domination of the seas, Hitler wanted to inaugurate a new German Empire' (ibid.: 412). The third art Grint expounds is labelled 'martial', and concerns 'organizational tactics' (ibid.: 413–17). This procedural art largely involves devising ways of ensuring 'followers' competence can compensate for leaders' incompetence' (ibid.: 417). That is, it requires leaders to recognize others' expertise, and put in place institutional checks on their own self-will: something Grint judges Richard Branson more successful at than Henry Ford (ibid.: 414–15). The fourth and final art is that of 'performing', and consists in 'persuasive communication' (ibid.: 417–19). Here Grint gives a wide sense to 'communication', so as to include not only cognitive content, but also how a leader appears, how often he appears and what kinds of information he tries to suppress. This concludes Grint's 'four arts' of leadership, which he summarizes as, in turn, the 'who', the 'what', the 'how' and the 'why' of leadership.

Now the first element of Grint's analysis – viz. leadership's 'relational' nature – is well-taken, so far as it goes. He is no doubt right that there are structural or organizational conditions on leadership, as well as 'voluntarist' ones (to do with the leader's will and personality: Grint 2000: 291). Likewise, Grint may well be right that there are various 'arts' or techniques that leadership incorporates, or tends to draw on. But what is striking is precisely what is absent from his analysis: namely, any mention of leadership as having a constitutive moral direction, or being under any systematic moral constraints. After all, merely adverting to the necessarily relational nature of leadership does not establish what that relation is *for*, or whether it must proceed *within* certain bounds. Conceivably, it might be aimed at the ultimate immolation of both leader and led, and proceed in a morally completely unconstrained way. (Hitler's rule – which, despite his title as *Führer*, I'll argue did not constitute leadership proper – may have been an instance of this.) And if we turn to Grint's purported 'arts' of leadership, we seem equally bereft of any moral weathervane. For none of them so much as gestures at any constitutive moral content to leadership: something borne out by the fact that he cites both Hitler and Martin Luther

King as adept at the supposedly 'philosophical' art. Grint may laud 'strategic vision', 'organizational tactics' and 'persuasive communication', but the (at best) relativistic and constructivist nature of these is palpable.[5] Is this ethically denuded conception of leadership simply par for the course, or does the history of Western philosophy provide reasons for construing leadership as something morally richer and more robust?

When put in the context of Western philosophy as a whole, Grint's notion of leadership appears ethically oddly truncated. For not only do philosophers right at the start of that tradition – viz. Plato and Aristotle – assume leadership's subordination to ethical norms, this normative conception held sway at least until the appearance of Machiavelli's *The Prince* in 1513. Moreover, even Machiavelli's work seems to acknowledge the existence of ethical norms: while he is keen to teach political leaders of his day 'how not to be good', he admits the existence of moral goodness, and at most denies that some of its norms apply within the political realm. In what follows, then, I will explore the prospects for a conception of leadership – specifically, political leadership – that is, *pace* Grint, morally structured. And to do this, I shall begin by going back to the roots of Western philosophy, i.e. to Plato and Aristotle, and asking: What argumentative materials does their work supply to show that (a) political leadership – *contra* sheer power-seeking – must have an ethically structured end or ends and that (b) it need not make use, in the achievement of those ends, of morally illicit means?[6] I shall start by addressing question (a).

Plato and the ends of political leadership

If any philosopher has the reputation of being a strong 'moralist' in political theory, it is Plato. His *Republic* elaborates a detailed educational programme for the prospective leaders of Kallipolis, his projected 'noble city', a programme that includes not only prescriptions for what these 'guardians' should study, and how they should exercise, but also stringent proscriptions on the types of entertainment and dramatic art to which they should be exposed.[7] This political training programme is embedded, moreover, in an ambitious metaphysics of the 'Good': Plato presents the moral education of the guardians as akin to a journey out of darkness, at the end of which they discover a superordinate 'Form of the Good', which conditions not only the possibility of knowledge, but also the very existence of the city or *polis* itself.[8] The upshot of this narrative is, despite the obscurity of the images it employs, clear: the end of political leadership is inextricably an ethical end, an end which Socrates refers to as *dikaiosunê*, more or less accurately translated as 'justice'. Although this political teleology is in a sense axiomatic for Plato, he is aware that it has its detractors – represented most brilliantly in the dialogue by Thrasymachus (whose name means 'quick fighter'). Thrasymachus, like Machiavelli centuries later, finds Socrates' political teleology profoundly naïve, or 'very high-minded simplicity' (348c). Instead, he proposes what is, in effect, a proto-Machiavellian end to politics – what he calls 'the advantage of the stronger' (338c). He explicates this as follows: since what Socrates calls 'justice' reduces to law-abidingness, and since laws promote the 'the advantage of the established rule' (339a) – such rule being, by definition, the strongest power in the state – justice itself reduces to whatever is in the interests of state power.

No doubt one can question Thrasymachus' reduction of justice to legality, and of legality to the power-advantage of political rulers. But the issue he raises is a genuine one: What can Plato do to show that political leaders are bound to promote justice – construed as the *common* good – as opposed to their *own* power and 'glory' (to use Machiavelli's term)? Is there anything a philosopher, that is, as opposed to a mere moralist, can do to show that political leadership, properly understood, has a constitutive, ethical aim? The end of *Republic I* contains a series of arguments for this conclusion and, although of variable quality, I think they point in very fruitful directions. Socrates begins by asking whether rulers should always be obeyed, to which Thrasymachus responds in the affirmative, given his high doctrine of state power (339b). But on Thrasymachus' own premises, this is clearly too quick. As Socrates suggests, if the maintenance of established rule is one's overriding aim, then there are likely to be norms, or something approaching a craft – in Greek, a *technê* – of how to achieve that aim. And this is so *a fortiori* if the aim is not merely to preserve one's power, but to enhance it: after all, it is not as if power can be gained in any way – there must, it would seem, be ways of achieving it that are more propitious than others (what Grint would call the 'how' of leadership). But if one concedes this, then it follows that rulers can make mistakes: as Socrates puts matters, they are 'liable to error' (339c), and even by Thrasymachus' lights it would be wrong in every instance to obey them. In other words, if power per se is structured, and thus subject to the constraints of a *technê* or *technai* (crafts), the idea of a ruler with ineluctable power is a myth: even the most gifted political leader has to acknowledge that his dictates are defeasible, and liable to correction.

So far, so good – perhaps. At least Socrates has shown that Thrasymachus' initial assumption (or gambit?), namely that state law must conduce to state power, has been undermined. State power is conditioned, and actual laws may flout those conditions.[9] But all this demonstrates, I take it, is that leaders need to have a degree of humility, recognizing when they are wrong and being willing to accept correction.[10] As yet we have no reason to think their overall *telos* must be the common good, as Socrates supposes. It is this ambitious 'must', however, on which Socrates sets his sights in his second argument (*Republic* 341c–5d) – which, like his opening argument, draws heavily on analogies with the professions or 'crafts'. Essentially, Socrates' strategy is to confront Thrasymachus with various professions, and to ask him to specify their constitutive ends. As Thrasymachus acknowledges, medicine (for example) aims at the health of patients, navigation at the safe passage of sailors and ships and horse-breeding at producing well-bred horses. These are the constitutive *erga* or 'products' of their respective crafts. Having got this far, though, Socrates takes a step too far: he adjures Thrasymachus to concede that, in light of these examples, the '*technai* [are] by nature set over [their respective subjects] to seek and provide what is to their advantage' (341d). And he takes a corollary of this to be that 'no one in any position of rule, insofar as he is a ruler, seeks or orders what is advantageous to himself, but what is advantageous to his subjects' (342e). As Thrasymachus is quick to point out, this is a false induction. For as he neatly retorts, 'you don't even know about sheep and shepherds' (343a): shepherds may fatten their sheep and 'take care of them' (343b), but only with a view to their *own* good. And the same applies, he suggests, to political rulers – they 'think about their subjects [no] differently than one does about sheep' (343b).

It seems, then, that Socrates has failed to show that political leadership is directed essentially at the common good, and that Thrasymachus' reduction of it to gaining and maintaining power-advantage over others (or what he calls 'outdoing' them, *pleonektein*) is successful. Nonetheless, I think Socrates has managed to move the argument on, and valuably so. What he has shown is that just as the political leader is under certain cognitive constraints – he is not omniscient – he is also under certain practical constraints. Even if he wishes to rule unconstrainedly, he must at least beware of contravening the basic interests of his subjects, or offending them unduly. In terms of Thrasymachus' analogy, the well-being of the sheep sets limits to the shepherd's ambitions. For even if he wants to eat or sell them (ultimately), not only will they not tolerate such an end being publicized – on pain of rebellion – they will not be fit to eat or sell if they are treated in systematically harmful ways. Furthermore, the obverse of this point also plays into Socrates' hands. For if we grant that very few, if any, political leaders seek the utter immolation of their 'flocks' – how would that rationally conduce to their success or 'glory'? – it would seem that most, if not all of them must seek (most of the time) to keep most of their people in at least a reasonable state of well-being. (If this has the added dividend, moreover, of contributing to their leader's 'glory', then so be it: no discernible harm is done thereby.) The core point is, then, that those (so-called) leaders, like Nicolae Ceauşescu, who genuinely seek to profit and succeed and gain glory *at the direct expense* of their people, will not have an easy time of it. At best, they will continually have to suppress dissent, which in turn will threaten their peace of mind, and require their quasi-sequestration from others. At worst, they will find themselves trampled by their own sheep.[11]

To this line of argument there are three clear and immediate objections. First, by pitting the well-being of the populace against the power of Thrasymachean 'leaders', am I not assuming a false dichotomy? For aren't there other conceivable political ends, such as that of the obsessive, for instance, who devotes all the state's resources to removing right angles from buildings, with the upshot that many of his people starve? Or take the simply incompetent ruler, who despite his best intentions fails to secure even basic living standards for significant sections of his people. Surely these both constitute unjust forms of political rule, but ones that do not involve the deliberate pursuit of one's own power. To this objection I would concede that the 'advantage of the stronger', let alone the continual enhancement of one's political power, are only limiting cases of unjust political ends (and hence ones that preoccupy thinkers like Plato and Machiavelli). There are, demonstrably, other unjust political *telê* or outcomes of policy that – to the degree they conflict with the common good – thereby conflict with what I have called the constitutive end of political leadership. But it is not a necessary condition of such conflict that injustice be deliberately or consciously pursued. All that is necessary is that injustice be the systematic upshot of policy; to the degree it is, leadership, rightly understood, is under threat.

Second, it might be objected that the facts are against me. That is, the empirical record is replete with examples of 'leaders' who undermine the common good, yet at no serious cost to themselves (Robert Mugabe comes to mind). And if so, my hypothesis is disconfirmed, and strongly so. But the demand for empirical proof here is, I contend, misplaced, and shows a failure to attend to the gravamen of Socrates' argument. For as he contends further on in *Republic I*, what is salient is that the 'just person doesn't outdo [or "get the better of"] someone like himself but someone unlike himself, whereas an unjust person outdoes both like and unlike' (349c–d). In other words, the fundamental *tendency* of injustice is to seek ends irresponsibly and without sufficient regard to the good of others. It thereby tends to cause dissension and disharmony, and the more it is given free rein, the more it does so.[12] As Socrates notes, this is why bands of robbers find it hard to co-operate and achieve a common goal: 'injustice … [is] incapable of achieving anything as a unit, because of the civil wars and differences it creates … mak[ing] that unit an enemy to itself' (351e–2a). But to affirm this is not to commit oneself to determinate, empirical laws concerning exactly how and when various kinds of unjust 'leadership' will come undone. All one is committed to here is the inherent *nisus* of such leadership, which is towards disintegration and dissolution. It turns out, then, that Hitler's increasing tendency to isolate himself from and denigrate his advisers was (on my account) no accident (see n. 4). It bore witness to a personality bent on power without limit, which ultimately made him 'his own enemy, as well as the enemy of just people' (352a).

Third, it may be objected that even if the cognitive and practical constraints I've outlined are genuine, and hence have effect in the real world, they still add up to no more than *prudential* constraints on political leadership. What Socrates has not demonstrated is that such leadership is necessarily under *moral* constraints, or displays what I called an ethical constitutive end. And with this objection I would readily concur. But I would also deny it has devastating force. For the dichotomy between 'prudential' and 'moral' reasons is an artefact of post-Kantian moral philosophy: it has little resonance among ancient philosophers, and certainly not in Plato and Aristotle, who saw no great gap between happiness or well-being and the good. So I would counter this third objection by saying that the constraints I've outlined are both prudential *and* moral, and that positing any large or significant gap between the two is unjustified.

Plato and Aristotle on power and political leadership

What Plato discovered about political power, or rather helped discover – viz. that it must be subordinated to the common good, on pain of dissension and ultimate incoherence[13] (i.e. that it must become leadership) – Aristotle systematized. Drawing, like his teacher, on the model of the *technai*, Aristotle presents the *polis* as a vast structure of professions or crafts, at the summit of which is the craft of political rule (*hê politikê technê*). As he puts things at the start of the *Nicomachean Ethics*, political science is 'the most authoritative art … the master art … for it is this that ordains which of the sciences should be studied in a State[;] … since it legislates … what we are to do and what we are to abstain from, the end of this science must include those of the others, so that this end must be the good for man' (1094a26–b7). When Aristotle holds that political 'science' (or better, 'expertise') 'includes' the ends of medicine, navigation, generalship, etc., he does not mean that political leaders must be experts in all fields. What he means is that their job is specifically to co-ordinate activities in the state, with a view to the common good (the 'good for man') – a good that transcends and is not a function of those activities taken singly. It follows that *hê politikê technê* is both far more difficult and more crucial than any subordinate expertise – for while the variables involved are legion, their harmonious co-ordination is essential (and in a sense tantamount) to the good of all. As Aristotle comments, 'though it is worth while to attain the end merely for one man, it is more noble and godlike to attain it for a nation or for city-states' (1094b9–10).

Now there are two points I want to highlight on the basis of Aristotle's analysis, one positive and one critical. First, although political 'skill' is to a degree indeterminate,[14] owing to its vast subject matter, it is nonetheless structured and has constitutive norms. These norms are derived from the virtues it takes to establish and maintain a just, well-ordered and harmonious *polis*: virtues Aristotle spends most of the *Nicomachean Ethics* elaborating (such as courage, temperance and justice itself). By contrast, there is, despite how things may initially appear, no real art or skill of sheer power-seeking. Thrasymachus and Machiavelli proceed on the assumption there is, but ultimately, as I've suggested, this is an illusion (albeit a very glamorous one).[15] For in Plato's and Aristotle's terms, power per se has no *logos* or internal, rational structure: whereas the common good sets a limit (*horos* or *peras*) to political power, and shapes it in relatively determinate directions, power itself is essentially limitless, and thus liable to degenerate into a more or less arbitrary policy of self-assertion and wilfulness. Admittedly – and this brings me to my second point – this fact is often masked, at least for a time, by the way in which political 'leaders' can turn their wilfulness or power-urge outward, towards other states. The needs of war, in particular, have a certain determinacy and structure, and can lend power-seeking a good deal of coherence: one has only to think of Hitler's brutal and sustained assaults on surrounding nations. But ultimately the coherence bestowed on polities and their leaders by the external pursuit of power gives way: either they must come to terms, and work for a new, cosmopolitan common good, or give themselves up to permanent, internecine strife at the international level. Plato and Aristotle are guilty on this score, I take it, since they confine the common good to within the bounds of the *polis*, and even then only to certain of its members (the Stoics alone, in the ancient world, clearly saw the need for a cosmopolitan good). Nevertheless, the logic of their arguments points beyond these bounds, and in a way that Machiavellian power-politics wholly fails to register.

In sum, then, we have seen that, right at the start of the Western philosophical tradition, there are arguments which indicate why *politikoi* (political leaders) who devote themselves to power per se are flouting the constitutive end of their own practice or profession. They are, in effect, pseudo-leaders, seeking as an end something which is at best a mere means, the 'glory' of which properly and lastingly supervenes only on the common good. Having explored the *telos* of political leadership, I now want to tackle its methods. Can Plato and Aristotle help us think more clearly about whether there are any constitutive ethical limits on *how* political leaders pursue their ends? This question of means is a vital one, since it is faced by such leaders every day (even the most laudable ends can be pursued using unacceptable means).[16] In order to answer it, I will first investigate the state of the debate over 'dirty hands'.[17] At least since Machiavelli, philosophers have been drawn to the idea that political success, even if it doesn't properly *warrant* the use of immoral means, in some sense *requires* them. As I'll document, there is a spectrum of views here, from the hyper-Machiavellian to the minimally Machiavellian. But at whatever point on the spectrum such views fall, I shall argue there is more wisdom to be found by returning to the ancients.[18]

Three Machiavellian views of dirty hands

Michael Ignatieff stakes out a position at the hyper-Machiavellian end of the spectrum (see Ignatieff 2013). As he notes, it was Machiavelli's contention that 'when public necessity requires actions that private ethics and religious values might condemn as unjust and immoral', those actions should be taken. But Ignatieff goes further than Machiavelli, who, as Jacques Maritain points out, 'never calls evil good or good evil' (Maritain 1953: 139). For Ignatieff, 'evil deeds cease to be evil if urgent public interest makes them necessary'. Furthermore, because morally bad acts somehow become good under such conditions, Ignatieff infers – in the spirit of Machiavelli's 'brutal candour' – not only that 'politics demands dirty hands, but that politicians shouldn't care'. One might demur at the inconsistency here in maintaining both that some evil deeds cease to be evil, and that doing them nonetheless generates 'dirty hands' (whence the dirt? – this is an inconsistency I shall come back to). But in fact Ignatieff's position seems to be that, because the realm of politics (i.e. that of 'public necessity') is concerned with a supreme, overriding good – one he refers to as 'the health of the republic' – talk of 'dirty hands' in that realm is never more than 'moralizing claptrap'.

Ignatieff's view that 'dirty hands' are either clean, or not worth worrying about, is a philosophical outlier. But there are views which approximate it, notably Kai Nielsen's 'weak consequentialism' (Nielsen 1996: 1). Whereas 'strong consequentialism', Nielsen claims, commits one to maximizing benefit, his position merely denies 'absolutism', viz. the view that 'there can be ... *justified categorical denials of permission to act to avoid the lesser evil*' (ibid.: 3). On Nielsen's view, the 'right thing to do' can hence involve wrongs,[19] where these constitute the 'lesser evil' – but once factored into an 'everything considered' judgement about what to do, those wrongs cease to be action-guiding (ibid.: 2). What they generate instead is a psychological residue, in the form of remorse or feelings of guilt (ibid.: 1). Nielsen is keen to stress, however, that such feelings do not indicate *actual* guilt: since the action was to-be-done, and all-things-considered 'right' (he is a consequentialist), actual guilt is unwarranted. Our psychology nonetheless registers some degree of uncancelled – even if overridden – harm (ibid.: 6). And it is this psychological tendency we have, Nielsen remarks, that leads us to admire 'saints' or 'heroes', viz. those who – acting on 'supererogatory' norms (ibid.: 2) – try to avoid wrongdoing altogether, even when it amounts to the lesser evil. When it comes to how much 'evil' can be tolerated before it precludes action, Nielsen is vague. We should be 'morally conservative' on this front (ibid.: 2), he counsels, but still allow 'very considerable' evils (ibid.: 3), if need be – the final answer always depending on context, and likely proximate outcomes (ibid.: 6). We are left with the impression, then, of a theorist tempted by an Ignatieff-type dismissal of dirty hands, but who draws back in the face of residual moral psychological scruples. Whether these scruples are sufficient to separate his position substantially from Ignatieff's is, however, open to doubt.[20]

Curzer moves a step closer to affirming that political decision-making presents a conflict not just between ethical demands and our psychology, but between contradictory ethical demands. He holds that while action to save the polity from catastrophe can be 'admirable' and 'great' (echoing Ignatieff), it can simultaneously be 'morally repugnant' and a 'terrible thing' (Curzer 2006: 34–5). Unlike Nielsen, though, he does not confine this repugnancy and terribleness – of having to torture an innocent, say – to the realm of mere psychology. Rather, such descriptions capture the fact that torturing innocents is offensive to what Curzer calls 'virtue'. This stands in systematic contrast to 'duty', which correlates with what 'morality' demands, whereas virtue amounts to 'a sort of high-mindedness, a refined moral sensibility' (ibid.: 48).[21] As he summarizes his position, 'the act of refusing to torture is admirably immoral because it is a virtuous, morally wrong act. And the act of torturing is a case of dirty hands because it is a vicious, morally required act' (ibid.). So Curzer's position is ethically more hard-hitting than Nielsen's, since he understands our qualms about actions like torture as indicative of virtue, not merely some form of ingrained scruple. But equally, he wants to resist the further, and in his view unlicensed, claim that virtue is in a biconditional relation with moral duty. Far from it. According to Curzer, 'the dirtiness of torturing provides no evidence for the inconsistency of morality, since torturing and refusing are not conflicting duties. Torturing is required; refusing is just evidence of virtue' (ibid.). This clash between 'the dispositions of virtue and the demands of duty' (ibid.: 49) may spell a disturbing discontinuity between how we are habituated to act, and how we may be required to act. But for Curzer, this is a price worth paying. It simply reflects the (albeit rare) phenomenon of morally inescapable, yet vicious action.

Where Curzer sees a deep tension, but not a 'direct contradiction' (Curzer 2006: 48) between moral 'reason' and our 'habituated desires' (ibid.: 51), Michael Walzer sees straightforward inconsistency or incoherence _within_ our moral thinking. In his seminal paper 'Political Action: The Problem of Dirty Hands' (Walzer 1973), he argues that in the 'terrible competition for power and glory' (ibid.: 164), politicians are liable to and even inevitably involved in severe wrongdoing or 'moral crime' (ibid.: 167). In contrast to both Nielsen and Curzer, then, Walzer does not relegate our sense of wrongdoing to a mere inherited scruple or a sub-'moral' form of virtue: instead, that sense all too accurately reflects the moral facts. As Walzer puts matters, 'When [moral] rules are overridden, we do not talk or act as if they had been set aside, cancelled, or annulled. They still stand and have this much effect at least: that we know we have done something wrong even if what we have done was also the best thing to do on the whole in the circumstances' (ibid.: 171). Having conceded there is ineliminable wrongdoing in politics, Walzer nevertheless refuses to go down the Weberian path[22] of consigning political leaders to a tragic realm, in which there is an 'irreconcilable conflict' between the demands of their job and the 'god of love', making the loss of their 'souls' inevitable (ibid.: 177). Instead, he contends that they are under an obligation to do 'penance' (ibid.: 178) in some publicly recognizable way, and thereby expiate their transgression. It is not good enough, Walzer implies, to speak of political 'vice' (à la Curzer), or feelings of 'remorse' (à la Nielsen), if these have no upshots in action. Rather, when the _politikos_ transgresses, he or she should be punished, and the more severely the severer his or her crime. Only paying this 'price' (ibid.: 180), Walzer concludes, fits the gravity of dirty hands.[23]

We have seen, then, a range of post-Machiavellian responses to the problem of dirty hands. From Ignatieff's hyper-Machiavellianism all the way to Walzer's minimal Machiavellianism, most modern philosophers who address the problem end up affirming the need for political leaders sometimes to transgress ethical norms in pursuit of their goals. It is probably also true that most of these philosophers take positions at the Walzerian end of the spectrum. Bernard Williams, for instance, although he eschews Walzer's moral gravitas in favour of more Oxonian language – he speaks of politics as an arena of the 'morally disagreeable' or 'unpalatable' (Williams 1978: 55, 59) – agrees with Walzer that political wrongdoing leaves behind 'uncancelled' harm (ibid.: 63), which must at least be 'explained' (ibid.: 61) to those wronged. Even Raimond Gaita, despite his 'absolute conception' of good and evil, believes that political leaders must do evil to protect their communities against threat. It is just that, according to him, this 'necessity' does not entail or constitute justification for such evil (Gaita 1991: 260). We are left, he concludes, in the unenviable position of having to acknowledge, whether we like it or not, that political hands always have been and always will be dirtied (ibid.: 262).[24] Notwithstanding the austere and disillusioned tone adopted here, I suggest we are still very much on the Machiavellian side of the debate. Is there anything pre-modern philosophers can do to extricate us from it? Or is this modern consensus on the inevitability of dirty hands inescapable?

Plato and Aristotle on dirty hands

What is striking about Plato's and Aristotle's approach to the problem is precisely that they don't approach it explicitly.[25] As is evident from Plato's city-soul analogy in the *Republic* (434d–49a), and the ethical training programme he devises for the city's guardians, he makes no strong distinction between 'public' and 'private' ethics. Indeed, *êthos* in Greek just means 'character', and there is no word cognate with our 'moral' (where this is opposed to 'political'). Granted, 'practical wisdom' (*phronêsis*) is, as Aristotle claims, more 'noble and godlike' when it operates at a political – rather than merely individual – level (*Nicomachean Ethics* 1094b9–10), and no doubt there is need (as Plato saw) for some kind of training peculiar to *politikoi*. But there is no real difference in *kind* between political and non-political applications of *phronêsis*.[26] Furthermore, there is no solid evidence that either Plato or Aristotle concedes the need, ethical or otherwise, for political leaders to engage in actions that are 'evil' (in Gaita's terminology), or have 'important moral costs' (to use Michael Stocker's phrase; see Stocker 1990: 18). While it is clear that Socrates countenances (rather than recommends) the use of a 'noble falsehood' (*Republic* 414b–5d) – viz. the 'myth of the metals' – to bolster his hierarchical conception of a just society, it is doubtful whether Plato considered such deception deeply vicious or absolutely forbidden, at least if entered into rarely and for good reason.[27] Furthermore, the cases usually cited to show that Aristotle accepts the inevitability of dirty hands are unconvincing (*pace* Stocker 1990, Ch. 3; Curzer 2005). First of all, they do not address the decision-making of *politikoi* as such: throwing goods overboard in a storm (*Nicomachean Ethics* 1110a9–11), committing a 'base' act to save one's family from death at the hands of a tyrant (ibid.: 1110a4–7) and Alcmaeon's matricide (ibid.: 1110a25–9) are not treated as specifically political acts. And second, none of these 'mixed' (voluntary-cum-involuntary) acts conform to clear dirty hands criteria.[28]

Are we to conclude, then, that neither Plato nor Aristotle has anything to contribute to the dirty hands debate, the outcome of which is key to determining the moral standing of political leaders? Are we just dealing with philosophers who inhabited far smaller, technologically less advanced *poleis*, and hence failed to see that the demands on leadership in large-scale modern States are different in kind? This would be far too quick. To begin with, their view that – although the virtues are sometimes expressed differently in the family sphere (say) and the sphere of 'grand politics' – ethical and political theory are essentially continuous with each other, forming a coherent whole, is instructive. It alerts us to the fact that Machiavellianism, of whatever stripe, helps itself far too quickly to a distinction between private and public political norms. For instance, Reinhold Niebuhr speaks of 'irreconcilable elements in the two types of morality, internal and external, individual and social' (Niebuhr 1932: 258), and of 'personal morality' or 'individual ideals' as opposed to the 'needs of an adequate political strategy' (ibid.: 273). Isaiah Berlin declares that 'There are two worlds, that of personal morality and that of public organization. There are two ethical codes, both ultimate' (Berlin 1997: 54). And Stuart Hampshire's edited volume is entitled *Public and Private Morality*.[29] But the salient question to ask here is: Where exactly are the boundaries between private and public norms, and how are they determined? If there is a clearly delineated sphere of 'family' norms (let us suppose), how should we classify the norms that apply to a school's parent–teacher association? Or those that govern the decision-making of a local authority district? Are these private, public or a mixture of the two? Given the grave consequences of how one answers these questions, it is not sufficient merely to point out that there are clear cases of public political decision-making, leaving 'borderline' cases until later. Those living under (for example) a particular local authority, whose lives or livelihoods depend upon the justice of its decisions, will not take this as an adequate response.[30]

Our thinking about dirty hands can also be helped by reflection on Plato's and Aristotle's political teleology. As I outlined, they both take it that the constitutive aim of political leadership is the common good, even if they have differing conceptions of this. As Aristotle puts matters, 'governments that have a regard to the common interest are constituted in accordance with strict principles of justice, and are therefore true forms. But those that regard the interest only of the rulers are all defective and perverted forms, for they are despotic; whereas a State is a community of freemen' (*Politics* 1279a18–21). This pits Plato and Aristotle against the Machiavellian view that political leaders properly aim at their 'own' power and glory (even if these are constituted by the power and glory of the state). But it is a corollary of the latter view that dirty hands are inevitable, since the *telos* Machiavelli posits for politics simply cannot be achieved without them. It is interesting to note, then, how even minimal Machiavellians assume – rather than argue for – something like the Florentine's political teleology. Walzer, for example, avers that political leaders are necessarily involved in the 'terrible competition for power and glory' (Walzer 1973: 164), a sentiment echoed (albeit more gingerly) by Weber, who describes such leaders as 'ventur[ing] to lay hands on the spokes of the wheel of history' (Weber 1978: 212). But it remains unclear why one should endorse such sentiments. Thomas More, for one, did not: Writing in 1516, only a couple of years after the appearance of Machiavelli's *The Prince*, his character Raphael Hythloday holds that 'princes ... are generally more set on acquiring new kingdoms by hook or crook than on governing well those they already have' (More 1989: 14). Yet he does not infer from this that they *must* have this aim, as if subject to some kind of 'necessity'. Contrast, once again, Walzer, who asserts that, when it comes to governing political communities, political leaders find themselves under 'the rule of necessity' (Walzer 1977: 254). But this resurrection of the Greek notion of *moira*, 'fate', remains under-explicated and under-defended. While Aristotle recognizes the existence of 'force', *bia*, and its capacity to coerce agents – as when a wind blows one off-course (*Nicomachean Ethics* 1110a1–3) – he finds no application for the concept of *moira*.[31]

To this it might be responded that there is indeed a kind of necessity – viz. moral or political – which operates when political leaders are faced with (to take Walzer's modern example (Walzer 1973: 166–7)) an imminent terrorist attack. In such cases they *must* dirty their hands – not in order to achieve power or glory, but rather because the protection of an overwhelming good is at stake. But at this juncture the following question presses: Are there any bad actions that are so bad they are absolutely prohibited, however good their (supposed) consequences? Although Aristotle says far too little on this topic, he does make a start: he affirms there are types of action it is never right to do (*Nicomachean Ethics* 1107a9–26), of which one, as we have seen, is matricide.[32] But when it comes to those who argue for the inevitability of dirty hands, there is either merely an *assumption* that any act can be required, if the (often imagined, or stipulated) stakes are high enough, or an otherwise unconvincing argument for this. Curzer, for example, argues that any distinction between wrongs – e.g. 'evil' and 'non-evil' ones – is 'arbitrary', since good consequences can outweigh any wrong (Curzer 2006: 39). But this is odd, since there seems a clear difference between the disvalue of (e.g.) throwing out goods in a storm, and that of matricide. Nielsen refuses to be drawn on the issue, maintaining that a 'lesser evil' must be 'very considerable' before it becomes unthinkable (Nielsen 1996: 3). It is unclear, however, whether his consequentialist framework really permits the notion of absolutely prohibited acts in the first place. And several philosophers, perhaps following Weber, gesture at the idea that some forms of 'violence' or 'force' are the most intolerable aspects of political action[33] – but it remains obscure which forms might be straightforwardly impermissible.

Concluding thoughts

In general, and as Tony Coady puts it, it seems that 'much of the point of invoking dirty hands comes from an ambiguous attitude to absolute moral prohibitions, combining a rejection of them with a certain wistful attachment to their flavour' (Coady 2014: Preface). But as we've seen, what this 'wistful attachment' actually leads to is incoherence: it leads to Curzer's contrast, for instance, between what 'morality' demands and a 'refined moral sensibility' (Curzer 2006: 48), to Nielsen's claim that those who resist dirtying their hands fail to do the right thing, but are nonetheless 'saints' or 'heroes' (Nielsen 1996: 2), and to Ignatieff's view that evil can become good, yet nonetheless generate 'dirt' (Ignatieff 2013). Unless the ascriptions of refinement and sainthood and dirt here are wholly ironic, we are up against theories that are enmired in and struggling with inconsistency. In order to overcome this inconsistency, it is not good enough to pass the buck on to the 'world' or 'reality', which several philosophers we have looked at refer to as itself 'messy', or even 'evil'.[34] Instead, what is necessary is to get one's *philosophical* hands 'dirty' (in a good sense), by carefully exploring various options that neo-Machiavellian philosophers tend to ignore, or deprecate. Gaita, for example, dismisses the distinction between the 'intended and unintended consequences' of political action (Gaita 1991: 257; cf. Nagel 1979: 60–1), perhaps in reaction to misuses of 'double effect' reasoning to justify (e.g.) the use of the atomic bomb. But he, among others, should be more attentive to inmates of the Nazi death camps, many of whom later claimed that political leaders would have been thoroughly justified in bombing those camps, even at the expense of their own lives. And Gaita, once again, should take seriously Alan Donagan's argument that torture can, at least in cases where a person is 'deliberately allowing innocent persons to be killed and mutilated by withholding his knowledge', be unequivocally justified.[35] For in short, if double effect reasoning and Donagan's argument are cogent, they would erase large swathes of 'dirt' that neo-Machiavellians view as clinging ineluctably to political leaders' hands.

In conclusion, I hope I have shown how debates about the ends and means of political leadership can benefit from a renewed look at ancient philosophy, especially that of Plato and Aristotle. Although it is too much to hope that current political leaders will practise politics in the sense of genuine *politikê technê* – it is far more likely that most of them will draw on Grint's pseudo-'arts of leadership', which float free of the common good – I hope, nonetheless, to have made some headway in showing that this *technê* is both desirable and possible. If so, the way lies open for political leaders not only to avoid Weber's tragic realm, but also to reaffirm their vocation as a truly honourable one: one in which they can pursue their proper end, namely justice, and without inevitable transgression along the way.

Notes

1   See, for instance, Sun Tzu 2008.
2   See Grint 2010 and Grint 2000. Recent books with 'leadership' in their title
     are too numerous to mention, and concentrate overwhelmingly – despite the
     non-specificity of their titles – on business leadership.

3   I use this term in preference to 'followers', since the latter implies a strict
      dichotomy between leader and led of which Grint is critical.

4   Grint makes the argument that Hitler displayed the advantages and disadvantages
      of charisma *par excellence* (see Grint 2000: Ch. 8). On the one hand, he could
      inspire his subordinates to 'work towards him' (318–22), thereby achieving initial
      military success with a series of lightning attacks (336, 340). But in the longer
      term, he proved incapable of working with others, arrogating all law-making
      powers to himself (316), ditching cabinet meetings (328) and refusing to listen to
      military advice (336, 342).

5   While Grint affirms some notion of 'fairness', he appears to relativize it to culture:
      'fairness is only an appropriate criterion for judging leaders in contexts that are
      culturally associated with fairness' (Grint 2010: 70). Note also his emphasis on
      'constructing' identities: the implication is that the 'strategic vision' of leaders need
      not incorporate any substantive, predetermined ethical goals.

6   Something Grint appears to deny, when he speaks of 'the necessarily grubby
      compromises of power' (Grint 2000: 311). This suggests he believes political
      leaders inevitably have 'dirty hands'.

7   See, especially, *Republic* books II–IV.

8   See *Republic* 514–21.

9   A good example might be Margaret Thatcher's Poll Tax laws, which inspired
      a nationwide revolt, severely undermining her authority and that of her
      government.

10   As Grint agrees: see his notion above of the 'martial art' of leadership.

11   A misleading aspect of Thrasymachus' analogy is that people, especially under
      modern conditions, tend to be less ill-informed and docile than sheep.

12   Cf. Jacques Maritain: 'justice and righteousness *tend by themselves* to the
      preservation of states, and to … real *success* at long range … injustice and evil
      tend by themselves to the destruction of states, and to … real *failure* at long range'
      (Maritain 1953: 154).

13   Note Socrates' words to Thrasymachus: 'unjust men … would never have been
      able to keep their hands off each other if they were completely unjust … for those
      who are all bad and completely unjust are completely incapable of accomplishing
      anything' (*Republic* 353c).

14   As Aristotle notes, 'We must be content … in speaking of such subjects and
      with such premises to indicate the truth roughly and in outline, and in speaking
      about things that are only for the most part true and with premises of the
      same kind to reach conclusions that are no better' (1094b19–22). Grint also
      acknowledges that leadership is a relatively 'indeterminate skill' (see Grint 2000:
      419).

15   Hence the misleadingness of the view that there is or could be a *technê* of power.

I granted this above, when explicating Socrates' first argument, but this was *pro tempore* and for dialectical purposes only.

16 The Allied bombing towards the end of World War II is often taken to be a limiting case of this. Although the Allies' goal was above reproach – viz. the elimination of the Nazi and Japanese régimes – the destruction of Dresden and the use of the atomic bomb (to name only the worst cases) were, arguably, a means too far.

17 A metaphor used by Sartre in his play *Les Mains Sales* (Sartre 1989). Walzer (1973) drew on this metaphor in discussing the problem of legitimate political means, and the label has stuck.

18 In some respects only, I should add. I shall not be defending strictly hierarchical class structures (à la Plato) or Aristotle's arguments for slavery as essential to the common good.

19 Sometimes Nielsen, following W. D. Ross, speaks of these as '*prima facie* wrongs' (Nielsen 1996: 5) – thereby indicating a certain shakiness about how to characterize so-called 'necessary evils'.

20 This is so especially since the scruples in question are not action-guiding, and do not, according to Nielsen, track the moral truth.

21 For the moment, I'll leave the occurrence of 'moral' on both sides of this contrast to one side.

22 See Weber 1978.

23 Like Walzer, Stephen de Wijze thinks political leaders can be under a duty to do wrong, which when done should lead to 'tragic-remorse' (De Wijze 2005: 463). But he also thinks that, even when such remorse is accompanied by forms of reparation, 'in some cases, no amount of restitution or atonement can fully alleviate the guilt and shame or remove the moral stain' (ibid.: 465). Walzer seems more sanguine on this score, given his talk not just of fitting punishments, but also of their constituting *expiation* (Walzer 1973: 178). Still, it may be that, ultimately, he agrees with de Wijze.

24 Whether this ostensibly purely descriptive approach to dirty hands is fully honest is doubtful. Gaita goes on to say that governments have the responsibility to 'do evil' out of 'loyalty to the conditions of political communality' (Gaita 1991: 262–3). This invocation of a virtue, viz. loyalty, undermines Gaita's earlier denial that 'necessary evil' can be justified. In short, where Curzer talks of political wrongdoing being justified by moral duty, Gaita implies it is justified by moral virtue – despite his claims to the contrary.

25 It does not follow that their ethical-cum-political theories have nothing to contribute to the debate: far from it, as I'll argue below.

26 This is borne out by the fact that Aristotle views his political treatises as the 'completion' of his ethical treatises (see *Nicomachean Ethics* 1181b14–15), not as

introducing a new or rival genus of wisdom. The *politikos* simply is the *phronimos* (man of practical wisdom), but one who applies the virtues constitutive of *phronêsis* at the political level.

27   As I'll come back to, the notion that lying is absolutely forbidden is an artefact of later, mediaeval philosophy. See, for example, Aquinas 2006, II–II, question 110, article 3.

28   Aristotle maintains that although there are contexts that 'overstrain' human nature – plausibly, e.g. the tyrant case – submitting to such pressures is at best forgivable, never praiseworthy or justified. Matricide, he holds, can never be excused: even death must be chosen in preference to it. And throwing goods overboard in a storm is viewed by him (wholly reasonably) not as a serious offence.

29   It should be noted, however, that Hampshire himself denies any absolute distinction between these supposed types of morality (see Hampshire 1978: 52).

30   I would reiterate here that there are aspects of a political leader's life that do clearly distinguish it from other lives: e.g. the degree to which such leaders wield influence, and set precedents for the future (if the lawyer does both of these, the *politikos* does so on a far larger scale). But this simply indicates that political leaders need to be far *more* careful about the ethical contours of their lives than most of us.

31   Beyond non-veridical poetic contexts, that is.

32   Interestingly, lying is not on the list, as it is for Aquinas. It may well be that the mediaeval scholastic discussion of absolute prohibitions has dissuaded modern philosophers from taking them seriously. It is worth noting here that an advantage of the ancients' focus on virtue, rather than moral laws, is that it becomes possible to engage in (e.g.) unjust, cowardly or intemperate action, at least on occasion and to some minimal degree, without thereby becoming (respectively) unjust, cowardly or intemperate oneself.

33   See Weber 1978: 217, 221–2; Niebuhr 1932: 233; Hampshire 1978: 49; Williams 1978: 71; Ignatieff 2013.

34   De Wijze, for instance, writes that 'inescapable moral wrongdoing' is 'a pervasive and important aspect of our moral reality' (De Wijze 2005: 469; cf. Nagel 1979: 74), a view implied also by his later claim that 'sometimes our ethical lives can be complex, messy and difficult. And from this there can be no escape' (De Wijze 2012: 895). Cf. Coady 2008.

35   See Donagan 1977: 188. For Gaita's hasty dismissal of his argument, see Gaita (1991: 257–8). It should be noted that Donagan argues, further, that torture should nevertheless be *outlawed*, not because it is intrinsically evil, but on grounds of its likely proliferation (and hence use in inappropriate cases).

Bibliography

Aquinas, T. (2006), *Summa Theologiae* (ed. T. Gilby). Cambridge: Cambridge University Press.

Aristotle (2002), *Nicomachean Ethics: Translation, Introduction, Commentary* (ed. S. Broadie and C. Rowe). Oxford: Oxford University Press.

Berlin, I. (1997), 'The Originality of Machiavelli', in *Against the Current: Essays in the History of Ideas*. London: Pimlico Press, pp. 25–79.

Coady, C. A. J. (2008), *Messy Morality: The Challenge of Politics*. Oxford: Oxford University Press.

—(2014), 'The Problem of Dirty Hands', in *Stanford Encyclopedia of Philosophy*. Available at http://plato.stanford.edu/entries/dirty-hands

Curzer, H. J. (2005), 'How good people do bad things: Aristotle on the Misdeeds of the Virtuous'. *Oxford Studies in Ancient Philosophy*, 28 (1): 233–56.

—(2006), 'Admirable immorality, dirty hands, ticking bombs, and torturing innocents'. *The Southern Journal of Philosophy*, XLIV: 31–55.

De Wijze, S. (2005), 'Tragic-remorse – the anguish of dirty hands'. *Ethical Theory and Moral Practice*, 7 (5): 453–71.

—(2012), 'Punishing "dirty hands" – three justifications'. *Ethical Theory and Moral Practice*, 16 (4): 879–97.

Donagan, A. (1977), *The Theory of Morality*. Chicago: University of Chicago Press.

Gaita, R. (1991), *Good and Evil: An Absolute Conception*. London: Routledge.

Grint, K. (2000), *The Arts of Leadership*. Oxford: Oxford University Press.

—(2010), *Leadership: A Very Short Introduction*. Oxford: Oxford University Press.

Hampshire, S. (ed.) (1978), 'Public and Private Morality', in *Public and Private Morality*. Cambridge: Cambridge University Press, pp. 23–53.

Ignatieff, M. (2013), 'Machiavelli was Right', in *The Atlantic*, December edition. Available at http://www.theatlantic.com/magazine/archive/2013/12/machiavelli-was-right/354672

Machiavelli, N. (2008), *The Prince* (trans. Peter Bondanella). Oxford: Oxford University Press.

Maritain, J. (1953), 'The End of Machiavellianism', in J. Maritain (ed.), *The Range of Reason*. London: Geoffrey Bles, pp. 134–64.

More, T. (1989), *Utopia*. Cambridge: Cambridge University Press.

Nagel, T. (1979), 'War and Massacre', in *Mortal Questions*. Cambridge: Cambridge University Press, pp. 53–74.

Niebuhr, R. (1932), *Moral Man and Immoral Society*. New York: Charles Scribner's Sons.

Nielsen, K. (1996), 'There is no dilemma of dirty hands'. *South African Journal of Philosophy*, 15 (1): 1–7.

Sartre, J.–P. (1989), *No Exit and Three Other Plays*. New York: Vintage International.

Stocker, M. (1990), *Plural and Conflicting Values*. Oxford: Clarendon Press.

Sun Tzu (2008), *The Art of War* (trans. J. Minford). London: Penguin Classics.

Walzer, M. (1973), 'Political action: The problem of dirty hands'. *Philosophy and Public Affairs*, 2 (2): 160–80.

—(1977), *Just and Unjust Wars: A Moral Argument with Historical Illustrations*. New York: Basic Books.

Weber, M. (1978), 'Politics as a Vocation', in W. G. Runciman (ed.), *Weber: Selections in Translation* (trans. E. Matthews). Cambridge: Cambridge University Press, pp. 212–25.

Williams, B. A. O. (1978), 'Politics and Moral Character', in S. Hampshire (ed.), *Public and Private Morality*. Cambridge: Cambridge University Press, pp. 55–73.

2

Rulers, Moralities and Leadership

Anna Moltchanova
Carleton College

This chapter defines leadership and ethical leadership from the perspective of social ontology, which studies the basic structures and constitutive elements of social reality. In particular it looks at how individuals function as members of groups. At times, individuals may not be in sync with the group, which then appears to have a life independent of individual members. Or, they may enthusiastically join together in advancing shared group goals. This highlights that individuals can relate to group actions organized by those deemed leaders in different modes. The chapter argues that not all of these modes allow individuals to be influenced by leadership, let alone ethical leadership.

The definition the chapter provides applies to all kinds of leadership – that among friends or members of other informal groups, when the positions of leaders and followers can be exchanged among members, or that in more structured groups like businesses or political societies in which those who can potentially become leaders often have an institutionally higher rank or elected position. Writers usually focus on institutionally based leadership, but social ontology focuses on what kind of influence relation, involving individuals functioning as members of groups, leadership is. Hence, the notion can apply to small groups and include both institutionalized and non-institutionalized modes of interaction.

I define leadership as an influence relation that shapes individual motivation in action in a certain way: the actions of individuals are motivated by group goals associated with the project they share, and this happens in part because they perceive themselves to be members of the relevant group. Thus, leadership motivates individuals to act based on group purposes that they share as members of the group. Leaders may influence followers in a variety of ways: they may take initiative in identifying or formulating group goals, finding innovative ways to achieve the existing goals and direct the followers' behaviour by inspiring them to act, and so on. In all cases of leadership, leaders are able to convince their followers that they have shared goals and/or the shared goals should be their reason for action.

My view of leadership addresses a widespread confusion about the relation of ethics and leadership, when 'leadership' is equated with 'ethical leadership'. I agree with Jacqueline Boaks and Michael Levine that ethics and leadership do not have an intrinsic connection.[1] My definition of leadership, focusing on leaders being able to motivate the followers to act based on what they perceive as shared goals, allows that leadership may not necessarily aim at ethical or good outcomes: there are many examples of leaders rallying dedicated followers behind pernicious aims or potentially mistreating the followers. A political and military leader can inspire the followers to harm others, or a business leader can increase the followers' performance but by inspiring them to sacrifice some of their autonomy, and so on.[2] Moreover, there can be cases of relationships that are not leadership (like power or authority). My account allows these to be identified and distinguished.

Social ontology considers individuals as not isolated but encumbered selves and provides a nuanced view of autonomy that helps to evaluate whether leadership is ethical.

As far as ethical leadership is concerned, the social-ontological view is not about the good character of a leader or a follower, but about a good kind of relation between them and within the group as far as some basic moral norms are concerned. Leadership is ethical when, in addition to inspiring individuals to promote mutually shared goals, this influence relation does not diminish these individuals' autonomy. Finally, leadership is ethical when, in addition, the achievement of the shared goals it promotes does not interfere with the autonomy of non-members, both individuals and groups, provided non-members do not forfeit their right to self-determination.

Not all types of individual actions in advancing the goals of the group are characteristic of either leadership or ethical leadership. I will now clarify how leadership relates to other kinds of influence relations, such as power or authority. Both leadership and ethical leadership can be instances or aspects of formal authority, business management or some other influence relationship, but the latter notions cover much broader social phenomena that do not always function either as leadership or ethical leadership. For example, stopping for a stop sign is an act of routine obedience of the rules promoted by the corresponding formal authority. However, if a local community starts a campaign 'come to a complete stop and proudly honk', to increase public safety, stopping because of being motivated by the campaign goals may constitute an instance of being influenced by the leadership of those who started the campaign. This requires that the follower recognize the goals of the campaign as those of the community and oneself as a member of the community. Or, projects like contributing to a war effort lead by a country's chief executives may mobilize individuals around what they perceive as a common goal as members of their society; the individuals then would be motivated by their membership and the desire to achieve the common goal. Since they are inspired to act by the way their formal authority relates to them, this influence relation would constitute an instance of leadership influence. Thus, societal mobilization to achieve a shared goal articulated by those in elected positions could become a case of leadership influence and not merely an exercise of legitimate authority in routine modes of functioning under the rule of law. Many other important social processes that involve changes to the way the society functions, like the introduction by leaders of new policies such as universal health care, or organizing a nation-building effort, definitely stand out as involving leadership.

Authority and power have many contested definitions, but for the purposes of this chapter I will use Robert Paul Wolff's notion that defines authority as having the right to command and be obeyed.[3] In contrast, he defines power as the ability to compel compliance, but power is not authority, because there is no corresponding right to command: a gunman has the power to extort money but has no authority to do so. On some views of power, it can be considered as capable of having instances of leadership, but the notion of power used in this chapter doesn't allow this usage.[4]

It should be noted that in many instances, authority, influence and management are not leadership, because individual actions are not motivated by being group members and by group goals associated with the project they share. For example, a pupil in a school can be motivated to do well for her own sake and perceive her teacher as authority; if the teacher succeeds in motivating the pupils to learn because they have a shared goal of learning as a community, the teacher becomes a leader (while remaining being a representative of authority). Thus, the ability to articulate shared group goals and motivate individuals to act because they are group members makes a leader. As I mentioned, there may be many cases of leadership that are not ethical leadership if individual autonomy is not properly preserved in actions motivated by group goals or if the group acts unethically with respect to others. Sometimes a perfectly ethical authority is not leadership: individuals acting under the rule of law in a democratic country live under an ethical authority, but most of the time they are not motivated in their compliance with the rules by the desire to achieve specific mutually shared group goals.

Leadership then is an influence relation that organizes a group's functioning (even friends constitute a group, a very small one) in a certain way, and there can be instances or periods in the existence of formal authority, management or any influence in general when these modes of interaction involve the relation of leadership.

A typical critic of defining leadership as a relation distinct from power is a Machiavellian sceptic, who would consider leadership to be the opportunity to seize power and who would deny that leadership might be limited by normative constraints. However, leadership requires being motivated by shared goals, power doesn't. Moreover, we can grant the critic that leadership does not necessarily motivate followers to achieve good goals or it can influence the followers in unethical ways: ethical goals and modes of influence are only required for ethical leadership, but leadership is still distinct from power.[5] We can also grant the Machiavellian critic that leaders may not necessarily be morally virtuous. My view does not focus on whether group members are individually morally virtuous (some morally virtuous people fail to lead), but instead on whether they stand in an appropriate relation to group goals and on whether this relation safeguards the autonomy of participants and those who are not group members. Hence, my account pays attention to the mode of interaction of leaders and followers, based on how individuals relate to the group goals they help engender. It separates power from leadership and leadership from ethical leadership on this basis. The definition is descriptive; however, we can apply an ethical norm for the assessment of the interactions of group members. I use the norm accepted as foundational by most ethical theorists – the value of individual autonomy to determine whether leadership is ethical.

Preliminaries

My social-ontological definition applies to leadership in various kinds of groups, but it would be helpful, in order to situate it with respect to existing literature and show that the philosophical view I present is not unrelated to debates in other disciplines, to start with a brief overview of one very common genre of such literature offered by Joanne B. Ciulla: the literature on organizational leadership. She presents how the focus in defining leadership changed throughout the twenieth century from what looks mostly like managerial power to what we would now more likely refer to as leadership.[6] Looking at her review I identify the elements that have been recurrently involved, albeit in different functional roles, in defining leadership regardless of the features of leadership the definitions highlighted.

Definitions of organizational leadership changed significantly throughout the twentieth century. Older notions of effective leadership, like those from the 1920s, emphasize that leaders are both empowered to lead and responsible for achieving group goals, but they concentrate on a leader's ability to impress their will on those led and induce obedience, respect, loyalty and co-operation. In the 1930s, leadership is viewed as a process in which the activities of many are organized to move in a specific direction by one. This appears to be more managerial power than leadership, because the definition says nothing about the motivation of the followers. In the 1960s leadership is most commonly viewed as acts of a person that influence other persons in a shared direction. While the type of influence is not specified, the shared direction is a new development that introduces the perspective of the followers in the definition. But even in the 1980s, when the notion of leadership introduces the notion of inspiration – another new development with respect to the status of the followers – it emphasizes that the followers are inspired to undertake some form of purposeful action as determined by the leader.[7]

The end-of-the-century definitions, like Joseph Rost's definition from the 1990s, are more likely to reflect the followers' perspective on the actions under-taken in the process of leadership and indicate the goals as shared, which doesn't exclude the goals being generated with the followers' help: 'leadership is an influence relationship between leaders and followers who intend real changes that reflect their mutual purposes.'[8]

All of these definitions indicate that thinking about leadership involves a group goal of which all members are aware, and that the members also know that their joint action or their participation is a means to achieve the goal by which they are motivated. How the goal is set and in which way individuals are motivated in acting to achieve it are different in different definitions (for example, the origin of the shared goal changes from having been set by the leader who acts in a managerial style to being established through a more collaborative method and based on the shared perspective of all group members). My definition states that the influence relation of leadership happens when individuals are motivated by the shared goal and do not consider their actions as being based on purely individual goals. Individuals identify with the group in the members' joint effort to achieve the shared goal. The leadership relation is ethical if the autonomy of the followers is respected and the group follows moral norms in actions affecting non-members. This rules out, for example, toxic and despotic leadership. I will say more about this later in the chapter. Given the history of definitions and the focus of my own, I am now going to consider the standing individuals may have with respect to shared group goals.

Individuals and group goals

It is non-controversial that individuals do not always endorse group goals that they help to promote. The problem of influence over autonomous human beings is demonstrated well by philosophical anarchists. I will consider how social ontology can shed light on the problem of autonomy posed by Wolff. He is talking about authority in general, but looking at his discussion and identifying what his view overlooks helps me explain how leadership is viewed from the point of view of social ontology.

Wolff considers autonomy as the ability to choose and be responsible, which involves one's knowledge of motives and outcomes. Autonomous individuals must decide to obey an authoritative command for themselves – not because of the authority the command rests on:[9] '[t]he autonomous man ... may do what another tells him, but not *because* he has been told to do it.'[10] For the autonomous man there are no commands – that commands are expected to be obeyed is a fact to be taken in his deliberations of how to behave.[11] Wolff gives an example of obeying a captain on a sinking ship not because of his authority but because of the consideration that not obeying will be generally harmful. In what he viewed as a conflict between authority and autonomy he saw one's primary obligation to be to one's autonomy. The mode of functioning Wolff envisions for individuals is very different from being motivated in actions due to group membership and by agreeing with group goals for the group's sake.

Wolff's picture of autonomy is based on looking at persons as essentially solitary and unencumbered agents. However, it seems more true to the nature of how individuals are in social environments to consider persons as essentially social and their autonomy as not exclusively individualistic. Wolff's conflict between authority and autonomy comes with a rigid perception of individuals opposed to the system of social influences, instead of seeing individuals as being an integral part, willingly or unwillingly, of how this system functions.

Social ontology takes group membership into consideration; thus, reconciling individual and group actions is not a problem on my account.

Wolff concludes that individuals only follow rules autonomously when they, from their individual perspective, accept that the course of action prescribed by the rules is the right way to proceed in the circumstances. Wolff's individuals may preserve their autonomy even if they decide that it is right for them to join an organization that binds their future autonomy, like an army. By deciding that joining is the right way to proceed for them, the individual consents to the rules of engagement, unless the orders issued in accordance with the rules of engagement are blatantly against the principles or some major legal rules that the individual endorses. Before joining, the individual may want to assure themselves that there is an exit clause for cases like these. This individual also needs to be aware that they will be bound by the agreement. The awareness of the outcome and an exit clause make this individual self-governing rather than just obeying authority in following the rules.

Wolff's view of autonomy, a paradigm of an individualistic view, illustrates how viewing individual motivation in action as never shaped by group goals is problematic. His claim about individual autonomy is important, but there are more nuanced ways of looking at how individual autonomy relates to group rules and goals. Wolff ignores some ways in which the presence of collective environments motivates individual actions. These modes of functioning are important for ethical leadership. Wolff would say that individuals should not follow rules because they are issued by the authority, but act based on their judgement of what they perceive as beneficial for them in the circumstances. There are also cases, however, when individuals follow rules because they perceive themselves not as individual and isolated selves but as group members whose duty it is to follow the group's rules.[12] It may appear that these individuals may act out of self-interest, but I clarify below how their motivation in action is different, and that we are indeed faced with two different modes of functioning for individuals, one based on their self-interest as an isolated self, the other based on their self-interest as a member of a group.

For example, it is a common experience that friends can influence each other but if we consider friends only as a group of individuals each of whom is acting based on self-interest, one's friends would not amount to more than just part of one's calculation of what is beneficial in terms of self-interest. This is contrary to how we think of friendship. We do things *because* our friends have asked us and because we think that we are their friends.

I will now consider various views on individual motivations and autonomy that social ontology offers which challenge the exclusively individualistic view of the self. This will clarify how different kinds of motivation work and shed light on the nature of leadership.

There is a range of motivations individuals can have in joint actions. Consider two individuals playing a board game: they both intend to play and, acting on their intentions, they are jointly playing the game.[13] It could happen, very much in line with Wolff's view of individual motivation, that one of the joint actors is a reluctant co-operator, because she depends on her partner in an affair unrelated to the game. She may hate playing the game but nonetheless intend to co-operate in playing it with her partner. Thus, they both seem to work towards a shared goal, but at least one partner's motivation in action, although she intends to play the game, is not to promote the shared goal of game-playing, but her personal goal. She also wouldn't think there is a 'we', a mini-group above the two interacting individuals. In the examples of friendship below, we will see that joint actions and corresponding motivations can include other varieties of co-operation and individual motivation. An individual can co-ordinate an activity with her partner because she likes and wants to accommodate the partner, but there can in addition be the sense of the 'we' that shares this goal. The specific issues of leadership connected to this are that there are different modes of individual functioning – as a self in relation to others and as part of the 'we'.

Let us start with leadership in friendship to consider cases of the different degree of association individuals experience with collective persons in being motivated by shared goals. When leadership exists among friends, it is a relationship in which most people take turns in being leaders and followers.

Friendship is the relation in which friends share and shape each other's thoughts, feelings and lives.[14] To show how friends can influence and motivate each other, Bennett Helm introduces the idea of plural agents (which can be understood as a mini-version of a group agent). Such an agent includes individual agents that are accountable to other members of their group to act, care and feel on behalf of the group, as *one of us*.[15] In this way, group members can lead each other, in turn, in common projects, because they have shared goals. In addition to goodwill, which leads friends to modify their individual evaluations to accommodate each other, friends can interact at a higher level, by sharing a joint perspective. This means that when members constituting a plural agent deliberate, there is no competition among individual evaluative perspectives. Even if each friend has a slightly different idea of group aims, there is only one evaluative perspective from which they attempt to come up with a decision for shared reasons. When one member tries to impose a personal view, it is an abuse of the joint evaluative perspective.[16] Thus, each friend cares about the other *and* has an affection for, and commitment to, the plural agent; each friend identifies her or himself as part of this agent.[17] Some friends, usually close friends, in addition to shared projects, may have a joint conception of the kind of life worth their living together and so have, in this sense, a joint identity as a plural person, not just plural agent. These friends exercise *joint autonomy*.[18] In both cases, of plural agents with joint perspectives on shared goals and of plural persons with joint perspectives on the notion of the good, if one friend influences the other in terms of the maintenance of, or changes to, the plural agent's goals or the plural person's values, that friend is a leader because she articulates the changes in group goals and inspires the other to follow.

Some theorists, Marylin Friedman in particular, raised concerns about viewing friends as plural agents, because one friend's autonomy can be violated when friendship is viewed through the lens of the plural agent/person. For example, she criticizes Robert Nozick, who advances this view but with respect to love, that one friend's autonomy can be violated by the other, because the other friend may shape the plural agent's or person's perspective to his or her own advantage.[19] Thus, a balance of influence that allows both friends to exercise autonomy when being motivated to achieve the shared goals of the plural 'we' corresponds to the influence mode of ethical leadership in friendship. Each friend's autonomy is shaped and exercised in the interrelation of the friends' selves, and a proper autonomy-conferring manner of behaviour is only possible through being able to question, doubt, defend one's position, imagine alternatives, and so on, as an equal.[20] Since each friend self-identifies in friendship as part of the plural agent or person, their autonomy is shaped in this relation. A submissive friend may be led by his or her counterpart not in an ethical way. If the dominant friend diminishes the other friend's autonomy, they are not equals any longer. Their friendship is not virtuous and is not ethical. If one friend is more competent in a certain area and the other entrusts decisions to her in a manner that preserves the autonomy of both, the less competent friend's autonomy is not diminished, but exercised. This is why social ontology helps in defining ethical leadership – it doesn't exclusively concentrate on individual people but on the balance of their autonomies in their relation. Thus, asymmetry is fine as long as there is no autonomy violation.

Larger group agents and individual actions

First, let us define group agents that include more than two or several friends. Larger groups that I will discuss later in this chapter, political communities and businesses, can be defined as Peter French does, as collectives with an institutional organization and a decision procedure that are capable of purposeful action over time and have identity over time independent of particular membership.[21] In a corporation, for example, even if the personal reasons for voting that executives have are inconsistent with the established corporate policy, the corporation can be properly described as having done something: its decision structure *incorporates* intentions and acts of various biological persons into a corporate decision.[22] However, collectives may have nothing as formal as institutional organization: a national group without a state or a family may be two examples. A view that accommodates groups organized to various degrees is put forward by Raimo Tuomela. He states that a social group exists when the members of the group respect and promote the norms, practices and traditions of the group.[23] For example, even if members of a family disagree with each other on values, there may still be value in being a family with other corresponding shared beliefs and practices (a dysfunctional family may not be a group agent). Tuomela's idea of group agents includes a range of groups, directed by or functioning as the result of power, formal authority or management. Some instances of leadership are possible if a group functions in the right kind of mode, with the followers motivated to act by the group goals they share.

When groups persist, this comes about through joint actions of their members, but individual participants can adopt a range of attitudes to their participation. In joint actions that maintain a group, as Tuomela highlights, individual agents can act as group members or as private persons. Acting in the latter mode excludes performing the same action as a group member. Individuals act recurrently as group members if the group's goals give them motivating reasons for action. In this case, an individual believes that her actions will promote the ethos of the group and she is motivated to act by this knowledge.[24] The individual can be motivated by dangerous or toxic leadership to act as a group member, so there is no normative element to being a group member. The shared goals and values can be evil and unpalatable, and this is why considering group actions with respect to the normative notion of autonomy of members and non-members is important in identifying when leadership is ethical.

An agent is acting in a different mode – not as a group member but as a private person – when she finds it rational to co-operate in promoting the ethos of the group and accordingly co-operates, but is motivated to act by private reasons and may not accept the group reasons for actions as applying to her.[25] A group member whose values clash with the goals that the group pursues or the way in which the group functions in achieving these goals but who follows group rules may be acting in this mode. A Muslim teacher prohibited from wearing a headscarf at work may co-operate based on her self-interest in keeping her job. In Wolff's terms, her action is autonomous, because she reasons that not wearing the scarf is the best course of action for her. Hence, the teacher is not motivated by the group's aims if the majority's interests are formulated so that they cannot in principle be translated into the regulations that can accommodate her religious beliefs.

It is precisely the problem with an individualistic view of autonomy that it leads to the conclusion that there is no coercion in how her behaviour is shaped by society. With a more complex view of autonomy that social ontology offers, it is not the case – the person cannot in principle act as a group member in following the rule: their actions are self-guided in the wrong way for them to stand in relation to the group that can be described as fully preserving their autonomy in following the directives of authority. Thus, the authority does not engage them via the influence relation of ethical leadership. Moreover, provided it may be difficult for the teacher to be motivated by the goal of 'no religious expression in the workplace', she cannot at all be guided in her behaviour by the influence relation of leadership in attaining this goal, although she is guided by the state's formal authority or school management. Therefore, the view of individual motivation in group actions from the point of view of social ontology shows that there is more nuance to group inclusion as far as leadership is concerned than the individualistic approach to autonomy allows us to discern. Not all motivations in actions meant to achieve group goals position group members as followers in the influence relationship of leadership, let alone ethical leadership. They have to be motivated by group goals and their actions should not diminish their own autonomy and the autonomy of other members as well as non-members.

Summing up, leadership allows followers to act by being motivated by shared group goals as members of the group; if this mode is not available to the followers, there is no leadership, although individuals can still be influenced in other ways.

In the rest of the chapter I will consider in more detail the features of ethical leadership. The main features of ethical leadership I will look at in more detail below are:

(1) Leadership is ethical when an influence process motivates the followers to act based on the shared group goals in joint actions that bring about the outcomes, but it also allows the followers to preserve their autonomy ('group spirit and individual autonomy'), which includes that (2) leadership is not based on deception or manipulation to motivate the followers' actions, which would undermine or diminish their autonomy ('non-manipulation/non-deception') and (3) since the pursuit of group goals by group agents cannot be considered in isolation from their effects on non-members, the achievement of the shared goals motivated by leadership does not interfere with the autonomy of non-members, both individual and groups, provided non-members do not forfeit their right to self-determination ('ethical group').

In order to present in more detail the meaning of ethical leadership I will limit my consideration, for the reasons of space, to two areas of leadership, that of elected political leaders and of organizational leaders in business. Nevertheless, these areas lend themselves well to represent the defining features of the influence relationship that turns mere authority or management into ethical leadership.

The three features of ethical leadership

Group spirit and individual autonomy

Autonomy and ethics

That the preservation of individual autonomy when individuals are motivated to act based on group goals is important for ethical leadership presupposes that individual autonomy, or self-government, is important. So far I have offered a descriptive view of the modes of individual motivation in an action of achieving group goals, with acting as a group member motivated by shared group goals being constitutive of the influence relation of leadership. I will now briefly present reasons why autonomy is a foundational ethical notion to evaluate the character of leadership.

Most ethical theories connect individual autonomy to their notion of what is ethical, or at least in defining what relationships and actions are ethical. The idea of autonomy (that we have some capacity to set and pursue ends in a way that other creatures do not) figures centrally in Immanuel Kant's theory[26] and the subsequent Kantian accounts (for example, Christine Korsgaard's)[27] of why humans have dignity and why certain kinds of action (lying, coercion, and so on) are at least presumptively impermissible. Many consequentialists follow John Stuart Mill in taking something like autonomy, 'individuality' or 'self-direction' to be a fundamental constituent of well-being.[28] Thus, many actions will be wrong to the extent that they compromise autonomy (and so well-being). Something like autonomy figures centrally in neo-Aristotelian approaches to ethics, like Martha Nussbaum's.[29] One of the essential human capabilities worth promoting has to do with having the ability to form and pursue one's conception of the good, which grounds duties in others to respect this ability so long as their pursuit does not get in the way of other people's pursuits.[30] Thus, making the preservation of individual autonomy in group actions a requirement for a relation of leadership to be ethical is based on a foundational notion in ethics.

I will consider below how Plato's design of the ideal city limits the exercise of individual autonomy by conditioning, deception and a restriction of choices, although individuals are motivated by group goals set out for them by the rulers. I interpret his ideal city is an instance of leadership but not ethical leadership. I will then consider how actions towards non-members should be limited by autonomy for leadership to be ethical. In the rest of this section I will concentrate on the first feature of ethical leadership, and consider how individual autonomy relates to group goals in political and business environments.

Minorities and group values

The care of the followers with various views of the good is especially important for ethical political leadership to preserve the autonomy of all members. For example, an instance of Nelson Mandela's leadership in nation-building efforts involved the inclusion of a symbol important to the formerly dominant and unjust minority. His attention to the white minority's investment in the game of rugby helped to foster a better understanding between the minority and majority in the emerging 'rainbow nation' and increase the chances that the minority would be motivated by the nation-building goals and co-operate as citizens who share the nation with the majority.[31]

If a minority member (an immigrant, for example) is not happy with a rule or directive because it excludes or ignores her world view, and tries to voice her disagreement, the group needs to be careful in the evaluation of the validity of her claims. If this evaluation involves the perspective that presupposes that the minority member's values are unacceptable in public discourse or the reasons she is giving are deemed inadmissible in the public sphere, the rules of engagement make it difficult for the minority member to contest the rule or directive. Having no influence over the rule and disagreeing with its essence, she will have a hard time being motivated to follow it as a member of the group.

If a minority cannot be motivated by a group goal as members of the group, they will not be engaged by the related leadership relation altogether; or, if a minority member is motivated by the shared group goal that conflicts with her religion, her actions in accordance with this goal may hinder the promotion of her autonomy (as the formation and pursuit of one's conception of the good) and thus her engagement as a follower in the relation of leadership will not make for an ethical leadership. A similar situation could happen to some members born into a culture, such as anarchists, based on their political beliefs.

Hence, one of the challenges to leadership in dealing with minorities in a liberal-democratic society comes when some of a minority's values, practices and beliefs that they cannot give up clash with how the majority culture expresses liberal values. To enable proper membership and exercise of autonomy for minority members, if the conditions for their full inclusion are in principle attainable with reasonable modifications of the majority's ethos, they should be pursued.[32]

Business environments

Both political and business environments involve an authority's directives that carry penalties for non-compliance, although superiors in a business are most often not elected, and not seen as representing 'the will of the employees'. As political superiors can motivate the followers to act by the goals they promote, in the business sphere some managerial actions can have the same influence on the followers and thus also count as leadership. In addition, an ethical business leader not only motivates the followers to act based on the shared goals, but also feels accountable for interfering with the followers' views of good life and autonomy.

One crucial difference between the two spheres is that organizational superiors in a business have the power to decide the status of their employees, with respect to the continuation of their inclusion in the group. While an employee can sometimes be fired, by contrast, citizens can hardly ever be stripped of citizenship. Some may think that the very talk of business leadership is misguided: the threat of being fired or denied a promotion or pay raise if one does not please the boss excludes a truly free following of a superior as a leader. Even if following a business superior's instructions is not about 'pleasing the boss' but instead about doing one's job, this is likely to be done as a private person.

This is why we should say that only when the employees' reasons for following are motivated by the goals of the group action could the business superior be called their leader. An employee motivated to the greatest possible degree by the group goals while working to achieve these goals and at the same time being able to preserve their autonomy (on any definition of the term, as the capacity to set and pursue personal ends, or as self-direction, or as the formation and pursuit of one's conception of the good as far as their professional self-fulfillment goes) is a worthy ideal. The ethical mode of leadership in business has to do with the removal, as much as possible, of barriers to the participation of the followers in this mode. (I will explain in the next section that leadership can influence participants to pursue evil goals as members of the group and aim to safeguard their autonomy within the group, but that won't be ethical leadership.)

Research in business ethics identifies many forms of leadership that are positively influencing leaders, followers and their organizations, such as ethical leadership, authentic leadership, servant leadership, transformational leadership, and so on.[33] These contemporary views on leadership consider good leadership as the art of building and sustaining social and moral relationships between leaders and followers as well as everyone affected by their business activity. This leadership is based on a sense of recognition, a sense of care and a sense of accountability for a wide range of economic, ecological, social, political and human responsibilities.[34] However, while new forms of leadership seem to increase the chance of individuals being motivated by the shared goals as members of the relevant group, they come with the threat of the erosion of individual autonomy and thus can make leadership unethical. For example, transformational leaders influence their followers by developing and communicating a collective vision and inspiring them to look beyond self-interests for the good of the team and organization. Burns thinks that real transformational leadership takes place only if ethical aspirations of the participants are enhanced.[35] While the leaders may be able to influence the values of the followers, there is a danger to the followers' autonomy that needs to be taken into consideration. Being the influence relation that pushes the followers to look beyond self-interest, transformational leadership inspires them to act as group members, motivated by shared group goals. Nevertheless, while transformational leaders put their followers' needs above their own and emphasize the importance of moral consequences in key decisions,[36] this influence relationship can also diminish the autonomy of the followers because the close relations of care and inspirational self-sacrifice it fosters may alter the traditional boundaries of the self demanded by autonomy (which are based on individuality, personal interests and self-direction in formulating one's conception of the good). For example, the followers may feel pressured to pay less attention to their individual career goals when they act in the workplace.[37]

In contrast to transformational leadership, what is called in business ethics literature 'transactional leadership' influences followers by controlling their functioning through rewards of agreed-upon behaviours and corrective transactions applied to what those in charge regard as problem-ridden performance. This mode of influence does not qualify as leadership on my definition, because it would most likely make it impossible for the followers to be motivated by shared group goals as group members instead of just being motivated by personal interests as private persons. However, retreating to this mode of functioning safeguards the followers' sense of individual autonomy, which means that they are aware when their autonomy is impinged on.

Thus transformational leadership can be contrary to ethical leadership because it interferes with the followers' autonomy, but the style of management that is called 'transactional leadership' most of the time does not qualify for leadership. The transactional style is more likely to prevent individuals from being motivated in actions by shared group goals, but the transformational style encourages group-oriented motivation in achieving group goals by potentially diminishing the individuals' concern for their individual goals, which is not always good, or putting pressure on them to sacrifice their preferences to group interests, which may result in unethical leadership.

In order to avoid the violation of rights of the followers based on the diminishment of their will to attend to their own interests, a combined approach that is careful to introduce the new features of virtuousness, care, compassionate support and inspiration in the notion of leadership, but safeguard the transactional basis of interactions, will do best to engender ethical leadership. The essential elements of the transactional style of management ('leadership') are founded on the notion of rational and fair exchange between separate and autonomous individuals.[38] A mechanism of 'rational exchange' based on self-interest should be available for the rejection of the inspirational proposals of transformational leaders so that a follower, being motivated by the goals of the group, does not end up doing what is not promoting her own good. It should be noted that the shared group goals individuals promote might be unethical. I will deal with unethical group goals below.

There may be many strategies that would allow the followers to own their actions in the right mode, in which they can preserve their autonomy while being motivated by group goals. For example, having a process in which the followers can assess how their personal goals are fulfilled in group actions, where they stand in relation to shared group goals, would be helpful. This can involve creating a table in which the same actions are planned and evaluated both from the perspective of being a member of the group, and from the perspective of one's self-direction with respect to their job in advancing their conception of the good.

In the next two sections I will consider some modes of influence the leaders may not employ and the external goals groups may not pursue if their leadership is to remain ethical. The corresponding main features of ethical leadership that I described above are the second and third, 'non-manipulation/non-deception' and 'ethical group'.

Non-manipulation/non-deception

In the previous section we saw that some types of leadership raise questions about the modes of influence on the followers that can be considered ethical. In continuing talking about ethical modes of influence, I would like to discuss Plato's ideal city for which, according to my view of leadership, he did design a leadership scheme, but not an ethical leadership scheme.[39] This has to do with the methods his rulers employ to influence citizens. I will discuss how manipulation and deception diminish the followers' autonomy and are, therefore, contrary to ethical leadership.

Plato advocates rigorous conditioning of citizens narrowly tailored for the occupational positions into which they were placed by philosopher-kings. The rulers also limit citizens' access to knowledge beyond what is required for performing their jobs. Thus, Plato's societal design explicitly limits individual choices and reasoning and therefore their capacity to self-govern in society.

The wills of the citizens are directed at promoting the good of the whole. All citizens are taught to love the city that they share with their 'brothers'. Plato designs the city so that, due to their conditioning and circumstances, individuals have enough motivation as members of the group to do what they are assigned (the rulers place them into the occupations that, in the rulers' view, the citizens are ideally suited to do). The city overall is just, due to its balance: ideally, everyone does what they have to willingly and they do not imagine having any other goals in life and do not meddle into the affairs of other strata. However, it also seems that the wills of the lower strata, the producing class, are not really their own. Self-governance for Plato includes the use of reason and the lower strata, which he does not consider capable of fully developed rationality, cannot self-govern and need to be directed and conditioned from the outside, by those with the exercise of reason. Hence, the lower strata are not considered capable of autonomy as based on individuality, personal interests and self-direction in formulating one's conception of the good. This anachronistic introduction of the contemporary notion of autonomy into Plato's city shows that his leadership is not ethical, according to my definition: Plato's citizens are motivated to act for the good of the group as its members, but Plato's rulers cannot be considered as exercising ethical leadership over the lower strata because their autonomy is thwarted, in part by deception and educational manipulation. Plato's lower strata are deceived by a strategically designed myth concerning the origin of the division of labor (citizens are brothers, but all naturally have a different kind of metal in them, which assigns them to a different rank)[40] and by strict censorship of the information accessible to them. The myth that Plato formulates to be taught to the citizens and to which philosopher-kings can resort when administratively expedient is designed to keep citizens in place.[41]

My use of the *Republic* to demonstrate leadership that is not ethical may be contentious (Plato himself would think that the rulers are ethical, for example). However, there are a number of scholars who would consider Plato as not caring for the lower strata's autonomy.[42] C. C. W. Taylor agrees with Gregory Vlastos that Plato's theory is paternalist, and that to maintain it Plato needs to show that an adequate conception of a good life need not include any substantial measure of autonomy, but Plato makes no attempt to do so and even shows no sign of an awareness of the problem.[43] Gorman Beauchamp argues that since the ordinary citizens of the Republic can never know for themselves what is right or wrong (the rulers inculcate in the citizens 'correct' beliefs that serve to promote the stability of the state, not knowledge), their proper civic duty becomes unquestioning obedience to the philosopher-kings, which is a complete lack of autonomy.[44] The knowledge they are deprived of requires the practice of defending one's views. The discernment of the true meaning of things, or the world of Forms, in this manner is the activity only accessible to the higher strata.

Plato's citizens are motivated to act in such a way that philosopher-kings can be considered as exercising leadership in ruling their ideal city-state. Nevertheless, philosopher-kings are not ethical leaders because this motivation by collective goals as group members is the only mode in which citizens act:

they have no will separate from the good of the whole. Philosopher-kings hold the city together by eliminating the possibility of the followers' exercise of autonomy through strict conditioning, lies and the curtailment of choice.

The presence of deception or manipulation diminishes the followers' autonomy and thus excludes the influence relation from being ethical leadership. Mobilizing followers to act for the benefit of the group based on lies and manipulation curtails their autonomy because they cannot envision and assess their choices. As C. A. J. Coady points out, dishonesty is a form of injustice that is injuring the right of the followers to the truth (because knowing the truth is for their own good).[45] Generally speaking, not everyone always has the right to be told the truth, like a criminal inquiring about the whereabouts of the innocent victim hidden in your house (because committing the intended crime is not in the criminal's interest and her right to know the truth is trumped by the right of the victim to self-defense). However, group members who advance group goals that the rulers put forward definitely have the right to learn about the truth behind the goals of the group agency they are bringing about through their actions, otherwise they are not treated as autonomous individuals but just as a means to the achievement of the rulers' ends.

It seems that state secrets related to security may be an exception: for example, leaders may face moral dilemmas about delaying the release of information because it may harm citizens. But those will still be moral dilemmas – it is wrong for the rulers, all things being equal, to manipulate, deceive or be paternalistic towards citizens.[46] Hence, there may be some cases when the well-being of the followers would require deception temporarily, but it does not make deception a moral course of action. The citizens may agree to a set of rules that would allow the rulers, in extreme circumstances, to use deception, but also have checks and balances in place to limit the degree and duration of the leaders' prerogative. In other words, there has to be a clear and promulgated set of rules that guides the rulers' behaviour in such situations, ideally democratically accepted by citizens. In this way, their autonomy wouldn't be undermined.

Even in a business setting where the management may have increased access to information and understand it better, they would not be able to stand in the influence relation that qualifies as ethical leadership if they withhold appropriately adjusted information from their employees or deceive them about the goals and the standing of their organization.

Since ethical leadership enables the followers to be motivated by shared goals in a way that preserves their autonomy, and deception and manipulation diminish autonomy, ethical leadership would involve an unforced functioning of well-informed individuals. Thus, ethical leadership requires restrictions on the methods by which the participation of followers can be encouraged, and does not admit manipulation and deception.

Ethical group

Yet even if individuals are motivated to act by the goals of the group and the group leadership respects the autonomy of group members exercised within the group setting, the leadership may remain unethical. The fact that individuals share beliefs about the interests of their collectives and are motivated to act based on these shared beliefs does not fix the character of those interests. A certain state of affairs, the achievement of which the members of a collective perceive to be in its interest and around which they willingly mobilize, may be objectively *bad* for them, like waging an unjust war. The autonomy of group members is diminished if their actions bring about something objectively bad for them. Thus, the relationship of leadership in this case is not ethical. Mick Fryer emphasizes that a leader can even be altruistic with respect to the followers, but organize the group to harm those considered outsiders, sometimes members of other religions or nations.[47] The relation of leadership that brings about unethical outcomes implicates the followers who are motivated as members of the group in realizing group goals even if they themselves are treated well. This relationship of leadership is not ethical.

For example, a group of school bullies can be motivated by their leaders to achieve shared goals of humiliating their victims. Under the leadership of bullies within the pack, the joint value defining the kind of life they perceive as worth living together, as a group or a plural person, is based on their not caring about the worth of non-members. The bullies' friendship based on their mutual worth as bully-friends turns their mutual influence relation into leadership that is not ethical. The notion of 'good' leadership needs to include that leadership may not be aimed at ethically bad ends.

Leadership of groups waging wars of aggression is not ethical; even in a war of self-defence, some actions may not be motivated by ethical leadership. Michael Walzer argues that Britain's earlier bombings of German cities in World War II could be justified as self-defence in the face of supreme emergency,[48] but bombings later in the war were not justifiable in the same way. The same leadership that united a nation behind them in the war effort was within the doctrine of Just War and thus ethical in its bombing campaigns at the beginning of the war, but it stopped being ethical because of the treatment of non-members unmitigated by self-defence later in the war.

In groups larger than several school bully-friends, the bulk of care for the proper group standing with respect to non-members falls to the de facto group leaders. One may say that since the leaders organize the followers to express and implement their shared conception of group interests, they may not be in a position to know better than the followers. However, it seems that in decisions that leaders are both empowered and given responsibility to make on behalf of the group, their duty, as of those in charge, is to assess whether the group is heading in an ethically wrong direction (especially when, in a state of emergency, they, and not the public, have better access to information). So in the bombings in the later part of WWII the leaders were in a position to foresee that, in the absence of supreme emergency, the use of force at such a huge scale was excessive.

Groups normally assert their entitlement to various protections and privileges in relation to non-members. A group could claim a right not to be dominated or terrorized or otherwise wrongly treated by other group agents. For example, in international law, the right to self-determination protects the sovereignty of national groups over their affairs. Businesses are governed by market rules that equally apply to all similar groups and regulate their relation to consumers, each other and the environment, both economic and natural. By violating the rights of others, groups violate the very ethical and legal principles they want upheld in relation to them. It is inconsistent to justify their own demands of others by the norms they do not respect in their own behaviour.

Thus when leadership motivates members to act in ways that are harmful to non-members, it is not ethical, in part because of the character of the action and in part because the followers' moral standing and autonomy are compromised through partaking, as members of the group, in achieving a goal that is objectively not good for the group. So a national group's authorities can mobilize their population in a nationalistic mode to oppress, drive out or attack other national groups, and this act will constitute leadership, but not ethical leadership. Or, superiors in a business that motivate their followers to pursue projects that end up polluting the environment or motivate them to participate in practices that can negatively affect the economy can be called leaders but not ethical leaders, even if their leadership with respect to the followers and their autonomy within the group is impeccable. To practice ethical leadership, business superiors should focus their leadership practices not only on maximizing shareholders' wealth but also on the well-being of everyone whose interests are affected by the functioning of the business, including those outside of the group. In this way, they can help the followers self-actualize through their work and, as group members, respect the interests of all affected by their business activity.[49]

Conclusion

In this chapter, I explored the notion of ethical leadership from the perspective of social ontology and demonstrated that, in order to express the meaning of ethical leadership, the classic way of looking at willing co-operation needs to be qualified to highlight individual motivations for acting in accordance with the shared group goals and the preservation of individual autonomy in these actions.

While leadership requires that the followers be able to be motivated to act as group members in realizing shared group goals, the ethical modes of leadership ensure that the followers are not manipulated or deceived into acting this way and in general are not prevented from exercising autonomy. Ethical leaders also care about the influence of the group in their charge on non-members and take the enlarged view of the consequences of the group actions to include non-members and the parts of the environment that the group's activities impact into consideration.

Notes

1   Levine, M. and J. Levine (2014). 'What Does Ethics Have to do with Leadership?' *Journal of Business Ethics* 124(2): 225–42.

2   On pernicious kinds of leadership see: Newman, Levine and Cox 2009. The authors provide a psychoanalytic account of unethical leadership. For example, they give an explanation of how leaders can manipulate whole groups into accepting such defence mechanisms as projection or ego-defence to justify harmful actions towards non-members.

3   Wolff 1970: 4.

4   Two approaches to power are defining it as 'power-over' and 'power-to'. Robert Dahl's view of 'power-over' is that 'A has power over B to the extent that he can get B to do something that B would not otherwise do' (Dahl 1957). Hanna Pitkin notes 'that power is a something – anything – which makes or renders somebody able to do, capable of doing something. Power is capacity, potential, ability, or wherewithal' (Pitkin 1972: 276). In this sense, power-to can also belong to those

who are not ruling others. If power-over and power-to are balanced in group relations, there potentially can be a leadership relation, but it would not happen on the more common definition of power I use in this paper.

5   Boaks and Levine, 229.

6   For a summary of various definitions, see Ciulla 1998: 11.

7   Ciulla, 11.

8   Rost 1991.

9   Wolff argues that although men accede to the claims of supreme authority as a matter of fact, it is not obvious that they *ought to* accede. He points out that among most ancient demonstrations of the authority of the rulers is 'Plato's assertion that men should submit to the authority of those with superior knowledge, wisdom, and insight', (Wolff 1970: 16) and thus they are not autonomous.

10 Wolff, 14.

11 Wolff, 15.

12 This perspective may not be excluded by Wolff's account of action, but he never spells it out.

13 Here is a more technical way to describe an instance of joint intention: A intends that A and B do X together (say, play a board game); B intends that A and B play the board game together; A intends this because both A and B intend to play together and their subplans mesh; the same applies to B; each other's intentions and reasons for those are common knowledge among them. Acting on their intentions, A and B are jointly playing the game (Bratman 1993).

14 Helm 2009: 255.

15 Ibid., 267.

16 Helm 2008: 47–8.

17 Helm 2009: 275.

18 Ibid., 286.

19 Friedman 1998: 169–72.

20 Ibid., 169.

21 French 1984: 13.

22 French 1979: 207, 211, 214.

23 This list may also include, in some cases, the group's constitutive goals, values, beliefs and standards. See Tuomela 2007a: 182.

24 As Tuomela would put it, she acts in the we-mode. Tuomela 2007a: 92.

25 In this case, according to Tuomela, the agent is thinking and acting in the pro-group I-mode. Tuomela 2007b: 244.

26 Kant 1902: 400.

27 Korsgaard 1996: 120–1.

28 Mill 2002: 46–62.

29   Nussbaum 2006: 76–8.

30   I would like to thank Daniel Groll for a very helpful discussion of autonomy and ethics.

31   Carlin 2009.

32   I discussed strategies for accommodation of immigrant minorities in detail in Moltchanova 2011: 132–52.

33   Toor and Ofori 2009: 533–47.

34   Cameron 2011: 25–35.

35   Burns 1978: 20

36   Simola, Barling and Turner 2012: 229–37.

37   Sen Sendjaya highlights that transformational leaders' effects are more emotional than rational. For example, Lee Iacocca exhibited an inspiring, engaging and confident style of transformational leadership that helped to turn Chrysler Corporation around, but his willingness to promote ethical organizational decision-making was lacking. (Sendjaya 2005: 77).

38   Simola, Barling and Turner 2012: 231.

39   Plato 1981.

40   Ibid., Book III, 414d–15c.

41   Beauchamp 2007: 289. Beauchamp emphasizes that other types of utopias are also often governed based on deception and oppression. 'We are told that the electric fences in Walden Two, that keep the sheep enclosed, are meant as only a temporary measure; once the sheep (revealing synecdoche!) have internalized the limits, the fences can come down. But when they are taken down—the sheep escape. Despite all the equivalents of electric fences in *Utopia*, More appears to suspect, were they down, his sheep, too, would escape. Thus the fences stay up and the current stays on in Utopia, always and for everyone.'

42   I would like to thank Sarah Jansen for her very helpful discussion of different readings of Plato.

43   Taylor 1995: 295.

44   Beauchamp, 285.

45   Coady 2008: 106.

46   On the tension between morality and politics, and a good discussion on the permissibility of hypocrisy when a larger and justifiable goal is in mind, see Grant 1999: 2: '"Doing the right thing" may require compromise ... deception, or ethical posturing, or both; some forms of hypocrisy may be perfectly acceptable or even laudable".'

47   Fryer 2011: 18. Fryer gives Hitler as an example of a potentially altruistic leader whose leadership was the opposite of ethical. Ciulla (1998: 13) disagrees on Hitler as a leader.

48   Walzer 1976: 255–62.

49 This mirrors a broadly Aristotelian view (of leadership as a master virtue) that Boaks and Levine outline in their paper. The features of an ethical business leader that Mick Fryer identifies are a great example of how this is accomplished in organizational leadership. Fryer 2011: 194–203.

Bibliography

Beauchamp, G. (2007), 'Imperfect men in perfect societies: human nature in Utopia'. *Philosophy and Literature*, 31: 280–93, 289

Bratman, M. (1993), 'Shared intention'. *Ethics,* 104 (1): 97–113.

Burns, J. (1978) *Leadership.* New York: Harper & Row, p. 20.

Cameron, K. (2011), 'Responsible leadership as virtuous leadership'. *Journal of Business Ethics*, 98: 25–35.

Carlin, J. (2009), *Playing the Enemy: Nelson Mandela and the Game that Made the Nation.* New York: Penguin Books.

Ciulla, J. B. (1998), 'Leadership Ethics: Mapping the Territory', in J. Ciulla (ed.), *Ethics, the Heart of Leadership.* Westport, CT: Quorum Books, pp. 3–25, 11.

Coady, C. A. J. (2008), *Messy Morality: The Challenge of Politics.* Oxford: Clarendon Press, p. 106.

Dahl, R. (1957), 'The concept of power', *Behavioral Science,* 2: 201–15, 202–3.

French, P. (1984), *Collective and Corporate Responsibility.* New York: Columbia University Press, p. 13.

—(1979), 'The corporation as a moral person'. *American Philosophical Quarterly,* 16: 207–15, 207, 211, 214.

Friedman, M. (1998), 'Romantic love and personal autonomy', *Midwest Studies in Philosophy,* XXII: 162–81, 169–72.

Fryer, M. (2011), *Ethics and Organizational Leadership: Developing a Normative Model.* Oxford: Oxford University Press, p. 18.

Grant, R. (1999), *Hypocrisy and Integrity.* Chicago: University of Chicago Press.

Helm, B. (2008), 'Plural agents'. *Nous,* 42 (1): 17–49, 47–8.

—(2009), *Love, Friendship and the Self: Intimacy, Identification and the Social Nature of Persons.* Oxford: Oxford University Press, p. 255.

Kant, I. (1902), 'Groundwork for the Metaphysics of Morals', in *Immanuel Kants Schriften. Ausgabe der königlich preussischen Akademie der Wissenschaften,* vol. 4. Berlin: W. de Gruyter, p. 400.

Korsgaard, C. (1996), *The Sources of Normativity* (O. O'Neill, ed.). New York: Cambridge University Press, pp. 120–1.

Levine, M. and J. Levine (2014). 'What Does Ethics Have to do with Leadership?' *Journal of Business Ethics* 124 (2): 225–42.

Mill, J. S. (2002), 'Chapter III: On Individuality, As One of the Elements of Well-being', in *On Liberty.* Mineola, NY: Dover Publications, pp. 46–62.

Moltchanova, A. (2011), 'The general will and immigration'. *Journal of Social Philosophy*, 42 (2): 132–52.

Newman, S. Levine, M. and Cox, D. (2009), *Politics Most Unusual: Violence, Sovereignty and Democracy in the 'War on Terror'*. London: Palgrave MacMillan.

Nussbaum, M. (2006), *Frontiers of Justice: Disability, Nationality, Species Membership*. Cambridge, MA: Harvard University Press, pp. 76–8.

Pitkin, H. F. (1972), *Wittgenstein and Justice: On the Significance of Ludwig Wittgenstein for Social and Political Thought*. Berkeley, CA: University of California Press, p. 276.

Plato (1981), *Republic* (trans. G. M. A. Grube, rev. C. D. C. Reeve). Indianapolis, IN: Hackett Publishing Company.

Rost, J. (1991), *Leadership for the Twenty-First Century*. New York: Praeger, p. 172.

Sendjaya, S. (2005). 'Morality and leadership: Examining the ethics of transformational leadership'. *Journal of Academic Ethics*, 3: 75–86, 77.

Simola, S., Barling, J. and Turner, N. (2012), 'Transformational leadership and leaders' mode of care reasoning', *Journal of Business Ethics*, 108: 229–37.

Taylor, C. C. W. (1995), 'Plato's Totalitarianism', in G. Fine (ed.), *Plato 2: Ethics, Politics, Religion and the Soul*. Oxford: Oxford University Press, pp. 280–96, 295.

Toor, S. and Ofori, G. (2009), 'Ethical leadership: Examining the relationships with full range leadership model, employee outcomes, and organizational culture'. *Journal of Business Ethics*, 90: 533–47.

Tuomela, R. (2007a), *The Philosophy of Sociality*. Oxford: Oxford University Press, p. 182.

—(2007b), 'Cooperation and the We-perspective', in F. Peter and H.-B. Schmid (eds), *Rationality and Commitment*. Oxford: Oxford University Press, pp. 227–57, 244.

Walzer, M. (1976), *Just and Unjust Wars: A Moral Argument With Historical Illustrations*. New York: Basic Books, pp. 255–62.

Wolff, R. P. (1970), *In Defense of Anarchism*. London: Harper & Row. p. 4.

3

Authority and Leadership: The Ethical Obligations of Authority

Sarah Sorial
University of Wollongong

Introduction

The concept of leadership has received significant attention in the context of business ethics, management studies, politics and philosophy, and yet a review of this vast literature does not provide any definitive or unproblematic accounts of what leadership is. Leadership has been variously defined in terms of a dispositional set of traits (the trait approach); as something that emerges in crisis situations (the contingency approach); as a particular style of doing things that is appropriate to particular circumstances (the situational approach); and as an interpretative and constructive assessment of people and situations (the constitutive approach) (Grint 1997: 4–5).

In this chapter, I argue that (i) leadership is not a style, a disposition or a linguistic construct, but is an ethical way of acting in response to particular situations that require some kind of social co-ordination. Acting ethically means doing the right thing because it is the right thing, irrespective of the consequences, and treating others in a respectful way and not as 'means to an end'. 'Social co-ordination' is understood broadly to mean any problem that affects a significant number of people, and which typically requires the support of others to address; (ii) the person is able to influence other people's conduct or persuade others of the merits of adopting this way of acting; (iii) a person does not need to have any formal authority to exercise leadership; and (iv) in cases where a person does have formal authority, his or her leadership cannot be understood or evaluated without an understanding of the institutional framework or structure in which he or she operates. I suggest that these core features of leadership defined in (i) and (ii) are the same for different kinds of leaders, including politicians, business leaders, university leaders and persons who do not have formal authority; however, what they do will vary depending on the context. All leaders with some kind of formal authority will also be bound by institutional structures, although, again, the actual structures will differ depending on the organization.

Distinguishing leadership and authority, and understanding the ways in which they intersect is important for several reasons: first, it enables us to analyse people who do not appear to have authority or any kind of institutional support, but demonstrate leadership, in the sense that they see a problem for which they take the initiative and act in a principled way to solve it, and are able to bring others along with them. To act on principle is to do the right thing because it is the right thing, irrespective of the consequences, and to treat people in a respectful way as 'ends in themselves'. If we think leaders are influential because they are able to convince others of the merits of a particular course of action, it is important to define leadership in an ethical way. This definition is thus not a stipulative one, but is informed by a Kantian ethical framework. Second, understanding how leadership and authority intersect might enable us to see the constraints of authority in institutional settings, and why people in positions of authority might be constrained in ways that prevent them from being good or successful leaders. Third, it enables us to determine what it means to have authority on its own terms and why leadership might be important in certain areas of authority: why it might, for example, be important for politicians to also be leaders, and why they also might fail to achieve their objectives, despite their plans and their intentions.[1]

In the first section, I give an account of some of the ways in which leadership is defined in the literature, focusing in particular on the distinction between leadership and management, charisma-based accounts and constitutive accounts, with a view to highlighting the problems associated with each. In section two, I give an account of some of the structural features of authority in order to demonstrate that (i) leadership and authority are different concepts; (ii) one can be a leader without having any formal authority; and (iii) in cases where a person does have authority and is also a leader, they might fail or be constrained because of the institutional structures in which the person operates. The main advantage to defining leadership in this way is that it enables us to account for the many different instances of leadership that occur outside of business or political contexts, and it is able to explain the constraints that leaders may face, and hence their failure in some instances. In section three, I apply this account to some cases of leadership in order to demonstrate how it might be consistent with our intuitions about what leadership is. In the final section, I respond to two potential objections to this account.

What is leadership?

Leadership defined in opposition to management

In the 1980s and 1990s the difference between management and leadership was the basis of a new paradigm in leadership theory, referred to as either the 'new leadership school' (Bryman 1992) or the 'neo-charismatic paradigm' (House 1995). Researchers examining the ways in which executives and managers were involved in transforming their organizations devised notions of leadership by contrasting them with the role of management. A person in a managerial position might have to execute administrative functions for an organization, including the procurement and deployment of available resources to maintain the day to day running of the organization, and supervise employees in a way that enables the efficient and effective completion of goals and the meeting of organizational objectives. Management thus requires the achievement of short-term, operational objectives of the organization. Leadership functions, by contrast, require an executive or manager to formulate long-term objectives for the organization in a novel way. The necessary characteristics of leadership were considered to include challenging the status quo, engaging in a creative vision for the future of the organization and promoting appropriate changes in followers' values, attitudes and behaviours using empowering strategies and tactics (Conger and Kanungo 1998: 8).

The 'new leadership school' (Bryman 1992) argued that modern organizations were unable to adapt to the changing world because of too much management and too little leadership. There was a 'crisis in leadership' because there was not enough leadership talent and leadership, not management, was what was needed to solve the various problems facing the organization. This narrative concerning the crisis in leadership remains pervasive in the literature, although some of it continues to conflate the concepts of leadership and management. For example, according to a study by Maritz Research, trust in leadership is low: only seven per cent of employees believe that 'senior management's actions are completely consistent with their words' and only 25 per cent claim 'that they trust management to make the right decisions in times of uncertainty' (Maritz Research 2010: 1). Other studies claim that organizational leaders struggle in retaining follower trust (Heavey et al. 2011) and continue to use traditional leadership models that are often ineffective (Convey 2004) and that often become the source of many organizational problems (Pfeffer 1998). Freeman argues that 'our current maps and mental codes about leadership are failing us' (Freeman et al. 2006: 149) while Cameron argues that the leaders of tomorrow's organizations must raise their standards, demonstrate their character and meet the expectations of a cynical but increasingly complex world (Cameron 2003). The response to this alleged crisis has been to devise various models for effective leadership, including 'authentic leadership' and 'ethical leadership' models.

Authentic leadership has four main elements: balanced processing, internalized moral perspective, relational transparency and self-awareness (Peus et al. 2012: 332); ethical leadership is defined as 'the demonstration of normatively appropriate conduct through personal actions and interpersonal relationships, and the promotion of such conduct to followers through two-way communication, reinforcement, and decision-making' (Brown et al. 2005: 117). These two accounts are representative of these models, although there is no universal acceptance of these claims. While both emphasize the ethical dimensions of leadership, they fail to give an account of what constitutes 'internal moral standards and values', and so leave open the possibility that these may, in fact, be immoral standards.

In much of this more recent literature, there seems to be a conflation of the former distinction between leaders and managers, or an expectation that managers also step up and demonstrate leadership. If it is the case that the current models of leadership are failing us, this could be partly attributable to the models being outdated, but it also could be because the leadership models were too vague to actually mean anything or to guide behaviour in any genuine way. What, for example, does it actually mean to change people's attitudes using 'empowering strategies and tactics'? What are these tactics and how do we know they will work as intended?

There are three significant things to note about the distinction between leadership and management as it is made in the literature discussed above. First, while there is widespread recognition that leadership and management are distinct roles and that individuals can and do perform both, the focus of the literature is on the behaviours and characteristics relevant to being a manager or a leader. There is little analysis of the ways in which managers and leaders function in the context of various institutional frameworks. This is relevant because institutional frameworks can often constrain or limit what people are able to achieve, irrespective of the kinds of dispositions, traits, vision or skills the person may have. A more careful analysis of the institutional contexts that confer formal authority on managers and managers acting as 'leaders' may change our expectations about what managers and leaders are able to do.

For example, a newly appointed Dean of a university faculty may have great ideas about the direction of the Faculty and strongly believe that the University should treat its staff in a respectful way, but may be unable to execute some of this vision because it may conflict with that of the Vice Chancellor, or because the rules of the institution do not allow for such rapid change. Alternatively, the efforts might be stymied because of other external factors. For example, the Dean might value the quality of research over quantity, and want to encourage staff to take the time to explore new ideas and make mistakes. However, she might find herself in an institutional environment that emphasizes quantity *and* quality, thus compelling her to make her staff work even harder, and so come to see themselves as the means to the institution's ends.

Second, there is an assumption that we need leaders to solve various 'crises', and that we need leaders to head our nations and our organizations for them to function effectively. Leaders thus seem to have some kind of managerial role, but they also seem to have additional powers to managers, in the sense that they are expected to also have 'vision' and the power to execute that vision, and so leaders can do different kinds of things. On some accounts, leadership is conceived as a system of authority. As Spicker puts it, 'even if we accept that leadership is the more exciting, more adventurous, hotter younger brother of management, leadership still requires people to be in a position to exercise those qualities, and effective management requires people to respond to and adapt their circumstances. That implies that leadership can also be understood as management by a different name' (Spicker 2012: 35). While it is the case that some managers are also 'leaders', the two terms are regularly conflated and an assumption made that leaders must have some kind of formal authority. For example, Day argues that leadership is a system of authority identified with running an organization, being in charge or carrying responsibility for a collective function or a team (Day et al. 2004). There are two assumptions being made here: first, an assumption that leadership typically occurs in organizational settings, or that leaders are also CEOs. There is thus a narrow focus on what leadership is and the contexts in which it occurs. Second, there is an assumption that leaders have some kind of formal authority.

However, not all leaders (on the account I will defend) necessarily have formal authority in this way, but a person could nevertheless qualify as a leader because they take the initiative to solve a social co-ordination problem in a principled way. Moreover, because a leader can lack formal authority, it is not always the case that he or she will be successful in what they set out to achieve; in the case where a leader does have formal authority, they might also be unsuccessful because of the institutional context in which they operate. This does not, however, mean they are failed leaders; a person can be a good leader even though he or she fails in what they set out to achieve, as I will explain later.

Finally, even if leaders do have special skills, like vision or some other trait that distinguishes them from managers, those skills and that vision are not always relevant in crisis situations. Sometimes those situations may call for better management or better administration rather than charisma or vision. For example, a business 'leader' may have vision and other great ideas for how to make a flagging business profitable, but the problem might be that the resources are mismanaged, the staff unhappy and the accounts are not properly kept. In these cases, the impending crisis (perhaps insolvency for the company) might be averted with better administration and organization.

Spicker's analysis of the ways in which leadership concepts and attributes cannot simply be transposed to all situations is instructive in this regard. For example, leadership concepts are not easily applicable in the public service, where the objective of agencies is not to innovate but to provide a consistent, reliable service. Civil servants are required to make recommendations about policy, not to decide on the policy themselves; because public management is necessarily political, managers need to be sensitive to the political implications and the dimensions of the work they do (Spicker 2012: 40).

This does not mean that people working in government departments or executing policy cannot act as leaders, especially as I am defining leadership. It may require that they solve various social coordination problems in an ethical way, and convince others to do the same. But it does mean that they need not be leaders in the ways leadership is typically defined in the literature. For example, they need not have an innovative vision of the future of the organization. Leadership and management thus seem to be different: they require different skill sets and attributes, yet there is an assumption that leaders and managers also have authority and operate within the same institutional environments. For example, the focus tends to be on CEOs and heads of companies rather than on the ways in which leadership can occur at many different levels, as I will demonstrate. While there seems to be some clarity in the literature about what managers do (probably because it is closely associated with various adminis-trative tasks), there is less clarity and consensus about what leadership is. Two of the more influential accounts that offer definitions of leadership are charisma-based accounts and constitutive accounts.

Leadership and charisma

Charismatic leadership emerged in the context of Max Weber's account of authority. According to Weber, the charismatic leader is a specifically extraordinary person:

> Set apart from ordinary men and is treated as endowed with ... exceptional powers and qualities ... [that] are not accessible to the ordinary person but are regarded as of divine origin or as exemplary, and on the basis of them the individual concerned is treated as a leader (Weber 1947: 358–9).

The charismatic leader emerges during times of emergency or distress 'whether psychic, physical, economic, ethical, religious, or political – were neither appointed officeholders nor professional in the present day sense, but rather the bearers of specific gifts of body and mind that were considered supernatural' (Weber 1978: 112). A charismatic leader need not be appointed a leader, or emerge from any kind of formal organization or bureaucracy, but seems to emerge naturally to address various kinds of crisis situations. The relationship between leaders and followers is intensely emotional, irrational and unstable (Adair-Toteff 2005: 195).

Since Weber, charismatic accounts of leadership have focused on the leader's personality traits, and the dynamics between leaders and followers. Charisma is a crucial factor in accounts advocating 'transformational' leadership. Burns' model of transformational leadership distinguishes between 'transformational leadership' and 'transactional leadership' (Burns 1978). For Burns, leadership is essentially about exchange: 'leaders approach followers with an eye toward exchanging' (Burns 1978: 4). Transformational leadership is not simply about followers' compliance; instead, it involves changing or transforming their beliefs, needs and values: 'the result of transforming leadership is a relationship of mutual stimulation and elevation that converts followers into leader and may convert leaders into moral agents' (ibid.).

Transactional leadership, by contrast, is based on a different kind of transactional relationship, consisting of instrumental exchanges: 'the relations of most leaders and followers are transactional – leaders approach followers with an eye to exchanging one thing for another: jobs for votes, or subsidies for campaign contributions. Such [instrumental] transactions comprise the bulk of the relationships' (Burns 1978: 4). Burns does not provide an adequate account of what constitutes a 'moral agent'. What, for example, are the kinds of behaviours or actions that are relevant? And why would followers need to have their 'higher order needs' realized by another person? Why wouldn't they be able to achieve these needs themselves?

Bernard Bass attempted to give more concrete examples of the kinds of behaviour relevant for transformational leadership. These behaviours include: charisma or idealized influence; inspiration; intellectual stimulation; and individualized consideration (Bass and Steidlmeier 1999: 182). According to Bass, charisma is crucial because it enables the leader to influence followers by arousing strong emotions and facilitates identification with the leader. Emotional arousal creates a sense of excitement for the mission, while identification with the leader reduces followers' resistance to change (Conger and Kanungo 1998: 14). By failing to distinguish between ethical and unethical charismatic forms of leadership, Bass falls foul of the so-called 'Hitler problem' (Ciulla 1995: 13): Hitler qualifies as a successful leader, despite our intuitions against classifying him as such. If it is the case that leaders are able to influence followers in this way, it seems important to define leadership with some reference to a normative ethical framework. Value neutrality could leave open the possibility that leaders can influence their followers in morally dubious or evil ways, and that followers will act unethically more easily if they strongly identify with a leader in the ways Bass is proposing.

Charisma-based models have been criticized for producing negative outcomes for themselves and for their organizations. For example, in a study on some examples of charismatic leaders (defined as leaders who had vision and followers who identified with them) such as Edwin Land, inventor of the Polaroid camera, and Robert Lipp, former president of Chemical Bank, Conger found that problems could arise with respect to the charismatic leader's vision, their impression of management, their management practices and their succession planning. With respect to vision, leaders can sometimes have an exaggerated sense of the marketplace opportunities for their vision or they can significantly underestimate the resources they need to accomplish their aims. For example, Robert Lipp had a vision that was too far ahead of his time with his concept of home banking, and Land failed to see what the market needed because he was too focused on his own personal ambition. The success of a leader's vision thus depends on a realistic assessment of the opportunities and the constraints in the organizations and sensitivity to constituents' needs. If the leader loses sight with that reality and the needs of the organization, the vision can become a liability (Conger 1990: 45). Charisma in these contexts can unreasonably sway followers to support flawed or unachievable visions. It is even more pernicious if it sways followers to support or commit evil or immoral acts. In this sense, charisma seems even more problematic for political leaders, given the kind of power and authority they have.

Charisma can also be used to evil ends when it is not constrained by any normative ethical framework, or where the charismatic person believes that what they are doing is consistent with ethical principles. Hitler, Pol Pot and Saddam Hussein all had charisma, although on the account of leadership I am proposing, they were not leaders, because they failed to solve the problems they were faced with in any normative ethical way; while they did succeed in convincing others of their vision and the justifiability of their actions, the vision and the actions themselves were fundamentally immoral.

Charisma can also prevent us from making informed assessments about whether a political leader was in fact able to solve a social co-ordination in a principled way. For example, the former Australian Prime Minister, Kevin Rudd, had huge personal charisma when he was elected in 2007, and he had vision on a range of important issues, including the need to issue an apology to the Stolen Generation and his proposal to implement an Emissions Trading Scheme (ETS) to address the problem of climate change. On his first day in office, he gave a moving apology to the Aboriginal and Torres Strait Islander people who were forcibly removed from their parents and their families under previous governments. This remains one of the defining features of his government, but it also obscures his party's failure to act on an election promise for constitutional recognition of Aboriginal people in Australia. Similarly, the personal charisma of US President Barack Obama has prevented the public from making an informed analysis of the failure to close Guantanamo Bay, despite this being one of Obama's election promises.

These problems with charismatic leadership or leadership 'styles' can indicate that we are looking for the wrong sorts of traits in our leaders if these traits can be exploited or used for evil ends in the ways outlined above, or if they can inhibit our capacity for critical analysis. It might suggest that we need to rethink our understanding of leadership in a way that excludes Hitler and Pol Pot from being used as examples of leadership. Bass and Steidlmeier attempt to rethink transformational leadership in a way that would exclude these cases by distinguishing between authentic transformational leadership and inauthentic or pseudo-transformational leadership (Bass and Steidlmeier 1999), but their account remains committed to the view that a leader must also have charisma.

Given the highly irrational nature of the relationship between charismatic people and their followers, it might cause people to act for the wrong sorts of reason.

This may mean omitting charisma from a definition of leadership. Leadership does involve 'bringing people along', as it were, but not by blindly and uncritically following a leader. It also suggests that because leadership involves some kind of influence, it is important to define leadership as involving ethically good conduct, where ethically good means doing the right thing because it is the right thing, irrespective of consequences, and treating people as ends in themselves. On this account, people who convince others of morally dubious actions (for example, adopting discriminatory policies) or who achieve various ends by violent means or by harming others, even if those ends are good ones, are not leaders. Charisma-based definitions of leadership suggest that we are looking for the wrong sorts of traits and dispositions in our account of leadership. An alternative approach is the 'constitutive' approach to leadership, which resists defining leadership in any explicit way. Instead, assessments of whether one is a leader are ultimately decided by popular or prominent interpretations of a person as being a 'leader'. This account is also problematic in a number of important respects.

Constitutive leadership

The constitutive approach to leadership is based on constructivist theories in social science. The core idea is that an objective determination of whether a person is a leader or any kind of definition of leadership as a concept is not possible because all accounts are derived from linguistic reconstructions. They are not objective and transparent reproductions of the truth. Instead, Grint argues that what the situation and leader actually are is a consequence of various accounts and interpretations, all of which compete for domination. This means there are no objective criteria with which we can judge whether or not someone is/was a leader; our only judgement is based on a particular assessment or interpretation of the person that has achieved prominence. Grint writes:

> ... My account of a popular individual may be that he or she is an incompetent charlatan, but if the popularity of this person rests upon the support of more powerful 'voices' (including material resources), then my negative voice will carry little or no weight. The critical issue for this approach, then, is not what the leader or the context is 'really' like, but what are the processes by which these phenomena are constituted into successes or failures, crises or periods of calm ... (Grint 1997: 5–6).

Leaders themselves can be responsible for shaping, constructing or interpreting these assessments. As Grint argues, it is leaders themselves who shape our interpretation of the environment, of the challenges, the goals, the competition and the strategy, and they try to persuade us that the interpretation is both correct and true. Because of the emphasis on interpretation, this account deems leadership more an art rather than a science, and suggests that our difficulty with defining leadership is partly attributable to the scientific framework that is typically adopted. The more scientific the methods of analysis are, the more obscure the object of the analysis becomes because leadership cannot be defined in any precise way (Grint 2002: 4).

There are, however, several problems with this account. First, just because a particular interpretation of a person as a leader has taken hold, it does not mean that this interpretation is correct or that we cannot assess whether it might be mistaken. Second, the account seems to assume that leadership is simply a product of power rather than something people actually do. That is, it is not so much the actions of individuals or their conduct, including their treatment of others, that matters, but *how* they are perceived. For example, people within an organization may have formed the view that a person is a good leader, and so give that person more responsibility simply based on a perception or an interpretation, however that interpretation may be mistaken. The person might, in fact, be a bully, treat people abominably and engage in ethically dubious conduct. It seems mistaken to suggest that the person's actions do not count as relevant and that we cannot be mistaken about whether someone is a leader (and in this example it seems right to say that others in the organization were simply wrong about this person).

Third, it cannot account for those cases of 'everyday' leadership or cases where a person might exercise leadership without any formal authority or institutional support. Does the fact that there are no powerful people with material resources to reconstruct a narrative of these peoples' actions mean that they have not exercised leadership? In this respect, there seems to be a failure to distinguish between leadership and the exercise of formal power, as well as a failure to pay sufficient attention to people's *actual* conduct.

Moreover, while Grint acknowledges the gap between a leader's vision and his or her execution of it, he attributes this either to followers seeking to pursue their own interests, and so not complying with the leader's strategy, or to the leader's inability to summon the necessary resources to achieve his or aims (Grint 2002: 18). There is little acknowledgement of the various institutional structures within which most people in positions of authority operate, and the ways these might constrain the person's vision or their ability to execute it.

A survey of the most influential literature does not, therefore, bring us any closer to understanding what leadership is. We can either conclude that leadership is rare or 'extraordinary', or it is merely a social invention, or it is too heroic or ambiguous to really mean anything at all. As Spicker argues (Spicker 2012: 34), despite the vast amount of literature on leadership, the concept remains contentious, poorly theorized and is often uncritical. It is not clear why the supposed roles, tasks or qualities of 'leadership' either need to be or should be concentrated in the person of a leader. For example, the tasks involved in 'leading' an organization are not in fact the tasks of motivation, influence or direction of others, and there is no reason to suppose that leadership is a primary influence on the behaviour of most organizations (Spicker 2012: 34), although it might be more relevant in some organizations than others. These seem to be the tasks of management. Moreover, it is possible that leadership is not, in fact, most visible in organizational contexts.

In the following section, I propose that it is possible to define what leadership is, and I offer the following definition: (i) leadership is assuming responsibility for a social co-ordination problem in an ethical way; and (ii) a leader is someone who can convince others that this is, in fact, the best way of acting in the given circumstances. My aim in defining leadership in this way is threefold: first, I think it is important to distinguish leadership from management in a more coherent way than in some of the literature examined in the first sections of this chapter. While many accounts do argue that leadership and management are different things, as has been demonstrated, there is also a tendency to assume that leaders are just better kinds of managers, with more vision, more power and more charisma. That is, leaders have the same, if not more, power and institutional authority as managers and in addition have charisma, but nothing more. On the account I defend, leadership is not the same as management, and leaders, in the sense in which I am using the term, need not have any formal authority at all. Second, distinguishing between the two enables us to see the constraints of authority and why people in positions of authority might be constrained in ways that prevent them from being good leaders, as I will demonstrate in the following section. Third, it enables us to determine what it means to have authority (both formal and informal) on its own terms and why exercising leadership might be important in some areas of authority. Finally, the account I offer gives some criteria by which to distinguish who a leader is without relying on a person's character traits or dispositions. So if it turns out that Hitler fails as a leader or Churchill succeeds, in neither case do they do so because of their character traits and dispositions. The advantage of this approach is that it does not rely on a person's charisma, and so avoids the problems with charisma-based accounts.

Features of formal authority

There is a rich literature in philosophy addressing what authority is, and revisiting this literature might shed light on some of the differences between authority and leadership (Austin 1962; Langton 1993; McGowan 2004; Sorial 2011; Marmor 2011). There are roughly four main features of formal authority: (i) a person with authority is able to give directives or deliver different kinds of speech acts; (ii) the person has standing or power to make those speech acts; (iii) they create obligations on the part of others by uttering those speech acts; (iv) they come to have that power by virtue of institutional frameworks and procedures which identify the scope of the person's power and set limits to what persons can do (McGowan 2004; Sorial 2011).

The term 'formal authority' refers to our ordinary, everyday understanding of authority as being the capacity of a person to change the normative situation of another person (Marmor 2011: 239). Typical examples of this include various kinds of legal authority, the authority of employers over their employees, the authority of parents over young children, the authority of a referee over players in competitive games, the authority of a religious cleric over a congregation and the authority of teachers over students. We would regard someone as being a person of authority if she is in a position to impose an obligation on another person by expressing certain directives and that the person ought to act in accordance with those directives. As Marmor puts it:

> An authoritative directive purports to make a difference to the reasons for action that the authority's subjects have by way of recognising the directive itself as a reason to do as directed. Authoritative directives are speech acts, of the kind that purport to motivate conduct by way of recognising the utterance of the directive as a reason for action. (Marmor 2011: 240)

Persons who have authority are thus able to do certain things with their speech acts. In his work in philosophy of language, J. L. Austin (1962: 151) classifies the kinds of speech acts persons in positions of authority can perform as being 'verdictive' speech acts and 'exercitive' speech acts. Both kinds of speech acts require that the speaker have authority over the domain in question for the speech act to be successful or to secure 'uptake'. Second, as Maitra and McGowan have argued, both are significantly obligation-enacting (Maitra and McGowan 2007: 41–68). The authoritative role of the speaker in a certain context gives the utterance a force that would be absent were it made by someone who did not occupy that role.

To be in a position of authority is to have the power to do various things: it is to have the power to choose from a range of options whether, and how, to introduce changes in the 'normative landscape that prevails in the area of one's authority' (Marmor 2011: 243). Having this kind of power enables the authority holder to introduce changes, dictate how those changes will occur, determine who is subject to them and how those changes will be enforced within the context of the institution in which the person operates (ibid.). The powers can be wide reaching or quite limited depending on the kind and extent of power the authority holder has. This is typically determined by certain institutional structures. The second relevant feature of power is that the introduction of change by the power-holder is unilateral, subject to the discretion or decision-making of the power-holder (ibid.).[2]

Finally, persons with formal authority have the power and standing to secure uptake in these ways because of particular institutional structures that confer power to them. The authority of persons is thus closely bound up with certain institutional facts. Authority, and the kind of power it confers, is thus only granted by power-conferring norms, or by some rules or conventions, and these power-conferring norms are institutional in nature. To summarize: '(1) to have practical authority is to have normative power of a certain type; (2) power, in this sense, is granted or constituted by norms, that is, some rules or conventions; and (3) power-conferring norms are essentially institutional – they form part of some social practice or institution' (Marmor 2011: 241). The norms of an institution will enable authority holders to impose obligations on others and to initiate changes, but they will also constrain her in various ways. An understanding of the institutional background against which an authority holder acts can enable us to see the limits of authority and why people in positions of authority might be constrained in ways that prevent them from realizing or executing their vision.

The point here is that not all people with authority are leaders because there are people who have these statutory powers that we would not want to call leaders (because on my account, they do not solve social co-ordination problems in an ethical way, and bring others along with them), and others without such powers who are leaders and are perceived as such by others. Leadership can occur in cases where a person does not occupy a position of formal authority (i.e. they do not have the necessary institutional support) but nevertheless are able to co-ordinate conduct or change norms in some way.

Application

In this section, I consider some examples to illuminate this definition of leadership. First is the case of an employee who has no formal authority to issue directives or impose obligations on others, but decides to do something about the workplace culture of sexual harassment, with a view to changing the normative landscape about the acceptable and ethical treatment of women in her workplace. This could be conceived as a social co-ordination problem, given the number of people affected and the number of people necessary to actually bring about change. The employee could do a number of things, including speak to an equity officer, report the behaviour to managers higher up in the organization, organize other employees in order to gain critical mass and agitate for change in various other ways. This employee might risk losing her job as a consequence of her actions, but we would typically consider the employee to have acted as a leader, even though she does not have formal authority. The employee took the initiative to solve a social co-ordination problem in a principled way, and was able to convince others of this course of action, despite not having any formal authority to do so. In this case, the person in question is able to influence the normative landscape in significant ways, despite a lack of institutional support. The lack of institutional support is not necessary for leadership, although it may require more effort on the part of the leader to bring about change. What is necessary is the ability to convince others of the course of action or to 'bring them along'. Had the person only spoken to an equity officer, this would not have been sufficient for leadership. What makes this example one of leadership is the person's capacity to bring along a critical mass of people, which in turn can foster more productive change.

Thus not every leadership position a person successfully assumes is an exercise in practical authority; instead, as Marmor argues: '[a] leader is typically one who can deliberately influence others' conduct without having the requisite authority or regardless of the authority one does have' (Marmor 201: 246). A leader may not have the power to impose obligations on others to follow their directives, and they might not have any authority over anyone, but they are still able to change the normative landscape. In either case – whether a leader has formal authority or whether they do not – a distinctive feature of being a leader is that the person takes the initiative for solving social co-ordination problems in a principled way, and is able to convince others that this is the best course of action. Recall, acting in a principled way means doing the right thing because it is the right thing, irrespective of consequences, and treating others as 'ends in themselves'. This account excludes people who bring about change in the 'normative landscape' through vigilantism or violent action.

It also may be more difficult to be a leader without authority; for instance, the culture of workplace sexual harassment could have been more easily addressed if the person with the authority (the manager) had done something about it. His or her failure to act, despite having formal powers to do so, is also a failure to exercise leadership and may be more blameworthy, given the person could have acted but chose not to. By contrast, a person might have the ability to convince others of a particular course of action but chooses to do nothing. Returning to the above example, the employee who takes the initiative might have a colleague who can see the extent of the problem and who is also well respected in the workplace and so would be able to convince others. She chooses, however, to do nothing. In this case, she is not a leader or is not exercising leadership but is still not as blameworthy as the manager.

A more familiar example from the leadership literature is that of Martin Luther King, who is typically held as a paradigm case of exemplary leadership. While King had formal authority, in the sense that he had a small organization – the Southern Christian Leadership Conference – of which he was president, and informal authority to a bigger circle of hundreds of thousands of people in the form of moral authority, these are not what define him as an exemplary leader (Heifetz 2011: 305). King was a leader because the people he wanted to lead were not the ones over whom he had formal or informal authority, including African Americans who were not members of his church but sympathetic to his cause, white Americans who were sympathetic and also white Americans who were hostile. These were the people whose values he wanted to change. As Heifetz notes: 'he was leading beyond his authority into constituencies over whom he had no authority at all – people who would never have considered themselves followers' (ibid.). King took the initiative to solve a social co-ordination problem and tried to convince others or bring them along, especially those who were most resistant. While not many of us have the opportunities King had, we nevertheless regularly face or come across various social co-ordination problems that may require us to take the initiative, act in a principled way to solve the problem and bring others along to this way of acting. Leadership in this sense can thus occur on both small and large scales: we can exercise it in the ways we might resolve disputes between our children, the way we deal with situations that arise in our workplaces or in our political culture more generally.

Consider, as another example, the actions of Australian GetUp! founders, Jeremy Heimans and David Madden. The organization GetUp! was founded in 2005 with the aim of keeping the then Howard Liberal Government accountable to the people. At that time, the Conservative Government held a majority of seats in both the lower and upper houses. This meant that it had the numbers to pass legislation in both houses with minimal resistance or oversight. The fact that it held a majority in the Senate presented the problem of accountability because the Senate provides critical scrutiny and oversight of proposed bills before they are passed into law. Heimans and Madden did not have any formal authority, but took the initiative to solve this social co-ordination problem by setting up an online community activist group, which used email, petitions and traditional media to put pressure on the government and to promote a more 'progressive Australia'. The organization provided citizens with a way to remain politically engaged and put pressure on their elected representatives on a range of issues, including controversial anti-terrorism legislation and changes to industrial relations law among other initiatives. Despite not having any formal authority, the organizers exercised leadership in solving a social co-ordination problem in an ethical way, and were successful in bringing others along with them (this is evidenced by the number of people who sign online petitions, send emails, etc.). They acted ethically insofar as they pursed an ethically good outcome (holding government to account) and did so in a way that did not use people as a means to an end, or through destructive or violent means. This ethical dimension is constitutive of leadership. Had the organization been used to pursue morally dubious ends (like promoting discriminatory or racist policies), the organizers would not be considered leaders on this definition of leadership.

So far, I have been examining cases of people who do not have any formal authority, but nevertheless exercise leadership. My aim has been to demonstrate that having authority and being a leader are not the same thing. But people in positions of authority can also be leaders. In these cases, it is necessary to understand the institutional background against which an authority holder acts. This can explain why people in positions of authority might be constrained in ways that prevent them from acting to solve a social co-ordination problem in an ethical way and why they may fail to convince others of this course of action.

In business, this may mean a person is unable to execute their plans to solve a particular issue because they are constrained by the business constitution, or other institutional structures that make it difficult to achieve change. In the tertiary sector, a head of school or Dean might have creative ideas of how to build a research culture in the Faculty or address issues associated with gender inequity, but their efforts might be stymied by others higher up in the organization, like Deputy Vice-Chancellors, who may have different ideas about how things should be done. In these cases, we could still say that the people in question exercised leadership, even though they did not ultimately succeed in executing their plans, and even though they failed to convince people higher up in the organization of the merits of their action. That is, a person can be a leader but nevertheless fail in what he or she sets out to do. Leadership need not require success.

The same kinds of institutional constraints are apparent in politics, where people may exercise leadership in how they identify a problem, take the initiative for solving it, but fail to convince all relevant persons of the merits of this course of action. For example, consider the actions of the then opposition 'leader' (i.e. head) of the Liberal Party, Malcolm Turnbull, who crossed the floor to vote with the Rudd Government to pass the Emissions Trading Scheme (ETS). Turnbull publicly supported the ETS even though the majority of members of his party did not. He publicly denounced his party's failure to address this major problem, and risked and lost his formal leadership over it. The Bill passed in the lower house, but failed to pass the Senate. The failure in this respect is partly attributable to the institutional structures of both the Liberal Party and the structures of Parliament (for example, in Australia, a bill has to pass both the House of Representatives and the Senate) within which all politicians must operate.

In this case, Turnbull had formal authority and exercised leadership, and yet was constrained because of various institutional structures and party politics. Leaders who do have formal authority must operate within these institutional structures, and these limit them in ways that might prevent them from executing their vision. Turnbull exercised good leadership in this case because he took the initiative to solve a social co-ordination problem; he also managed to convince others of the merits of this course of action,[3] although not the conservative members of his party. However, he was ultimately constrained by various institutional structures, including those of his own party. This suggests that a person can be a leader even though they do not succeed, and that persons with formal authority often do not succeed because of institutional constraints or for other reasons beyond their control.

Objections

There are, however, at least two possible objections to this account. First, how much success in solving a problem is necessary to constitute leadership? Can a person repeatedly fail and yet still remain a leader? Second, how many people does a person need to convince to meet the second condition for leadership, (being able to influence other people's conduct or persuade others of the merits of adopting this way of acting)? By drawing attention to the institutional structures that constrain people's actions, the idea of failure is already built into this account. Leaders do sometimes fail to solve the problems they take the initiative for. Given the aforementioned constraints, perhaps assessments about whether a person is a leader should be based on whether they take the initiative for solving a problem, rather than their success or failure in actually doing so.

With respect to the second objection, a person does not need to convince every single person of the merits of the proposed action to qualify as a leader; they do, however, need to convince a significant number of people that there is at least a problem to be solved or they need to generate some public awareness of the issues, whether those issues arise in businesses, workplaces or in political life. Building momentum about a particular issue might be sufficient for leadership, especially for complex or entrenched problems that can only be solved over a significant period of time.

Convincing others of a proposed course of action also demonstrates why leadership might be necessary in domain-specific areas of authority, in particular political authority. We expect our politicians to 'show leadership' by acting in an ethical way to solve problems and by convincing us that this is the best way of dealing with these issues. For example, we expect our politicians to distribute resources equitably and to provide everyone with equal opportunities to access education and health care. Moreover, we expect politicians to bring us along with them by arguing their case for the various policies they propose, rather than offering us empty slogans in place of arguments or convincing reasons. Politicians who routinely fail to act ethically to address problems and fail to convince the electorate are not exercising leadership. Note here that the failure to execute policy is a different issue to the failure to take the initiative to solve a problem and convince people. A politician who takes responsibility for solving a problem in an ethical way and tries to convince the electorate by offering good reasons, but nevertheless fails to secure uptake for the policy, is different to one who proposes to address a problem in an unethical way and fails to explain him or herself to the electorate. The former is an example of the type of leadership I am defending, while the latter is not.

A leader is able to identify a problem, address it in a moral way and bring others along with him or her. The demands of leadership are thus quite high, and so might be difficult to achieve. Nevertheless, there are some advantages for defining leadership in this way. First, this account does not rely on the problematic idea of charisma; some people may or may not have charisma, but this is not why they qualify as leaders. Second, a person need not have any formal authority in order to be a leader: all that is required for leadership is for a person to take the initiative with respect to a social co-ordination problem, act in a principled way to solve it and influence others to do the same. As such, this definition is able to account for diverse instances of leadership, including leading one's family or one's sporting team. Finally, even if a person has formal authority *and* is a leader some of the time, they can still fail because of the institutional structures in which they operate. This seems to be especially the case for political leaders.

Notes

1   In this respect, my account shares some essential features with Heifetz 2011, but differs in focusing on how people not only solve social co-ordination problems with respect to issues that they care about, but that they do so in an ethical way.
2   My aim here is to explain the formal features of authority, and I will leave to one side the ethical dimensions for the moment.
3   The Liberal Party did negotiate with the Labour Government to pass the Bill, and there was support, including from Joe Hockey. The right-wing faction could not, however, be convinced, given their view that climate change is not human-made.

Bibliography

Adair-Toteff, C. (2005), 'Max Weber's charisma'. *Journal of Classical Sociology*, 5 (2): 189–204.

Anding, J. M. (2005), 'An interview with Robert E. Quinn: Entering the fundamental state of leadership: Reflections on the path to transformational teaching'. *Academy of Management Learning and Education*, 4 (4): 487–95.

Austin, J. L. (1962), *How to Do Things With Words*. London: Oxford University Press.

Bass, B. (1985), *Leadership and Performance Beyond Expectations*. New York: Free Press.

Bass, B. and Steidlmeier, P. (1999), 'Ethics, character, and authentic transformational leadership behaviour'. *Leadership Quarterly*, 10 (2): 181–217.

Bennis, W. G. and Nanus, B. (1985), *Leaders: The Strategies for Taking Charge*. New York: Harper & Row.

Brown, M. E., Trevino, L. K. and Harrison, D. A. (2005), 'Ethical leadership: A social learning perspective for constructive development and testing'. *Organisational Behaviour and Human Decision Processes*, 97: 117–34.

Bryman, A. (1992), *Charisma and Leadership in Organisations*. London: Sage.

Burns, J. M. (1978), *Leadership*. New York: Harper & Row.

Burns, B. and Todnem By, R. (2012), 'Leadership and change: The case for greater ethical clarity'. *Journal of Business Ethics*, 108: 239–52.

Caldwell, C., Dixon, R. D., Floyd, L. A., Chaudoin, J., Post, J. and Cheokas, G. (2012), 'Transformative leadership: Achieving unparalleled excellence'. *Journal of Business Ethics*, 109: 175–87.

Cameron, K. S. (2003), 'Ethics, Virtuousness, and Constant Change', in N. M. Tichy and A. R. McGill (eds), *The Ethical Challenge: How to Lead with Unyielding Integrity*. San Francisco, CA: Jossey-Bass, pp.185–94.

Ciulla, J. B. (1995), 'Leadership ethics: Mapping the territory'. *Business Ethics Quarterly*, 5 (1): 5–37.

Conger, J. A. (1990), 'The dark side of leadership'. *Organizational Dynamics*, 19 (2): 44–55.

Conger, J. A. and Kanungo, R. N. (1998), *Charismatic Leadership in Organisations*. London and California: Sage.

Covey, S. R. (2004), *The 8ᵗʰ Habit: From Effectiveness to Greatness*. New York: Free Press.

Day, D., Gronn, P. and Salas, E. (2004), 'Leadership capacity in teams'. *Leadership Quarterly*, 15 (6): 857–80.

Elgie, R. (2002), 'The arts of leadership'. *Organization Studies*, 23 (1): 159–61.

Estlund, D. (2008), *Democratic Authority*. Princeton, NJ: Princeton University Press.

Grint, K. (2002), *The Arts of Leadership*. Oxford: Oxford University Press.

—(1997), *Leadership: Classical, Contemporary, and Critical Approaches*. Oxford: Oxford University Press.

Heavey, C., Halliday, S. V., Gilbert, D. and Murphy, E. (2011), 'Enhancing performance: Bringing trust, commitment and motivation together in organisations'. *Journal of General Management*, 36 (3): 1–18.

Heifetz, R. (2011), 'Debate: Leadership and authority'. *Public Money and Management*: 301–8.

House, R. J. (1995), 'Leadership in the Twenty-first Century: A Speculative Inquiry', in A. Howard (ed.), *The Changing Nature of Work*. San Francisco: Jossey-Bass.

Hunter, S. (2012), '(Un) Ethical leadership and identity: What did we learn and where do we go from here?' *Journal of Business Ethics*, 107: 79–87.

Langton, R. (1993), 'Speech acts and unspeakable acts'. *Philosophy and Public Affairs*, 22 (4): 293–330.

Maitra, I. and McGowan, M. K. (2007), 'The limits of free speech: Pornography and the question of coverage'. *Legal Theory*, 13 (1): 41–68.

Marmor, A. (2011), 'An institutional conception of authority'. *Philosophy and Public Affairs*, 39 (3): 238–61.

Maritz Research (2010), 'Managing in an era of distrust: Maritz Poll reveals employees lack trust in their workplace' http://www.maritz.com/Maritz-Poll/2010/Maritz-Poll-Reveals-Employees-Lack-Trust-in-their-Workplace

McGowan, M. K. (2004), 'Conversational exercitives: Something else we do with our words'. *Linguistics and Philosophy*, 27 (1): 93–111.

Newton, L. (1987), 'Moral leadership in business: The role of structure'. *Business and Professional Ethics Journal*, 5 (3–4): 74–90.

Peus, C., Wesche, J. S., Streicher, B., Braun, S. and Frey, D. (2012), 'Authentic leadership: An empirical test of its antecedents, consequences, and mediating mechanisms'. *Journal of Business Ethics*, 107: 331–48.

Pfeffer, J. (1998), *The Human Equation: Building Profits by Putting People First*. Cambridge, MA: Harvard Business School Press.

Searle, J. R. (1999), *Expression and Meaning: Studies in the Theory of Speech Acts*. Cambridge: Cambridge University Press.

Spicker, P. (2012), 'Leadership: A perniciously vague concept', *International Journal of Public Sector Management*, 25 (1): 34–47.

Weber, M. (1947), *The Theory of Social and Economic Organisations* (trans. A. M. Henderson and T. Parsons, ed. T. Parsons). New York: Free Press.

Yukl, G. (1999), 'An evaluation of conceptual weaknesses in transformational and charismatic leadership theories'. *The Leadership Quarterly*, 10 (2): 285–305.

Zaleznik, A. and Kets de Vries, M. F. R. (1975), *Power and the Corporate Mind*. Boston: Houghton Mifflin.

Part Two

Some Concerns About Leadership

4

Must Leadership Be Undemocratic?

Jacqueline Boaks
University of Western Australia

Theories of leadership and democracy and their underlying assumptions both speak to our relationship to power. The core question common to discussions ranging from political legitimacy, to democracy, to Machiavellianism, to Platonism, is what, if any, power that some individuals have over others is (morally as well as legally) legitimate and why? At one extreme are cases such as Machiavellianism and political realism, which come close to suggesting that whatever actual power individuals or states can maintain as just is legitimate. At the other extreme is the sceptical position that believes no power of individuals over others is legitimate. Theories of leadership and democracy both offer alternative kinds of answers to this question, both accepting that some types are legitimate and with limiting factors. Both democracy and leadership can be seen as centrally including claims for the right and safe allocation of power. This chapter will explore what, if any, the connections are between the norms of democracy and the norms of leadership.

As I have argued elsewhere,[1] to make sense of the term 'leadership' and to allow the term to serve the normative functions that we so often demand of it, leadership must be grounded in a sense of the good. This grounding involves knowledge of what is needed for the flourishing of both the followers and leaders. It also involves servicing that need – advancing those interests. . This results in an understanding of leadership as a broadly Aristotelian master virtue.

What does it mean to conceive of leadership as a virtue? The term 'virtue' in the Aristotelian context belongs to the conception of ethics known as virtue ethics, traceable to the ancient Greeks. This conception of ethics and the virtues that are a constitutive part of it are grounded in the idea of 'eudaimonia' or human flourishing. Eudaimonia can be loosely translated as a state of well-being in which human beings become what they should by living as they should. It is the end or proper goal of the master art of living virtuously and it is also the only way, on an account such as Aristotle's, to achieve real happiness. Paul Taylor describes it as:

> the good of man as man. Happiness (eudaimonia, well-being) is the kind of life that is suitable or fitting for a human being to live, and a human being is one who exemplifies the essential nature (or essence) of man. Thus happiness is not to be identified with any kind of life a person might actually want to live. Instead, it characterizes the kind of life we all would want to live if we understood our true nature as human beings. Happiness, then, may be defined as that state of the "soul" or condition of life which all human beings, insofar as they are human, ultimately aim at.[2]

The virtues are those traits of persons that serve human flourishing. Unlike the ethical rules or duties that ground other systems of ethics, the virtues are traits of persons (excellences) that make human lives go well. Having the virtue involves elements of skill, disposition and judgement. Virtues lie on a golden mean between two extremes and judgement is what allows the virtuous person to act correctly. For example the virtue of courage lies between the extremes of foolhardiness (too much) and cowardice (too little), and involves acting with the correct amount of courage, in the correct manner, at the correct time. 'Correct' in this sense is that which serves human flourishing.

Rosalind Hursthouse shows how the maxims of virtue ethics are grounded in this conception of human flourishing. Thus it is here that we find both the limiting factor on what is a virtue and also the content of virtue ethics: the virtues are those traits that foster just this particular human flourishing.[3] Grounding leadership in flourishing is one possible way to make sense of the claim that leadership just is ethically good leadership, and demonstrates what a grounding in virtue ethics can offer to leadership studies.

This account of leadership includes several key elements – such leadership must not be coercive and must respect the interests (the flourishing) of persons. Further, being a broadly Aristotelian virtue, leadership on this account contains a strong sense of good judgement about the good of followers and leaders as well as how to achieve this. Just as the Aristotelian virtuous agent shows the right amount of courage (being neither reckless and foolhardy nor timid), at the right time and in the right (that is, skilful) manner – so the individual who displays the virtue of leadership in this broadly Aristotelian sense leads in the right way at the right time towards the right goals. They do so because part of what it is to have this virtue is to know how to pursue this goal, and to be motivated and able to.

This is what is required to ground the sense of 'leadership' as distinct from mere populism, or from those who would use personal and charismatic power for evil. It is also where the potential lies for a tension with democracy . As we shall see below, any substantive definition of democracy involves or should involve respect for individuals to articulate, pursue and defend to others their own interests and conceptions of the good. Democracy is committed to equal respect for persons' own conceptions of the good, or in Thomas Christiano's terms, to the equal consideration of the interests of all.[4] This is why it is generally taken to be uniquely compatible with liberalism and its pluralist commitments. It represents a way of an understanding of leadership that means we would not apply the term to Hitler but we would to Gandhi or Martin Luther King, Jr. (thus addressing what Ciulla succinctly refers to as 'the Hitler problem':[5] that is, whether we consider Hitler to have been a leader). However, the concept of leadership is grounded in a potentially essentialist idea of the good for persons – one that does not recognize a plurality of goods or therefore *prima facie* any need for the equal consideration of persons' judgements about the good and their interests. There may thus be a conflict between the notion of democracy which recognizes the need for equal consideration and a plurality of goods on the one hand, and the notion of leadership that insists (in some essentialist manner) on one overarching notion of the good that ostensibly takes persons' interest (that is their 'real' interest) into account. This chapter will explain and then explore this potential conflict, before proposing a resolution.

In the case of democracy, Robert A. Dahl rejected the idea of rulers who know better than those ruled with a specific nod to Plato's model as the paradigm case of these. 'Guardians, Plato called them (that) has always been the major rival to democratic ideas.'[6] For Dahl, outlining a common thread of thought, given the absence of such experts and the historically evidenced dangers of instances where just such authority has been claimed, democracy is a constraint on just such claims to power: '… full inclusion in a democratic state is the only desirable outcome.'[7] Thus he writes:

> If no persons are so definitely better to govern that they should be entrusted with complete and final authority over the government of the state, then who is better qualified to participate than all the adults who are subject to the laws?[8]

This is fine as far as it goes, given Dahl's premises (that is, that there are no such persons who are better qualified to govern than we are). But given a conception of leadership as a virtue that serves human flourishing, that by definition includes knowledge of what is best – in fact that the concept of leadership only performs the conceptual work we want it to if it is grounded in knowledge and pursuit of the good – why should such a person not rule? That is, in terms of Dahl's conditional, the antecedent does not hold. The broadly Aristotelian leader *is* such a person. Our question is two-fold:

1. Is such a person and such ideal leadership compatible with democracy?
2. Would such an ideal ruler rule democratically? (*Could* they?)

That is, the key questions for our purposes are whether leadership as I have conceived it, as a broadly Aristotelian virtue, is compatible with democracy. More specifically, the question is whether there are conceptual links between the idea of democracy and the idea of the virtue of leadership, or whether they are compatible merely in the way that an ideal ruler could perhaps rule – that is, democratically. This latter kind of compatibility I will refer to as 'minimal compatibility'. It does not tell us much about any overlap between leadership and democracy. An ideal ruler or leader would rule *ideally* (*whether or not* that means democratically). They would do so even in circumstances where they are given more power and latitude than democracy permits given its checks and limits on power. The ideal ruler has no limitations on their power – such as those that motivate and define democracy. By definition the ideal ruler is not motivated to misuse power by applying it to self-interest or to ends other than the well-being of followers and is fully capable of advancing the well-being of followers. That is, they simply would not be a tyrant even if given licence and scope to be one[9] – thus avoiding one of the dangers that democracy can be seen as a safeguard against. However, one can easily imagine an ideal ruler, whether a philosopher-king, Gordon Graham's sense of an ideal and just but unelected ruler,[10] or Mill's benevolent dictator,[11] who is not democratic either in the regime they head or in the manner in which they rule. It would be wishful thinking to think otherwise: that is, that the ideal ruler must rule democratically (effectively relinquishing their power and position as ideal ruler). The question, as Graham succinctly put it, is whether the fact of this ruler's not being democratic would matter, whether we should still prefer a democratically elected ruler to such an ideal but unelected ruler and on what grounds we might do so.[12] Moreover, there is the second question raised above. We want to ask, in the context of our discussion about leadership and democracy, whether in fact our posited Aristotelian ideal leader *would* be democratic – that is, not whether such a ruler *could* rule democratically if such requirements were in place, but whether they *would* rule democratically even in the absence of such requirements. The answer is that they would be democratic (or better: would rule in a democratic manner) *only if such a democratic rule was good for us and our flourishing*. Why would this be the case? Because the ideal Aristotelian leader as we have defined them, who possesses the qualities of leadership as an Aristotelian master virtue, and who is motivated, and able, to subjugate all other goods to what serves the flourishing of his or her followers, both knows and pursues what serves our flourishing. In this case the question is one of whether democracy serves our flourishing. Thus, if democratic rule itself serves our flourishing, then the ideal ruler will rule democratically. If it does not, then the ideal ruler will not rule democratically, instead prioritizing our flourishing and subjugating other interests or goods (in this case including democracy) to that flourishing. Of course, given what Graham refers to as the problem of 'lack of candidates', then we may prefer democracy in the (presumably ongoing) absence of an ideal ruler, but we would not have a special reason to think that democracy is conceptually linked to the ideal beyond minimal compatibility.

What distinguishes leadership from formal power or authority is that, unlike the latter, leaders do not have the ability to coerce others to act as the leader wishes. Leaders *qua* leaders cannot use the formal, institutional powers that are constitutive of formal power to affect persons and oblige them to act or not act as the leader wishes. Leaders must rather appeal to followers to act, speak or think in a certain way or to adopt goals based on methods that are more voluntary on the part of followers. Given the central role of consent and voluntariness in the concept of ideal leadership, and the persistent and widespread normative preference for democracy at least in the West, the question of compatibility is important. Leadership's central appeal to followers, especially in the case of leadership as distinct from formal positions of authority, seems *prima facie* to mesh well with democracy, but leadership, with its valorizing of one individual, meshes perhaps too well with totalitarian and other forms of government that do not share the egalitarian commitments of democracy. Thus we need to ask if leadership is truly compatible with democracy or is this ideal leadership precisely one of the kinds of power that democracy aims to constrain? One indicator of compatibility – and not just the minimal compatibility described above – would be if the same underpinning concepts that justify democracy also justify leadership. Alternatively, a democratic style might be a qualifier of normative or ideal leadership – that is, being genuinely influenced by the preferences of all followers equally (something like what is often referred to in the leadership literature as a 'consultative leadership style') might be one of the very elements that mark out 'good' leadership as 'good'. That is, morally good as well as effective. What specifically is meant by 'morally good leadership'? The question is not as simple as it might at first appear. Ciulla offers the most concise and useful account of what we might mean by 'good leadership' by outlining three main possible senses of 'good' leadership', or what she refers to as 'three general, obvious and completely interlocking categories for the moral assessment of leadership'.[13] First, Ciulla lists 'the ethics of leaders themselves' – their 'intentions … [and] personal ethics'; second, 'the ethics of how a leader leads (or the process of leadership …)'; and third 'the ethics of what a leader does – the ends of leadership'.[14] It may well be that democratic leadership answers to one of Ciulla's three criteria for 'good leadership', specifically leadership done in an ethically good manner, i.e *how* the leader leads. The intuitions that ground democracy in an equal respect for persons, their interests and their judgements might be the same as those that ground 'good' leadership in the good of followers.

What does 'democracy' mean?

It is important at this point to define what we mean by 'democracy'. Beyond the general, pre-theoretical concept of democracy as a kind of shared decision-making procedure that appeals to an equal counting of preferences, the finer details of what makes a community or state democratic are often nuanced and contested. For example, the role of equality of opportunity, distributive fairness, deliberative democracy and the level of participatory involvement by citizens in decisions are all contested aspects of democracy. It should be possible, however, to do what our discussion requires without taking a stance on these contested aspects of the definition of democracy here – to come up with a workable definition of what is common to accounts of democracy to allow us to meaningfully examine the relationship between leadership and democracy. To do this I will follow Thomas Christiano's account from his 'The Authority of Democracy'[15] and his 'Democracy as Equality'.[16]

Christiano identifies what he describes as two 'evaluative aspects' of democracy.[17] The first turns on the procedural element of democracy: that is, evaluations of decisions made 'from the point of view of how they are made or the quality of the procedure. We are concerned to make the decision in a way that includes everyone who by right ought to be included and that is fair to all the participants'.[18] The second turns on outcomes: that is, 'with whether the outcomes are just or whether they are efficient or protect liberty and promote the common good. This is sometimes called the substantive or outcome dimension of assessment of democratic procedures'.[19] I will follow Christiano and call these, respectively, the 'procedural' and the 'outcomes' aspect of our working theory of democracy. For Christiano, the meaningful and measurable element of substantive democratic outcomes is what he calls 'equal consideration of interests'[20] – that is, that advancing each person's interests should be treated as equally important as advancing that of every other person.[21] On Christiano's account (in part because we cannot ensure or measure or meaningfully compare the more direct measure of equal well-being[22]) this is best ensured by an equal share of resources in the democratic decision-making process (that is, an equal vote and equal resources to participate in collective decision making processes).[23] Thus, for Christiano, the two measures are interrelated – one (the substantive democratic outcomes, represented by justice, required equal consideration of interests[24]) grounds the need for the other. '[E]qual consideration of interests implies that individuals be given equal resources with which to understand, elaborate, and pursue their interests'.[25] This includes and requires equal resources to participate in collective decision making about aspects that affect persons, including but not limited to an equal vote[26] (that is, procedural fairness or in Christiano's terminology 'political equality'[27]). Thus, as we will see later, accounts that hold that the procedural element can meaningfully stand alone are slighter and do less justice to democracy correctly understood than it might first appear. Throughout – and to the extent that the procedural and the substantive (outcomes) elements of democracy can be separated – when I refer to the 'substantive democratic outcomes' or 'Christiano's outcomes criterion of democracy' it will be informed by this understanding of democracy as requiring the 'equal consideration of interests'.

Why might leadership and democracy not be compatible?

Graham is likely being unfair to procedural accounts when he refers to them as the 'opinion poll view of democracy'[28] (because as we have just seen, none beyond the most simplistic accounts of democracy assert it as a mere decision-making procedure that turns purely on a kind of majority rules), but it does suggest both an affinity that we suspect between democracy and leadership and why we might be concerned that personal popularity might undermine substantive democracy. One way to understand this threat is by the potential to lead to the 'mass irrational support' for a ruler or leader that E. B. Portis describes as a threat to political competition.[29] Another is the Weberian charismatic leadership that is based on an emotional and uncritical following of a (seemingly infallible) leader for their exceptional personal qualities that Tucker describes.[30] Such charismatic leadership can be used for good or for bad, but it is its ability to switch off followers' own critical faculties that makes us concerned about it as a threat to democracy and about its potential to lead to objectives and actions we would otherwise find unappealing or even repugnant. One reason we have to be concerned about the relationship between democracy and leadership is that these forms of leadership can easily be seen as a threat to democratic procedure and the well-being of persons on any plausible understanding of that term. This is even more true of substantive democratic outcomes – that is, the equal consideration of interests. This need not be because there is anything intrinsic about such kinds of leadership that necessarily undermines such outcomes. It is enough that the critical faculties of followers might be switched off or that the kind of public scrutiny and review of collective decisions can so easily be undermined where a disproportionate level of faith and trust (or some other kind of non-reflective, non-rational or irrational attraction) in the single figure of the leader is in place – and both of these mechanisms, the critical faculties of persons and the public debate over collective decisions, can be good protections against such undemocratic outcomes.

Charismatic leadership and democracy

The account of charismatic leadership, deploying so-called 'symbolic politics', that Portis describes[31] is closer to what prompts much of our scepticism about leadership than are the extreme cases of Machiavellian tyrants and charismatic demagogues. (And this is the case beyond the extremes of so-called 'toxic leadership' models proposed to account for very bad or wicked leadership by figures such as the dangerous cult leader or the bullying CEO that leads to often terrible outcomes.[32]) These other accounts such as Portis's are at least a significant enough threat to make us worry. Portis's claim stems from what she holds is 'the practical implausibility of classical theories of democracy in modern societies'.[33] This implausibility, according to Portis, occurs because such societies are simply not logistically conducive to a populace that is informed about matters of policy and is thus capable of participatory democracy in a way that is meaningful or desirable. In addition to this implausibility, Portis holds that in recent times 'the public, for better or worse, has found the symbolic awards more meaningful than specific policies', even where these specific policies contradict the symbolic messages. Thus, on this account, charismatic leaders can and should use symbolic politics as a way of achieving their ends of institutional stability and popular control.[34] This disconnection between a charismatic leader (in the case discussed by Portis, Ronald Reagan, whose symbolic politics is attractive to and supported by the public, while pursuing policies and objectives that the same public largely *disapproves* of) is an example of exactly the kind of risk that charismatic leadership and symbolic politics seem to raise, because of the gap it opens between public scrutiny of policy and endorsement of the symbolic politics. Think, for example, of the case of Barack Obama who talks of peace and reconciliation with nations previously hostile to the US and of scaling back the wars of the previous administration (sufficient to be awarded a Nobel Peace Prize) while increasing the frequency and locations of unpiloted drone attacks. The extent to which charismatic leaders can appeal to the public to 'follow' or support them based on these symbolic politics rather than the examination of their actual policies and objectives is the source of a more subtle but arguably more common problem we perceive with some purported instances of popular 'leadership': that it might distract from and minimize the examination of the goals and policies of a society that helps make it democratic. That is, that leadership and its personal appeal add something to the mix that undermines reasoned, rational discourse of 'what is to be done'. The appeal on this account attaches to the individual leader over any facts of the matter. This not only undermines the democratic values of debate and judgement by citizens but risks allowing the pursuit of wrong-headed or unethical goals and non-democratic values (whether immediately or in the future) by reducing the occurrence of, and the conditions for, public scrutiny of such goals and values. Such goals of course are antithetical to well-being on any account (though would-be leaders of this kind all too often claim otherwise). Both the procedural and the outcomes criteria for democracy that are described above in defining democracy can be violated and undermined in this way: the procedural because this can all too easily undermine the ability for rational discourse and debate that is necessary to equal consideration of interests; and the outcomes criteria because these goals need not serve the equal consideration of interests. What Portis depicts is the political version of the 'managing meaning' that Takala[35] and others in the business literature talk of as the role of leadership, disconnected from the goals and policies themselves. Portis, seemingly overlooking the requirements of an even minimally substantive definition of democracy over a purely procedural one, puts it like this:

> I argue in the following pages that if democracy in the classical sense of popular rule is to have much reality in the modern world, it will have to mean popular control of cultural meaning and cultural change. Furthermore, I believe that

significant popular participation in the determination of cultural meaning is
likely to occur only through the mediation of charismatic leaders.[36]

Far from ideals of deliberative democracy, Portis argues that democracy in
the current context of mass, technologically advanced cultures can only occur
through such symbols of meaning under the control of charismatic leaders
(and without offering much to define what such 'popular control' means).
Schumpeter held the same view. Schumpeter's model, as Mackie notes, is that
'The will of the people, usually, is not genuine, but is manufactured by the
leader. It is not true that voters control parliament, which controls its leader;
rather the leader manufactures the will of the people and followers accept it,
which is as it should be, since the judgement of a qualified[37] leader is generally
superior to that of parliaments and publics.'[38]

Of course, the mediating role of the charismatic leader that Portis describes
need not be seen as a dishonest role. If one accepts Portis's premise, that the
mass populations of large modern democracies are generally unwilling or
unable to have opinions on matters of political policy in a way that enables
meaningful participatory or representative democracy, then a mediation role
may well be seen as a way to salvage a form of democracy from this situation.
However, we cannot rightfully call such mediation 'leadership' without considering ethical aspects of it, and nor can we see it as compatible with democracy
without placing the kind of limits on it that Portis seems unwilling to do. For
the real danger is that this kind of 'charismatic leadership' undermines precisely
the role of the judgement of persons about matters of collective decisions
that are the hallmarks of democracy. That is, this account fails not only the
substantive outcomes element of democracy, but also the procedural element
correctly understood because it does not rise to the standard of decisions made
on the basis of informed and meaningfully expressed opinions held by citizens.
Portis may be correct that 'charismatic leadership, combined with a competitive
electoral system, can lead to a significant degree of popular control of symbolic
politics' (that is, of symbols of meaning mediated by charismatic leaders and
the narratives they tell) and she may even be correct that 'To be successful the
symbolic appeals of contenders for power will have to ... relate to real frustra-
tions, hopes and fears,'[39] but it is not clear that this 'significant' degree of popular
control will be a meaningful one nor that the symbolic politics themselves
will meaningfully relate to the actual politics and policies. Again, the example
of the Obama administration's military practices is instructive of the kind of
gap we have in mind here – where talk of reducing the wars and injustices of

the previous administration coexists with an *increase* in drone-strike killings and extrajudicial killings even of American citizens. The true danger of this account seems to be the real potential to undermine, to minimize meaningful democracy by reducing the extent to which members of the democracy can engage with and share in, or even influence, collective decisions. This kind of charismatic leadership, with its focus on personal appeal and symbols, moves away from objective formation and exchange of citizens' judgements about their interests and collective decisions, which makes some wary of leadership. This is echoed in concerns regularly expressed in modern mass democracies over the focus on the kind of personal charm- and personality-based election campaigns for elected office rather than, and in obstruction to, substantive debates about ideas and policies (let alone equal participation in these by ordinary citizens and highly financed lobby groups – though the two are very much related).

Further, even if we do accept Portis's claim that the mediation of charismatic leaders deploying symbolic politics is the most plausible path to popular control in mass democracy, it seems even more necessary that such leaders be moral, and make the right decisions regarding value and prioritizing goals, precisely because of the gap between these symbolic politics and the policies themselves. It is this that gives us concern that democracy might not be a good means of selecting 'good' leaders – especially when coupled with the claim that there is only symbolic and mediated connection between the political discourse and the actual issues and values discussed. Further, if we accept, per Portis and Schumpeter, that it is unlikely that the majority of citizens in a democracy will be politically savvy enough to make participatory democracy plausible – to participate in a meaningful way in discussions about concepts of the good and of justice – *and* that we want leaders who will at least do so in an ethically good manner and aim at or symbolically represent ethically good goals, then we risk a problematic paternalism: that is, the pursuit of the good without engagement with followers on what that good is. This omits one of the hallmarks of democracy – a respect for and engagement with people's judgements on the matter of the good.[40] Not all of these popular accounts of leadership will be compatible with democracy. So which accounts of leadership are preferable?

To do what we want the concept of leadership to do and to be coherent and non-stipulative, leadership needs to be conceived of as more than just popularity: it needs further grounding. We need to further explain what leadership is and how it relates to democracy.

Leadership, on both a pre-theoretical understanding and the broadly Aristotelian normative account above, is largely justified by appeals to the personal characteristics of the leader and their objectives. The ideal leader is the person who, *pace* Aristotle, by their very nature, can and does subjugate other interests to the flourishing of followers and themselves. Such a leader knows what the good of followers is and is able and willing to pursue it.

Rather than Graham's[41] question of whether an ideal (or at least more ideal) non-democratically elected ruler is more or less desirable than a less ideal democratically elected ruler, the question in our case is whether the ideal ruler *would* be democratic? Talcott Parsons notes that leadership's constitutive appeal for authority based on personal characteristics is 'a kind of claim to authority that is specifically in conflict with the bases of legitimacy of an established, fully institutionalized order.'[42] Here we have a potential opposition between the wellsprings of leadership and of democracy. The situation may even be worse than that democracy is *unlikely* to select good leaders. As we saw above in the case of Portis's symbolic politics and the kind of charismatic leader that Weber describes,[43] electoral popularity might be one of the very mechanisms by which democratic citizens and followers are led away from the ideal leader. As Tucker notes, for Weber the charismatic leader is a value-neutral term: 'To be a charismatic leader is not necessarily to be an admirable individual.'[44] Portis identifies well the concern here, with the case of 'mass irrational support' for a charismatic leader.[45] One particularly powerful way in which this can be instantiated is demonstrated in the Freudian approach outlined by Cox, Levine and Newman, who describe how in some instances leaders (or leading ideas) and the dynamic they share with followers can operate in neurotic ways, with followers at once (over)identifying with the leader and gaining psychological satisfaction from such emotional ties. Followers are reassured by the illusion that the leader, a kind of idealized father figure, bestows equal love on all followers.[46] The model operates at the level of (often unconscious) libidinal ties and sits closer to a shared neurosis than to any ideal leader or ruler. At best in such cases, Cox et al. (following Le Bon[47] and Freud[48]) tell us, such leader–follower group dynamics function and confer identities for followers in ways that are libidinal rather than rational and subdue the critical faculties of such followers (for example, by making followers susceptible to believe shared lies and not examine flawed shared 'truths' and reasons).[49] At worst, they lead to what Freud refers to as 'neurotic fear or anxiety'[50] when such groups and individuals are threatened and intolerance of others outside the follower group reinforces group identity and functioning.[51] It is just this 'cognitive deficit'[52] that Cox et al. describe as being a hallmark and product of some such group dynamics – this very impaired judgement about all matters that relate to the group and its beliefs but especially about the value of the (idealized) leader – that makes us right to be wary of an appeal to followers as a legitimating source of power. If this is indeed the nature of our attachment to leaders, then far from being the kind of 'honorific' that Ciulla describes, the normative value of such a status looks grim. So too does the question of whether we can call it 'voluntary' in any meaningful way. It's certainly not a candidate for respect for persons' interests and judgements because it undermines just those persons' ability to have reliable judgements about these interests. If this account is correct, it is particularly problematic for the view of leadership as a benign way of allocating power and of ordering such asymmetrical power relationships. We are likely to be led astray both in our choice of leaders and their goals. It is precisely the required connection between the judgement of followers required by both the concepts of leadership and the justification of democracy that these accounts call into question.

A similar picture to the Freudian account described by Cox et al. is given in the Weberian description of the 'charismatic leader'. Robert C. Tucker notes, in his account of Weberian charismatic leadership, that 'in a genuine case of charismatic leadership, it would be virtually inconceivable for a follower to contradict or disagree with the leader or to question his infallibility in any way'.[53] Such 'leadership' is explicitly described as embedded in an emotional fixation on the leader that echoes the Freudian approach outlined by Cox et al. According to Tucker, charismatic leadership is typically marked by 'the passionate devotion'[54] of followers to the leader, who personally embodies the hope of salvation from distressing conditions,[55] which explains 'the special emotional intensity of the charismatic response.'[56] Again, like the Freudian account, this kind of leadership is marked by strong, emotional attachment to an idealized individual (it is 'salvationist or messianic in nature'[57]). This emotional investment in and dedication to one individual fits exactly the kind of 'mass, irrational support'[58] that Portis describes (though often with less concern than we might have about it) and that is such a threat to a substantive, deliberative democracy – the procedural and the outcomes criteria of democracy – with its ideal of public discourse, the equal consideration of interests, the equal ability to participate in collective decisions and the nature of the good in the form of the justice of institutions, etc. This kind of attachment is crucial to my concerns. It is problematic for any account of leadership that wants to outline, as any good and useful account should, what kinds of leadership we should accept. We have a combination of a forceful, non-rational attachment and the power and pull of proffered ideas of the good – and in some cases of salvation. This kind of attachment undermines, if it does not preclude, a democratically adequate kind of evaluation. It does so because it shuts off the critical faculty required for such an evaluation of the would-be leader and their claims before us. This kind of concern yields the temptation to wariness of leadership *tout court*, especially if such influence coincides, or we have reason to think it coincides, with those who want to remake the world. The question again is whether this fulfils the requirements of democracy but not leadership; of leadership but not democracy; or of neither democracy nor leadership?

The role of the good

Central to this discussion is the role of the good with respect to power, to democracy and to leadership. Again, democracy and leadership may have different answers to this question. For Plato, the philosopher-kings should hold power not only because they best know how to rule but because they know and seek the good for those they rule.[59] On the Platonic account they do so undemocratically. Democracy is pushed to the side. It is unnecessary. It is detrimental. Virtue ethics and the broadly Aristotelian model of leadership place the good as central to leadership and to power – it is the knowledge and pursuit of the good of followers that we have used to ground and define leadership. At first glance, democracy seems to give a purely formal and value-neutral answer to the question of legitimate leadership – that is, without reference to the good. If a person is legitimately elected then they are the legitimate leader (ruler) – especially if we rely on what we described above as the procedural element of democracy. But this can be misleading. Any substantive account of democracy is in part defined by and grounded in the good of persons. In fact, neither of the evaluative aspects that Christiano refers to above as providing the authority for democracy – what we have called the procedural and the outcomes criteria – are neutral with respect to the good. The procedural aspect, as Christiano specifies it, is grounded in and gains its authority because of its treatment of the judgements of persons as equal in decision making, and not because we necessarily think they will come to the right decisions but because we think it serves the good of persons to respect equally the judgement of those persons.[60] Further, the equal consideration of interests is required. Following Christiano, this is how I have expressed the outcomes criterion, and which Christiano holds as our best measure in the absence of a meaningful measurement or comparison of achieving equal well-being of persons. This requires that each person has an equal say in collective decision making. This means treating the preferences of persons and thus treating persons themselves with equal respect – and in large part because such treatment is necessary for the equal consideration of interests that forms the basis of Christiano's substantive account of democracy, including the equal consideration of interests that is central to the outcomes criterion of democracy.[61] The substantive outcomes evaluative element – equal consideration of interests – turns on normative outcomes deemed to be good: outcomes such as equality. To think otherwise is to reduce democracy to the 'opinion poll' version of democracy invoked by Graham – the simplistic account of democracy as nothing more than a decision-making procedure where the majority rules. In part, theorists of democracy such as Christiano[62] argue that equality and equal respect for persons' judgements, as the best although still imperfect way to ensure 'equal consideration of interests', is the good to be pursued. However, the additional issue of neutrality with respect to what constitutes the good life, which as Chantal Mouffe notes is central to liberal accounts of democracy,[63] complicates this. At question is whether this neutrality with respect to the good life is incompatible with the central focus on the flourishing of followers that we have established as central to leadership as a master virtue. But we have begun to see above that democracy correctly understood is not value neutral.

As we noted above, the various accounts of democracy (and by extension the rulers it yields) offer different candidates as the defining and justifying criteria for democracy. However, there is a common thread – all address the good of persons. Thus, while some accounts such as Dahl's rely on the judgements of the governed, others such as Christiano's rely on equal consideration of interests requiring (but not perfectly guaranteed by) equal participation in decision making,[64] while others such as Machin refer to a democratic means of justifying differences in political power between citizens (what he refers to as 'the egalitarian challenge'[65]). All of these speak to the good.[66]

This makes clear the role of the good in at least substantive democratic accounts. On the above view political legitimacy of democratic processes, institutions and leaders comes not only from purely formal democratic selection processes or decisions justified by what Graham calls the 'opinion poll' form of democracy. Moreover, as noted above, even a meaningful equal count of preferences (that is, the procedural aspect of democracy) requires substantive outcomes to ensure that all have an equal opportunity and ability to participate in such preference counting. While an election procedure may be a necessary condition to political legitimacy of democratic rulers, it is not sufficient. Rather, on this justification, rule is democratic and legitimate to the extent that it serves the equal consideration of interests of subjects/citizens/followers. So, for example, a democratically elected ruler could act undemocratically by failing to ensure that substantive democratic outcomes (i.e. equal consideration of interests) are met. And here we find the question of the relationship between leadership and democracy sharpened. Would our ideal leader be democratic in this sense? Recall that the ideal ruler by definition will do what makes his or her followers flourish. Thus, if it serves our flourishing to have a leader/ruler with a democratic style of rule then he or she will provide and follow this. If it does not, they will not. The role of the good is thus a major site of the problem of the relationship between leadership and democracy because the requirements that both have towards the good, the way in which each of them is grounded in it, must be compatible if leadership and democracy are to be compatible. In part this is to be addressed by answering to what extent our flourishing, as the ideal leader would understand it, coincides with the equal consideration of our interests and the ways in which democracy pursues this.

The tension for leadership and democracy

The tension for leadership with respect to democracy is that it seems to at once both imply and preclude the kind of involvement in decision making (as opposed to equal consideration of interests or well-being) that Christiano tells us is the hallmark of democracy.[67] On Christiano's account, substantively democratic rulers and institutions can and should pursue the equal consideration of interests of persons partly by allowing persons an equal voice in public discussion of the questions of the good, of justice, etc., and to choose for themselves what is in their interests, but not measuring or comparing the well-being of followers. I have defined leadership as grounded in a knowledge and pursuit of the good for followers (and leaders). Thus, democracy's commitment to persons having the ability to choose what best serves their own well-being may well conflict both with its popular/majority rule and with the commitment and grounding of leadership as I have defined it in the knowledge and pursuit of the good of followers. Both leadership and democracy theory contain claims about popularity *and* about the nature of the good. This produces a tension both within and between the two ideas. Leadership in particular needs to reconcile the claims that the leader is qualified to rule because of their knowledge of the good, especially the good for followers, with two other facts. The first of these is the legitimating (justificatory) fact (which is at least partly indicative of leadership as distinct from more arbitrarily assigned power) of leaders' appeal to and selection by followers. The second is Dahl's advice that we are wrong to think that there are 'experts' who know better than we do and to whom government should be turned over. If we want leadership and democracy to be compatible, the outcomes condition of democracy places a limit on leadership that might help us to separate desirable leadership from what is posited as undesirable leadership, such as so-called 'toxic leadership' – or leadership that undermines the good of persons and the equal consideration of interests of persons. On this view, such leadership that does not further or that actively undermines the equal consideration of interests of persons which we have taken as a hallmark of democracy would not be leadership in this normative sense. This might well mirror the way in which the broadly Aristotelian idea of leadership as a virtue is grounded in its role in promoting human flourishing.

Prima facie, therefore, it is easy to think that there is some natural affinity between leadership and democracy (at least to a point) – and not only on the question of popular support as constitutive of legitimacy of both democratic rulers and of leaders but also with respect to the good. This is especially so if we see each individual's choice to 'follow' and thus legitimate a leader as akin to the resources to contribute to collective decision making that Christiano finds so necessary. Unconstrained, this choice to support a leader, to endorse them as a leader, is a 'resource' akin to voting for a decision or a ruler. It can seem to rule out concerns about a disconnection from the judgements of the ruled that Christiano describes as 'perverse',[68] as well as to other paternalistic accounts of power or ones that in other ways don't consider – in an equal way – the interests or judgements of followers. Above and beyond accounts of 'democratic' leadership *styles*, leadership can imply a reliance on the judgement of followers as the source of its legitimacy that implies both respect for the opinions of followers and a prevention of abuse of the ruled (for example, the protection of minority rights even in the face of a majority voting or lobbying against these). This tallies well with democratic theory, including the equal consideration of interests that ground the outcomes account of democracy outlined above, all of which can seem to sit well with leadership as distinct from mere power or authority.

In part, any accordance between this kind of leadership and democracy is no coincidence given that the aims of democracy also include the well-being of persons. We should not be surprised that a model of leadership that is defined as being capable and willing to pursue the well-being of persons accords well with it. Both have the same goals.

Of course, even if the kind of leadership discussed here marries well with democracy, the question remains how well it accords with leadership in other contexts. Does it, for example, carry over to business and other kinds of leadership? One difference here will be the extent to which such settings have the well-being of persons (including of the leader) as their goal, or the extent to which such goals are compatible with the well-being of persons. A common thread, for example, in what we might call the more optimistic accounts of leadership over scientific management in the business literature is what was referred to above as the 'good news story' that treating employees well and fostering their well-being also results in improved performance. But even if this is true in some cases it need not be. Perhaps this element of the context will limit the extent to which various kinds of leadership can approximate to the ideal, broadly Aristotelian model of leadership used here.

On the other hand, as we saw above, *contra* this apparent sympathy between leadership and democracy, various kinds of 'toxic', charismatic and symbolic leadership can raise problems with the idea of democracy as compatible with leadership as defined. These include populism, demagogues and an appeal to popularity over any substantive or just outcomes. But does a charismatic 'leader' who comes to power by appealing to an electorate in this manner fulfil the requirements of democracy? Specifically would the leader fulfil the procedural and the outcomes (equal consideration of interests) requirements I outlined above in our working definition of democracy? If not, what does this mean for the compatibility of leadership and democracy, including and especially on the grounds of what legitimates power? In fact an examination of this might well remove a potential discord between leadership and democracy. The concern here of course is that this kind of popular support might fulfil the procedural requirements of democratic power but not of ideal leadership. Leadership, as we described above, needs more grounding than that of mere popularity. On proper consideration, so too does democracy, as we saw when we came to define democracy above.

Leadership, undefined and open to interpretation as mere populism or charisma, can remind us of some of these excesses of populism unchecked by substantive democratic outcomes or by any focus on the justness of outcomes in part by reducing it to a form of pure, unconstrained influence on others. Recent world history is all too full of examples of the fact that such popular influence can lead us away from such substantive democratic ideals. This is true even when this is done with explicit popular support – and often on the grounds that moves away from such democratic ideals are temporary and needed in the face of supposedly extraordinary threats. Such examples remind us of the need for substantive democratic outcomes in our definition of democracy and our broadly Aristotelian model of leadership. A focus on being supported or liked by followers is both insufficient and potentially dangerous (for both leadership and for democracy). It is dangerous for leadership in that it threatens to reduce leadership to mere popularity. In addition, it loses the normative elements of leadership as I have defined it and requires that we solve what Ciulla refers to as 'the Hitler problem'. It is dangerous to democracy in that it threatens the substantive, equal consideration of interests aspect that I have followed Christiano in using as the outcomes element of democracy. Even if the ideal leader is possible (empirically as well as logically), undefined popular support just isn't the kind of thing that will pick out such a person. On the contrary, we are likely to be led astray and away from these normative and substantive aspects of leadership and of democracy respectively by just such characteristics that appeal to followers. Plato's ship-hands problem (of those who wrest control by force or mere popularity while the 'true' leader/navigator is overlooked) seems to recur. Accounts such as the psychoanalytic accounts explored in this chapter, as well as Portis's model of 'mass irrational support', and even the claims of the existence of so-called 'toxic leadership' are all examples, with varying levels of success and detail, of explanations of *how* we can thus be led astray. Further, none of these accounts meets the criteria of either a properly understood account of democracy (as including both the procedural and the substantive democracy outcomes elements), or of ideal leadership as we have now defined them.

So in fact a *prima facie*, unqualified definition of 'leadership' can seem both compatible with a *prima facie*, unqualified definition of 'democracy' that hews towards the procedural definition of democracy alone as well as a threat to substantive democracy. In part this is because both of these unqualified accounts can be reduced to mere popularity. On the other hand, a considered, qualified account of leadership as the broadly Aristotelian ideal leadership I have offered is not only less supportive of this 'mere popularity' or procedural account, but might also actually support democracy correctly understood as including the substantive as well as the procedural elements.

So what does this mean for the relationship between democracy and leadership? More importantly, what does it mean for the compatibility of democracy and the kind of leadership outlined above – namely leadership that is 'good' in all three senses that Ciulla outlines, that is, leadership that is done by an ethical character, in an ethical manner and for ethical ends?[69] Is there a natural fit between the two? Do they support one another?

The relationship between democracy and leadership reviewed

In light of the discussion of the nature of democracy and of leadership I have undertaken in this chapter, we are now in a position to outline in more detail the possible relationships between leadership and democracy. There seem to be four potential kinds of relationship between leadership and democracy:

First, we might hold that normative leadership as I have defined it – as a broadly Aristotelian master virtue that is founded in the flourishing of followers and leaders – is neutral or agnostic with respect to democracy – that in its various instantiations (i.e. various leaders) it can be more or less democratic, and it can be applied to support democracy, lead away from it or neither – but that it is constitutively neutral with respect to democracy. This need not mean that leadership is thus neutral with respect to all and any political systems. It might for example be incompatible with some or more compatible with others, but it would mean that there are no special affinities between leadership and democracy.

Second, we might think that particular *forms* of leadership are compatible with democracy, and more democratic than others, and if we have independent reasons to value democracy we should thus prefer these forms of leadership. Note that this view is not incompatible with the first view but it involves an extra commitment towards democracy that lends an appeal to the kind of leadership that complements democracy in this way. A particularly consultative style of leadership would be an example of this. That is, whether or not we think leadership is morally valuable, we might have independent reasons to prefer the kind of leadership that promotes and accords well with democracy. This would speak not only to the aims of leadership, but also to the way in which leadership is conducted. This, however, might have no bearing on what kinds of persons can be desirable leaders or it might only have bearing on this in instrumental ways. That is, it might give us reason to prefer the kind of leaders whose characters are likely and able to foster a democratic style of leadership *because* we (and very likely with good reason) value this style of leadership. Many accounts of democracy and leadership focus on exactly this – on the accepted styles or forms of leadership, which are the most democratic in their forms.[70] For example, we might prefer a genuinely consultative form of leadership that respects what Christiano calls political equality – that is, considers as equal (or as near to equal as possible) the point of view and preferences of all those affected to leadership styles that lack such hallmarks. In this case democratic values are ones that we use to evaluate the desirability of various forms of leadership.

Third, we might think that leadership is, in at least some of its forms and perhaps in the ideal form I have described, incompatible with democracy – either necessarily or contingently — in part because one of the roles of democracy is as a constraint against just the kind of unchecked power ascribed to the philosopher-king and to actual historical kings or some other forms of personal power unconstrained by the kinds of checks and balances as well as the commitment to equal consideration of interests that democracy institutes. That is, rather than it being contingently the case that some forms of leadership support democratic values and are done in democratic ways, a proponent of this view would argue that there is something about leadership that makes it by its nature incompatible with democracy. For example, models of democracy that limit the government's right to make decisions and judgements about what constitutes a good life seem *prima facie* incompatible with the claim that the ideal ruler, the broadly Aristotelian leader, by definition knows and pursues the good of followers. Much here will depend on how we conceive of 'the good of followers'. For example if the ideal ruler apprehends and pursues an understanding of the good of followers that is incompatible with a democratic style of rule then this incompatibly may well be true by definition, and thus unavoidable.

Fourth and last is what we might call the stronger case for leadership and democracy – that there is something about leadership that is especially or even uniquely compatible with democracy. That is, that leadership, properly understood, will in any instantiation comport well with democracy. How might this be the case? One option would be if democracy and leadership share some underpinning values in a way that would establish a conceptual relation between the two – an account of human flourishing that includes autonomy and an equal respect for persons might serve the purpose. Or it might contingently be the case that leadership as I have defined it happens to foster democratic values and practices, or foster the elements required for a substantive democracy.

Value neutrality

Leadership, as we have established, cannot be value neutral. The accounts of Burns and Ciulla, and the broadly Aristotelian account of leadership given in early chapters, have it that a coherent model of leadership as value neutral fails.

Nor, as we have seen, is democracy. It is not a purely procedural concept. Might the conflicts between the two concepts therefore disappear? For example, we might believe that democracy is perfectionist (and thus not value neutral) to the extent that it pursues more perfect forms of democracy – that is, in ways such as increasing the meaningful representation of all, including minorities, avoiding the tyranny of the majority, improving the quality of public discourse through education and other means, etc. We might call this a 'narrow perfectionism' – that is, a perfectionism that seems to instantiate a more perfect form of the kind of thing it is, in this case democracy. Might this be sufficient to allow a role for leadership, with its constitutive focus on the good, in democracy?

In part this raises the distinction between democracy and liberalism. As Chantal Mouffe notes, although the two are often held to coincide in practice, they are at least somewhat distinct.[71] But while liberalism is committed to a neutrality with respect to the good in many areas, as we saw above, democracy cannot be. That is, while some aspects of the 'interests' of persons that Christiano tells us democracy must treat as equally important for each person will consist of respecting their own conception of the good, other aspects of the equal consideration of interests are based upon a preformed idea of the good – the individual's autonomy, ability to freely choose, the self-respect and feeling of equal value that comes from equal opportunity to participate in discussions of the good and institutions that debate the conception and requirement of justice, etc. It is these that Christiano identifies, and the public equality and interest in this equality that represents the intrinsic justice, that are requisite for the authority of democracy. These aspects of justice, on this view, are independent of our individual notions of the good. Indeed, this justice requires that we be free to pursue our own notions of the good.[72] Each of the various accounts of the correct principle of state neutrality will require this.

That is, that there is something about democracy that not only instrumentally improves the well-being and flourishing of persons but, as Christiano notes, the egalitarianism of respect for the preferences and judgements of these same persons, is conducive to this well-being.[73] These are normative claims turning on the good of persons – and thus are far from value neutral.

As I outlined above, on Christiano's account of democracy that I have been using, any substantive account of democracy includes a commitment for the equal consideration of interests of persons.

One remaining problem arises if this democratic conception of the good of persons is incompatible with the conception of the good as outlined in the case of the broadly Aristotelian case of ideal leadership that understands (by definition correctly by the lights of the Aristotelian account) the good of persons as an essentialist concept of human flourishing. If democracy is constitutively committed to citizens having the right to choose for themselves what constitutes the good life, if this is in principle to be preferred to a ruler or leader choosing this for us, then this may represent a conflict with our conception of the ideal leader who by definition knows and pursues the good for all followers. If, on the other hand, democracy rejects paternalism in favour of citizens' right to choose what constitutes the good life merely because of the contingent historical fact that, as Dahl tells us, 'the preponderant weight of human experience informs us that no group of adults can safely grant to others the power to govern over them'[74] and judge and pursue what is best for them, and that it happens to be the case that 'no persons are so definitely better qualified to govern that they should be entrusted with complete and final authority over the government of the state',[75] then leadership as conceived here need not be incompatible with democracy in principle. The former – a principled rejection of paternalism even by those who are 'so definitely better qualified' is incompatible with even the philosopher-king.

As Steven Wall notes, theories of the kind of neutrality with respect to the good that the state should take vary from the claim that the state should take no actions to promote the good, through to claims that the state should not do so if the conception of the good promoted is subject to actual disagreement or could be subject to reasonable disagreement.[76] Leadership as I have defined it – as grounded in a knowledge of the good (flourishing) of persons – may be compatible with democracy but may not be compatible with the most strict of these definitions of the kind of state neutrality that liberalism (liberal democracy) might require. That is, leaders in such a democracy would violate this strict state neutrality even were they to foster and pursue the autonomy of persons and their ability to pursue the lives that they find meaningful. However, as we have seen, when we consider a substantive definition of democracy, we can see that this state neutrality with respect to conceptions of the good is nowhere near as absolute as it might seem to be. That is, even a substantive account of democracy that incorporates both procedural and outcomes elements (the equal consideration of interests) fails this strict state neutrality – and deliberately so. The equal consideration of interests is as we have seen constitutive of this account of democracy and is self-consciously an ethical feature.

Democracies regularly weigh the value of citizens' right to choose the good life for themselves (a justice claim) against the kind of things that limit this. For example, in most such democracies, fundamentalist religious communities are not permitted to prevent their children from receiving formal education or to allow them to marry before a certain age. Further, things such as public health campaigns encouraging people to quit smoking or to lose weight may seem to in fact be cases of the state prompting citizens to stop acting in ways that undermine their flourishing and their health (and not just the impacts on a government's health budget).

What of democracy and the question of perfectionism? Raz argues that perfect neutrality is neither possible[77] nor desirable.[78] For Raz, autonomy is both an intrinsic and instrumental good and governments (and presumably leaders) are justified and legitimate in acting to further autonomy and remove threats to it.[79] In fact, this accords well with the outcomes criterion of democracy I have used throughout – protecting individuals' autonomy, and doing so for all persons, accords well with the equal consideration of interests. If a key task of leadership is to select goals, and 'good' leadership requires the selection of morally endorsable, 'good' goals, there is no reason to think this is not compatible with pluralism about goals and goods, especially if such goals are subject to robust debate. Leadership is defined in terms of the virtue of advancing the good of citizens, but that is compatible with any number of limitations on what are the appropriate goods to be advanced. Just because something is good for a person doesn't bring it within the scope of a leader's *telos*. So there is room in the definition of leadership for restraint in deciding what goods are to be pursued and how they are to be pursued: restraints that make sense because of the autonomy and expertise of individuals and because of an endorsement constraint. People flourish best if they endorse the values they live by; a leader can't add to flourishing by imposing unendorsed goods upon citizens.[80]

On this view the role of normative leadership will often be to shape but not impose the goals and objectives of those led. On Burns' view transforming leadership is an activity whereby 'people can be lifted into their better selves.'[81] Transforming leadership occurs when leaders and followers raise one another to higher levels of morality. It is '*moral* in that it raises the level of human conduct and ethical aspiration of both leader and led.'[82] Following Burns, this position would argue that whereas transactional leadership operates and remains at the level of static, unchanged goals of individuals, transforming leadership rather interacts with followers to convince them of other, better goals and values.

And here of course the moral element seems particularly important – once we acknowledge the role of shaping and changing values in leadership, the moral element is an important restriction on normative leadership, in separating it from the kind of toxic leadership that is in part defined by the kinds of goals chosen. And this does seem to be consistent with the notion of genuine leadership in a democratic society. We want to avoid the so-called 'Hitler problem'[83] by avoiding the conclusion that toxic leadership is to be separated from 'good' leadership only by the fact that it chooses goals that followers endorse; but leaders can and surely must influence what goals are endorsed.

This fits particularly well with the model of the moral reformer that is also important for our intuitive idea of leadership. Danoff, for example, in discussing Abraham Lincoln's 'democratic' style of leadership, describes this as having consisted of not just accepting and acting on the existing beliefs and desires of the public but shaping (improving) them, in part because the existing beliefs on a subject such as slavery were not consistent with their other beliefs such as the value of liberty.[84] While appealing to public support, Lincoln, according to Danoff, maintained a commitment to improving these: 'Lincoln was deeply committed to majority rule, but he also believed – as Tocqueville did – that the "popular opinions and sentiments" of the majority needed to be educated'.[85] The echoes of Burns' model of leadership that improves ('educates') the opinions and judgements of followers are thus strong. Of course it matters that the moral elements of leaders and leadership are morals that we would endorse – many a misguided or even evil leader can make the claim of lobbying and 'educating for' moral values.

Leaders, understood on the broadly Aristotelian model of leadership that I have outlined as the correct way to understand ideal leadership, are circumscribed by a need to respect the autonomy, expertise and endorsements of those they lead. They may influence and educate by all means but they will not impose the 'best' goals without endorsement and consent. And this is because to do so does not serve the flourishing of followers or the leaders themselves. If human flourishing requires autonomy (and it does), then autonomy can trump what is best, even for (especially for) the Aristotelian leader.

Conclusion

So what does this mean for the relationship between democracy and leadership? The four options outlined earlier in this chapter were:

1. That we might hold that leadership is neutral or agnostic with respect to democracy .
2. That particular *forms* of leadership are compatible with democracy, and more democratic than others, and that, because we have independent

reasons to value democracy, we thus prefer these forms of leadership. As we noted above, this view is not incompatible with the first view, but it involves an extra commitment towards democracy that lends an appeal to the kind of leadership that complements democracy in this way.

3. That leadership is by its nature incompatible with democracy – either necessarily or contingently. That is, rather than it being contingently the case that some forms of leadership support democratic values and are done in democratic ways, a proponent of this view would argue that there is something about leadership that makes it by its nature incompatible with democracy.

4. What we called the stronger case for leadership and democracy – that there is something about leadership that is especially compatible with democracy. That is, that leadership, properly understood, will in any instantiation comport well with democracy.

Given that we have seen that democracy need not, and cannot, be value neutral, the third of these options is implausible. There is no reason to think either that leadership is incompatible with democracy because leadership cannot be value neutral while democracy must be, or that the kind of relation between leaders and followers that leadership requires does not meet Machin's 'egalitarian challenge'[86] in a way that democracy must.

Nor does the first of these options do justice to the reality because of the grounding in the good of persons that we have seen that both leadership and democracy share. Of course, this might be sufficient to make us prefer these forms of leadership, in accord with the second option, but even this underdetermines both the nature of leadership and its relation to democracy. Given the overlaps we have seen, there is enough for us to say that, properly understood, both leadership and democracy have a meaningful commitment to the well-being of persons in a way that includes autonomy and respect for persons to show that the relationship is more than these first or second options suggest. This 'meaningful commitment' is part of what grounds leadership in the sense we have described and a major component of the reasons why democracy cannot be understood in the reductive, merely procedural, 'opinion poll view of democracy'.[87] Neither democracy nor leadership, in the meaningful senses outlined here, reduce to mere popularity despite some *prima facie* affinities with (mere) popularity and it is not merely the case that some styles of leadership are compatible with democracy.

Which leaves the fourth option, the strongest case, that there is a compatible strong conceptual connection between the norms of leadership and the norms of democracy. It is important not to overstate this case however. There are of course forms of (even the broadly Aristotelian mode of) leadership that are not democratic (such as the forms of leadership found in organizational or other hierarchies), and there are all too many cases of holders of elected power in democracies who do not show leadership in any meaningful way. And just as the procedural element of democracy, with its grounding in the support of citizens, can map to the support of followers in choosing leaders, this same support can lead to an over-representation of the procedural elements of democracy over the substantive ones in a way that can all too easily yield bad or toxic leadership.

The relationship, while the strongest positive one of the four potential ones outlined here, is not a relationship of identity by any means. It merely means that there are similar underpinning norms and evaluative criteria for both leadership and democracy correctly understood and done well. We need to be open-eyed about this and aware of these underlying values and commitments in both cases in fleshing out our ideas of both leadership and of democracy.

The question I began this chapter with was: What are the connections between the norms of democracy and the norms of leadership? Our discussion has shown that what legitimates power in both cases is the good of persons and that both the broadly Aristotelian normative account of leadership and any democratic theory more substantive than a purely procedural or Graham's 'popularity' account share a grounding in the good of persons. Moreover, this understanding of the good of persons is, or at least can plausibly be seen to be, a compatible one. The broadly Aristotelian model of leadership, the only one that I believe can offer an account of leadership as normatively desirable and avoid the dangers of the ambiguity and potential for negative influence of the term and the attributed role of 'leadership', is grounded in and defined by its relationship to the good of persons. Democracy, at the political level, is similarly grounded.

Notes

1   Levine and Boaks 2013: 1–18.
2   Taylor, P. W. 1974. *Principles of ethics: an introduction*, Dickenson Pub. Co.
3   Hursthouse 1991: 225–6.
4   Christiano 2002.
5   Ciulla 1995: 13. See also Kellerman 2004: 11. Kellerman refers to this as 'Hitler's

Ghost'. In both cases the reference is to the familiar idea outlined above – the concern over whether we must categorize Hitler as a leader and what our answer to this question says about the concept of leadership.

6   Dahl 1998: 69.

7   Ibid., 79.

8   Ibid., 76.

9   Note that unchecked power need not be the same as tyranny. Unchecked power might be necessary for tyranny (or conducive to it) but it is not sufficient for tyranny. Tyranny is the use of unchecked power for personal gratification. That a non-democratic ideal ruler such as the one Graham (citation) asks us to imagine is conceivable demonstrates this.

10   Graham 1983: 91–102.

11   Mill 2011: 39.

12   Graham 1983: 94.

13   Ciulla 2005: 332. Of course, none of these refer to the effectiveness, the skill level of the leader *qua* leader. The intention here is to use these three useful criteria as a way of teasing out what is often conflated when we talk of ethically good leadership. Ciulla herself elsewhere addresses the requirement that leaders be 'good' in the sense of effectiveness, particularly in Ciulla 2004: 302–27.

14   Ciulla 2005: 332.

15   Christiano 2004: 266–90.

16   Christiano 2002.

17   Christiano 2004: 266.

18   Ibid., 266.

19   Ibid., 266.

20   Christiano 2002: 32.

21   Ibid., 39.

22   Ibid., 40–2.

23   Ibid., 45.

24   Ibid., 44.

25   Ibid., 44.

26   Ibid., 45.

27   Ibid., 45.

28   Graham 1983: 94.

29   Portis 1987: 232.

30   Tucker 1970: 73–4.

31   Portis 1987: 244.

32   See for example Lipman-Blumen 2005.

33   Portis 1987: 245.

34   Ibid., 245.

35   Takala 1998: 785–98.

36   Portis 1987: 232. Note of course that this account of leadership meets neither
     the substantive nor, properly understood, the procedural aspect of democracy as
     outlined by Christiano.

37   Note the ambiguity in the use here of the term 'qualified' to describe the leader.
     Amongst other things, and most salient for our discussion here, it is unclear
     whether we should take this to mean qualified because fairly elected or qualified
     for some other reason.

38   Mackie 2009: 129.

39   Portis 1987: 242.

40   A sceptic might argue that the kind of respect for persons' judgement in the
     form of a vote that in reality represents only one in many millions and is
     unable to meaningfully affect the overall outcome could be seen as equally
     symbolic. The difference is the equal treatment of such votes and the respect this
     implies. The difference I imagine my vote to make might be almost imaginary but
     the equal respect for it with respect to others' votes is real.

41   Graham 1983: 91–102.

42   Parsons 1947: 64.

43   Weber 1958: 7.

44   Tucker 1970: 73.

45   Portis 1987: 232.

46   Cox et al. 2009: 57–8.

47   Bon 1962.

48   Freud 1922.

49   Cox et al. 2009: 59.

50   Freud 1922: 97.

51   Cox et al. 2009: 58–9.

52   Ibid., 55.

53   Tucker 1970: 74.

54   Ibid., 80.

55   Ibid., 80.

56   Ibid., 81.

57   Ibid., 81.

58   Portis 1987: 232.

59   Plato, 347c–d, 412d–e.

60   Christiano 2004: 266, 273.

61   Christiano 2002: 44.

62   Ibid., 44.

63   Mouffe 2000: 3–5.

64   Christiano 2002.

65   Machin 2012.
66   Of course none of these speak to the good in the same way, and I will address this
     below in discussing perfectionism.
67   Christiano 2002: 38, 45.
68   Christiano 2012: 18.
69   Ciulla 2005: 332.
70   See, for example, the entry on 'Democratic Leadership' in Burns 2004.
71   Mouffe 2000.
72   Christiano 2004: 290.
73   Christiano 2002: 48–9.
74   Dahl 1998: 78.
75   Ibid.: 76.
76   Wall 2012.
77   Raz 1986: 133.
78   Ibid., 160–1.
79   Ibid., 417.
80   I am grateful to Damian Cox for pointing this out.
81   Burns 1978.
82   Ibid., 20.
83   Ciulla 1995.
84   Danoff 2005: 687–719.
85   Ibid., 719.
86   Machin 2012.
87   Graham 1983: 94.

Bibliography

Bon, G. L. (1962), *The Crowd: A Study of the Popular Mind*. London, Benn.

Burns, J. M. (1978), *Leadership*. New York: Harper & Row.

Christiano, T. (2002), 'Democracy As Equality', in D. Estlund (ed.), *Democracy*.
     Massachusetts: Blackwell.

—(2004), 'The authority of democracy', *The Journal of Political Philosophy*, 12 (3):
     266–90.

—(2012), 'Authority', *Stanford Encyclopedia of Philosophy*. E. N. Zalta, Stanford
     University.

Ciulla, J. B. (1995), 'Leadership ethics: Mapping the territory'. *Business Ethics Quarterly*,
     5 (1): 5–28.

Cox, D., Levine, M. and Newman, S. (2009), *Politics Most Unusual: Violence,
     Sovereignty and Democracy in the 'War on Terror'*. Basingstoke: Palgrave Macmillan.

—(2004), 'Ethics and Leadership Effectiveness', in J. Antonakis, A. T. Cianciolo and

R. J. Sternberg, *The Nature of Leadership*. Thousand Oaks, CA: Sage Publications, pp. 302–27.

—(2005), 'The state of leadership ethics and the work that lies before us', *Business Ethics: A European Review*, 14 (4): 323–35.

Dahl, R. A. (1998), *On Democracy*. New Haven, CT: Yale University Press.

Danoff, B. (2005), 'Lincoln and Tocqueville on democratic leadership and self-interest properly understood'. *The Review of Politics*, 67 (4): 687–719.

Freud, S. (1922), *Group Psychology*.

Graham, G. (1983), 'What is special about democracy'. *Mind*, XCII: 91–102.

Hursthouse, R. (1991), 'Virtue theory and abortion'. *Philosophy and Public Affairs*, 20 (3): 223.

Kellerman, B. (2004), *Bad Leadership: What it Is, How it Happens, Why it Matters*. Boston, MA: Harvard Business School Press.

Levine, M. and Boaks, J. (2013), 'What does ethics have to do with leadership?' *Journal of Business Ethics*: 1–18.

Lipman-Blumen, J. (2005), *The Allure of Toxic Leaders: Why We Follow Destructive Bosses and Corrupt Politicians – and How We Can Survive Them*. New York: Oxford University Press.

Machin, D. J. (2012), 'Political legitimacy, the egalitarian challenge, and democracy'. *Journal of Applied Philosophy*.

Mackie, G. (2009), 'Schumpeter's leadership democracy'. *Political Theory*, 37 (1): 128–53.

Mill, J. S. (2011), *Considerations on Representative Government*. Luton: Andrews UK.

Mouffe, C. (2000). *The Democratic Paradox*. London, New York: Verso.

Parsons, T. (1947), 'Introduction', in *Max Weber: The Theory of Social and Economic Organization*. New York: Oxford University Press.

Plato (1981), *Republic*. (trans. G. M. A. Grube, rev. C. D. C. Reeve). Indianapolis, IN: Hackett Publishing Company.

Portis, E. B. (1987), 'Charismatic leadership and cultural democracy'. *The Review of Politics*, 49 (2): 231–50.

Raz, J. (1986), *The Morality of Freedom*. Oxford: Oxford University Press.

Takala, T. (1998), 'Plato on leadership'. *Journal of Business Ethics*, 17 (7): 785–98.

Tucker, R. C. (1970), 'The Theory of Charismatic Leadership', in D. A. Rustow, *Philosophers and Kings: Studies in Leadership*. New York: G. Brazille.

Wall, S. (2012), 'Perfectionism in Moral and Political Philosophy', *Stanford Encyclopedia of Philosophy*. E. N. Zalta: Stanford University.

Weber, M. (1958), 'The three types of legitimate rule'. *Berkeley Publications in Society and Institutions*, 4 (1).

5

Plato's Paradox of Leadership

Damian Cox and Peter Crook
Bond University

Reluctant and willing rulers

This is a chapter about political rulers and what we can learn about leadership by examining conditions for good rulership. But what is the relationship between leading and ruling? A leader doesn't just exercise *de jure* authority over others, she *leads* others. Leadership is a success concept. To lead is to successfully bring others along with one; to lead is to successfully contrive others' co-operation in pursuit of a set purpose or goal that one has adopted. Of course, this can be done well or badly, through fear or inspiration, in a good cause or a miserable one. We use the term 'rulership' in a parallel way. To rule is to successfully impose one's will upon others in political matters and to do so with authority. A person who occupies a rulership position and fails to impose their will to a significant degree fails to rule. Just as an utterly indecisive leader fails to lead, an utterly indecisive ruler fails to rule. As we use the term, therefore, rulers are political leaders with the power and authority to impose their political will, to a significant degree, on an entire population. All rulers are political leaders, but not all political leaders are rulers. Political figures who lead by example and persuasion alone, for example, do not rule.

It is a commonplace observation that the best rulers are reluctant to rule. This is not to say that every person reluctant to rule would make a good ruler – many of us may be reluctant to rule because we know we are not up to the job. The thought, rather, is that reluctance to rule is a likely pre-condition of good rulership. There are no doubt exceptions, but in general, only those who are reluctant to lead are properly trusted to lead. The main reason for this has to do with motivation. Rulers too invested in ruling *per se* are likely to be ill-motivated. They are likely to be motivated by the sheer exercise of power and maintenance of privilege and this sort of motivation is unlikely to make for beneficial rulership. Just what might motivate a reluctant ruler is something we explore throughout this chapter.

What does it mean to say that a ruler is reluctant to rule? To a first approximation, a reluctant ruler is one who would genuinely prefer to be doing something else. In general, rulers rule willingly. Forced rulership implies a lack of a capacity to impose one's will. It is compromised, partially undone rulership. Even where they lack autocratic powers and rule at the behest of others, it seems always open to genuine rulers (rather than, say, figurehead rulers) to abdicate. Rulers rule willingly, but this willingness needn't be an uninhibited exercise of their will to rule. For one reason or another, including a sense of destiny or fear of retribution following abdication, rulers may feel that they have no real choice but to continue to rule. Even a sense of duty may cause a self-righteous but unpopular ruler to cling to power. For reasons such as these, willing but reluctant rulership is difficult to characterize fully. It is still harder to describe appropriate kinds or levels of willing reluctance among rulers. There seems little *prima facie* reason for subjects to prefer apparent diffidence to naked ambition: strong, competent and committed rulers are surely preferable, other things being equal, to weak, feckless or lackadaisical rulers. To be effective, it appears that rulers must share an appetite for ruling regardless of any degree of reluctance with which they might perform their allotted roles.

Our task in this chapter is two-fold. First, we seek to clarify the idea of the reluctant ruler by examining Classical Greek discussions of the issue. Plato is our primary source, for it is Plato who most clearly argues for the virtues of the reluctant ruler. Our second task is to expand on this Platonic account and demonstrate its relevance to contemporary struggles with the virtues of leadership. Rulership is but a special case of leadership. A ruler is a leader exercising sovereign power. A corollary of the ideal of reluctant rulership, therefore, is the ideal of reluctant leadership.

We also describe a closely related problem – we call it the Platonic Paradox of Leadership. This is realized whenever the conditions for assuming – or being granted – leadership preclude decent exercise of leadership. Ruthlessly ambitious rule is a special case of this. In a political environment where only the most ruthlessly ambitious achieve leadership roles, the qualities of leadership exhibited by the reluctant leader will be largely missing in action. The ruthlessly ambitious are among the worst of leaders, but they are also, often, the only possible leaders. This paradox generalizes. In many circumstances there exist qualities that are both necessary for achieving leadership and antithetical to good leadership: for example, willingness to make dodgy deals, flair for gaming systems, unempathetic ruthlessness, overconfidence, a projected sense of destiny, and so on.

Appetite and ambition as motive for rule

Ancient Athenians do not regard mortals as naturally altruistic. Proverbially, 'everyone is his own best friend' (Plato *Laws* 731df). 'No man hates his own advantage, nor does he place strangers' interests above his own' (Isaeus 3.66). Given this cynical (or perhaps realistic) view of human nature, how is one to understand motivations to rule? Here are some possibilities.

Philargyria: Appetite as motive for rule

For Aristotle (*Politics* 1310b14ff.), tyrants often start out as demagogues and he supposes (*Nicomachean Ethics* [*EN*] 1134b) that most men envy tyrants because they can selfishly and without restraint satisfy their appetites. Indeed, for Plato (*Republic* 580e) most men live to feed their insatiable appetites, pursuing wealth with that sole purpose. In terms of Plato's tripartite psychology, appetite certainly looms large in the *psyche* of the tyrant whom he thus distinguishes from other kinds of autocrat, emerging as he does from those states in which the appetitive, working class is sovereign. Plato (*Rep.* 347b, 391c) identifies *philargyria* (avarice or love of money) as the worst of two bad reasons for ruling. The second is *philotimia* (love of honour).

Philotimia as motive to rule: The timocratic man

Philotimia (or *thymos*) – or love of honour – is for Plato the less bad reason to rule. This is because, in the battle of the tripartite soul – that is, the enduring battle for control between the three elements of the human psyche: appetite, spirit and reason – spirit will tend to side with reason (*Rep.* 440b) and reason generates better rule than either spirit or appetite alone. Aristotle (*EN* 1095b23) identifies honour (*time*) rather than wealth as the usual goal of political life, and in Plato (*Rep.* 543a–545c), the best of the four degenerate political states (which, unlike the best state, actually exist) is the '*philotimos politeia*': timarchy or timocracy (Plato's own coinages: *Rep.* 545b). Plato (*Rep.* 544c) identifies

Sparta as an example of such. The Greek concept of honour (*time*) is very close to our own, though it incorporates the idea of glory won in battle and competition. This glory consists in public acclaim for excellence (*arete*) in battle, sport or politics. For Xenophon (*Hiero* 7.3f.), *philotimia* is the mark of the real man: it distinguishes the *philotimos* or timocratic man not only from beasts, but from lesser men.

Greek aristocratic culture is fundamentally agonistic. Competition informs all aspects of the Greek experience, and success in competition is the means by which both the individual and society are expected to progress. Strife (*neikos*) is the natural condition of life. Naturally, however, failure may always result in disadvantage and the outcomes of competitive struggles are not always just. For example, Xenophon (*Memorabilia* 3.4.1) reports that the experienced general Nicomachides complained of being beaten in an election to a generalship by a rich man ignorant of military affairs.

Furthermore, *philotimia* may easily degenerate into naked ambition or reckless arrogance. Even an excessive love of honour exhibited by those too eager to lead is a revelation of character weakness – the weakness of one too reliant on the acclaim of others or too eager for control. Aristophanes (*Acharnians* 595) doubtless speaks for the demos in decrying those 'anxious for command'. The dangers for ordinary mortals of *philotimia* so conceived are very considerable and the Greeks possessed a keen sense of the folly inherent in untrammelled pursuit of honour. For example, in Euripides' *Phoenissae* (530ff.), Jocasta addresses her warring son thus:

> Why, my son, do you so long for Ambition [*philotimia*], that worst of deities? Oh, do not; the goddess is unjust; many are the homes and cities once prosperous that she has entered and left, to the ruin of her worshippers; and she is the one you are mad for. It is better, my son, to honour Equality [*isotes*], who always joins friend to friend, city to city, allies to allies; for Equality is naturally lasting among men; but the less [i.e. Ambition] is always in opposition to the greater [i.e. Equality], and begins the dawn of hatred. For it is Equality that has set up for man measures and divisions of weights, and has determined numbers; night's sightless eye, and radiant sun proceed upon their yearly course on equal terms, and neither of them is envious when it has to yield. Though both sun and night are servants for mortals, you will not be content with your fair share of your heritage and give the same to him [i.e. your brother]? Then where is justice? Why do you honour to excess tyranny, a prosperous injustice, why do you think so much of it? Admiring glances are to be prized? No, that is an empty pleasure…

The thought Euripides expresses through Jocasta's speech is that a love of ambition conflicts with a love of justice. If ambition produces prosperity, it is only an unjust prosperity, unworthy of a timocratic man. Even if it leads to popular admiration, this amounts to a superficial and ultimately worthless pleasure.

Whatever the motive for seeking power, Athenian aristocrats were ruefully aware that tyranny begets hostility as readily as admiration and since ruling can so easily become tyrannical this is a strong motivation to avoid assuming a ruler's mantle. Thus in Sophocles (*Oedipus Tyrannus* 584ff.), Creon explains to a sceptical Oedipus his disinclination to reclaim the throne he has renounced:

> Weigh this first—whether you think that anyone would choose to rule amid terrors rather than in unruffled peace, granted that he is to have the same powers. Now I, for one, have by nature no yearning to rule as a king rather than to do kingly deeds, and neither does any man I know who has a sound mind. For now I attain everything from you without fear, but, if I were ruler myself, I would have to do much that went against my own pleasure. How, then, could royalty be sweeter to me to have than painless rule and influence? I am not yet so misguided that I desire other honours than those which bring profit. Now, every man has a greeting for me; now, all that have a request of you crave to speak with me, since in me lies all their hope of success. Why then should I give up these things and take those others? No mind will become false while it is wise. No, I am no lover of such a policy, and if another put it into action, I could never bear to go along with him.

The Greeks thus had an ambivalent attitude to ambition and the pursuit of honour. On the one hand, it was a central feature of their unapologetically agonistic culture. On the other hand, there was no shortage of rueful reflection in Greek literature on both the dangers and the unworthiness of an excessive love of honour. This is fertile ground for alternative ideas of motivations for rulership to grow.

Duty as motive for rule: Democratic conscription to office

Is there anything like a democratic motive to seek to rule? This is hard to answer because democracy is in part a matter of constraining the will to rule of would-be tyrants and demagogues. Even prior to the formal institution of democracy, the demos would as occasion demanded bestow autocratic powers on individuals with the expectation that those powers would be voluntarily relinquished in due course. But paradoxically, contempt for politicians who eagerly seek office may increase the popularity not only of appointed but also of hereditary leaders, leaders who may be regarded as reluctant rulers simply because they did not strive for office.

Popper (1966: 124) argues that there are two basic forms of government, democracy and tyranny, and that the former not only provides but is actually constituted by institutional safeguards against the latter. Tyranny is only a limiting form of oligarchy, and for all the obfuscation surrounding the precise number of different types of polity in Plato and Aristotle, both recognize that democracy and oligarchy are the basic constitutions from which all others are derived. Arguably, democracy is regarded by Athenians as a machine specifically designed to prevent citizens possessed by the will to power from fully realizing their aims. Such is the complaint of Callicles in Plato's *Gorgias* (483bff., 491eff.). But the fact that it was felt necessary to institute and (at least prior to the fourth century) exercise ostracism – the forced removal of citizens from the city on political grounds – gives testimony to a lasting hope of realizing demagogic ambitions even in a democratic environment.

Democracy sought to thwart ambitious politicians through filling public offices for one year at a time with reluctant citizens chosen by sortition, a system in which public officials are chosen by lot. The idea is that good men will respond to the challenge imposed upon them in this way. But how one responds to the challenges of imposed leadership is itself a critical test of character. In Sophocles (*Antigone* 175ff.), Creon avers that:

> Now, it is impossible to know fully any man's character, will, or judgment, until he has been proved by the test of rule and law-giving. For if anyone who directs the entire city does not cling to the best and wisest plans, but because of some fear [for his own interests] keeps his lips locked, then, in my judgment, he is and has long been the most cowardly traitor.

The democratic view is that justice in ruling is not or is not primarily a self-regarding virtue. Thrasymachus treats Socrates as a simpleton in apparently also advocating this view, addressing him thus (*Rep.* 343cf., trans. Shorey; cf. 392b):

> And you are so far out concerning the just and justice and the unjust and injustice that you don't know that justice and the just are literally the other fellow's good – the advantage of the stronger and the ruler, but a detriment that is all his own of the subject who obeys and serves; while injustice is the contrary and rules those who are simple in every sense of the word and just, and they being thus ruled do what is for his advantage who is the stronger and make him happy …

Thrasymachus (*Rep.* 343aff.) has invoked a traditional analogy between ruler and shepherd, and insists *contra* Plato that the shepherd does not, as a matter of fact, seek the good of his flock: he fattens them for his own (or his master's) advantage. Likewise, those rulers who deserve the name also seek their own advantage. Justice is 'other men's good', injustice one's own. The just man comes off second best everywhere, both in commercial and in political transactions. It is far more to one's own interest to be unjust than to be just as we may see from the case of tyrants, who represent injustice in its most perfect form. All men envy them. Injustice on a sufficiently large scale is at once stronger, more worthy of a freeman and more masterly and commanding than justice.

If, *contra* Thasymachus, ruling is about serving others and is not self-regarding, no one in their right mind would want to rule. Xenophon (*Mem.* 2.1.8ff.) portrays Aristippus as saying to Socrates:

> I do not for a moment put myself in the category of those who want to be rulers. For considering how hard a matter it is to provide for one's own needs, I think it absurd not to be content to do that, but to shoulder the burden of supplying the wants of the community as well. That anyone should sacrifice a large part of his own wishes and make himself accountable as head of the state for the least failure to carry out all the wishes of the community is surely the height of folly. For states claim to treat their rulers just as I claim to treat my servants. I expect my men to provide me with necessaries in abundance, but not to touch any of them; and states hold it to be the business of the ruler to supply them with all manner of good things, and to abstain from all of them himself. And so, should anyone want to bring plenty of trouble on himself and others, I would educate him as you propose and number him with 'those fitted to be rulers': but myself I classify with those who wish for a life of the greatest ease and pleasure that can be had.

The extent of any reluctance amongst the citizenry to fulfil their democratic duties is unclear but the use of the 'ruddled rope' (red-stained rope apparently used to herd citizens from market to the assembly meeting place) to achieve a quorum suggests that citizens may have been reluctant at times to attend the sovereign assembly. Doubtless in order to enable and encourage poorer citizens to attend, Athenians were paid for attending the assembly in the fourth century, in addition to receiving payments to perform jury service and various other duties of citizenship.

Socrates (*Rep.* 345e, trans. Shorey) invokes this contentious issue of payment for services rendered in challenging Thrasymachus' conception:

"Why, do you think that the rulers and holders of office in our cities—the true rulers—willingly hold office and rule?" "I don't think," he said, "I know right well they do."

"But what of other forms of rule, Thrasymachus? [Plato's examples include the rule of their respective clients exercised by physicians and pilots.] Do you not perceive that no one chooses of his own will to hold the office of rule, but they demand pay, which implies that not to them will benefit accrue from their holding office but to those whom they rule?"

Socrates (*Rep.* 346ef., trans. Shorey) informs Thrasymachus that:

... no one of his own will chooses to hold rule and office and take other people's troubles in hand to straighten them out, but everybody expects pay for that, because he who is to exercise the art rightly never does what is best for himself or enjoins it when he gives commands according to the art, but what is best for the subject. That is the reason, it seems, why pay must be provided for those who are to consent to rule, either in form of money or honour or a penalty if they refuse.

In relation to sortition, scholars commonly assume that candidates for all public offices must be self-selected (whether by adding or removing their names from lists for sortition is left unclear). Naturally, we might expect that those physically or mentally incapable of fulfilling official duties would be permitted to opt out. That anyone with any sense 'would rather be benefitted by others than take the trouble to benefit them' (*Rep.* 347d, trans. Grube/Reeve) does not, however, constitute any warrant for self-disqualification. It may serve perhaps as a justification for sharing the burden of office through rotation, but far from being consistent with democratic notions of personal liberty, opting out of the process altogether offends against Greek notions that the duties of citizenship are also privileges or rights of citizenship. So a sense of duty, a desire to serve rather than to pursue self-interest, might motivate those reluctant to rule through lack of ambition.

Although a sense of democratic duty is a plausible candidate for a motivation to rule, the Greeks were acutely aware of the limitations of such motivation. A reluctant ruler *might* be motivated to rule in this way, but is this the best available motive? Plato suggests that the best leaders need a different sort of motivation. And it is this motivation we turn to now.

Reason as motive to rule

If appetite and love of honour or ambition are poor motives to rule and a sense of duty is an insufficient one, might reason itself be a good motive to rule? A person who would otherwise be reluctant to rule, might be drawn towards rulership by the exercise of their reason. Rather than democratic fellowship, they might be motivated by a keen appreciation of what is best. This has the advantage of allying a motive to rule with a special kind of fitness to rule: wisdom.

Duty as a motive to rule is most thoroughly realized in the Athenian practice of sortition, but the problem with it as identified by Plato is that of wisdom: Aristophanes (*Knights* 180ff.) cynically asserts that ignorance is an actual qualification to rule in democracies. Sortition works fine as a demonstration of democratic commitment and as a test of character because it places people in situations where their character may come under immense pressure. But it is a test many, perhaps most, will fail because they prove unequal to the task assigned them. What are the prospects of wise leadership if duty, appetite and ambition flagrantly fail to furnish adequate motives to rule? Plato's answer is that reason itself must be a motive to rule.

Monarchs may be wise, or wise enough to consult sage counsellors, but no one before Plato appears seriously to have entertained the possibility that the pursuit of reason (*logos*) rather than wealth or honour might itself be the motive for seeking dominion over others. The pursuit of reason was generally regarded as incompatible with political ambition. Of pre-Socratic philosophers, tradition has it that Heraclitus abdicated in favour of his brother (Diogenes Laertius, *Lives of Eminent Philosophers* 9.1.6), Empedocles simply refused the proffered crown (ibid. 8.2.63) and Anaxagoras tells us that he felt obliged to reject a life in politics in order to pursue the philosophical life. Democritus squandered his family fortune in broadening his mind through travel and purportedly blinded himself so as not to be distracted from his thoughts. The lives of Socrates, Diogenes and even Epicurus broadly fall within this traditional category of the unambitious and reclusive or anti-social sage, those unambitious for worldly power or wealth.

In Plato's view, most people lack sufficient reason for it to constitute a motive for them. Temperance (*sophrosyne*) is the virtue of knowing one's place, the only virtue of which the appetitive man, the worker or slave, is capable. The temperate man knows himself and his station in life. A person is wise, on this view, only if they know their limitations. For Socrates, 'he who wields power ought to be aware of his ignorance' (Popper 1966: 269 n. 26), and Socrates set himself the task of disabusing democratic citizens of any delusions of knowledge. But for Plato 'he who wields power ought to be wise' (ibid.). This means that if reason is to be a motive to rule, it must be one restricted to an elite group: the wise.

In what does such wisdom consist? Although neither provided an adequate or convincing account of it, Plato and Aristotle both insist that there is a science of politics. Political practice is amenable to the development and deployment of specialized expertise. Naturally, a highly educated technician may be better placed than a layman in discerning effective means of achieving a common goal; however, the idea that politics yields to expert knowledge was disputed. When it comes to politics, Athenian democrats take the view that there simply is no science in which to become expert (cf. Plato, *Protagoras* 323a). Each is expert in their own affairs, in what is best for them; and everyone shares in political sensibility.

Even if there is widespread scepticism about the possibility of political expertise, an ambitious, confidant and decisive aristocrat may have an irresistible appeal to diffident and indecisive citizens only too conscious of their own limitations and mortal fallibility, more especially during periods of crisis. During the Peloponnesian war, Thucydides (3.82.4f.) claims that:

> Reckless audacity came to be considered the courage of a loyal ally; prudent hesitation, specious cowardice; moderation was held to be a cloak for unmanliness; ability to see all sides of a question inaptness to act on any … The advocate of extreme measures was always trustworthy; his opponent a man to be suspected.

If aristocratic over-confidence is dangerous, humility is not obviously the answer. The unmanly inadequacy of Aristophanes' self-deprecating assembly woman (*Women at the Thesmophoria* 383f.), who insists that 'It is not through *philotimia* that I have risen to speak', may well have provoked embarrassed laughter. The virtues of modesty and humility are not obviously compatible with the confident exercise of sovereign authority. Beyond aristocratic over-confidence and the inadequacies of the humble and temperate commoner lies the appeal of the wise and kindly saviour. And yet there is a counter-balancing democratic concern. The enduring power of the myth of the ruler as wise and kindly saviour doubtless owes much to the experience of carefree childhoods, but Athenian democrats appear to have recognized that its influence in tempting citizens to relinquish their sovereignty was pernicious.

The reluctant philosopher-king

The fundamental political problem, according to Plato, is to enable reason to function as a motive to rule. Only then will leaders be both wise and un-tyrannical; only then will they be neither humble nor reckless. This requires that expert and wise rule be combined with something to match the inherent (if only patchily successful) democratic safeguards against tyranny. Plato's answer is the reluctant philosopher-king.

Socrates addresses the following remarks to Glaucon and philosophers in general (*Rep.* 520cf., trans. Grube/Reeve):

> Thus, for you and for us, the city will be governed, not like the majority of cities nowadays, by people who fight over shadows and struggle against one another in order to rule – as if that were a great good – but by people who are awake rather than dreaming, for the truth is surely this: A city whose prospective rulers [i.e. those destined to rule] are least eager to rule must of necessity be most free from civil war, whereas a city with the opposite kind of rulers is governed in the opposite way.

Plato (*Rep.* 345e–347e) certainly argues that philosopher-kings rule, not for their own sakes as philosophers, but for the sake of their (ignorant) subjects.

> In a city of good men, if it came into being, the citizens would fight in order *not to rule*, just as they do now in order to rule. There it would be quite clear that anyone who is really a true ruler doesn't by nature seek his own advantage but that of his subjects. And everyone, knowing this, would rather be benefitted by others than take the trouble to benefit them. (*Rep.* 347d, trans. Grube/Reeve.)

This view, that not only the democratic citizen's rule but even the monarch's rule is actually 'serving', is now commonplace. Monarchs and democratic politicians alike routinely claim to be servants to their people or nation. But the aristocratic Plato very often talks with utter contempt for the working classes, and serving their needs is not the actual motive of the philosopher-king.

In Plato's *Republic* (347aff., trans. Shorey), Socrates refers to a penalty for not ruling. Glaucon does not understand:

> "What do you mean by that, Socrates?" said Glaucon. "The two wages [honour and money] I recognize, but the penalty you speak of and described as a form of wage I don't understand." "Then," said I, "you don't understand the wages of the best men for the sake of which the finest spirits hold office and rule when they consent to do so. Don't you know that to be covetous of honour and covetous of

money is said to be and is a reproach?" "I do," he said. "Well, then," said I, "that is why the good are not willing to rule either for the sake of money or of honour. They do not wish to collect pay openly for their service of rule and be styled hirelings, nor to take it by stealth from their office and be called thieves, nor yet for the sake of honour, for they are not covetous of honour. So there must be imposed some compulsion and penalty to constrain them to rule if they are to consent to hold office. That is perhaps why to seek office oneself and not await compulsion is thought disgraceful. But the chief penalty is to be governed by someone worse if a man will not himself hold office and rule. It is from fear of this, as it appears to me, that the better sort hold office when they do, and then they go to it not in the expectation of enjoyment nor as to a good thing, but as to a necessary evil and because they are unable to turn it over to better men than themselves or to their like ..."

A reluctant leader, therefore, is motivated by the thought that their sacrifice is necessary because alternative leaders are worse. Plato ameliorates the sacrifice of the reluctant leader by specifying a rotation of philosopher-kings' responsibilities.

If that is the nature of the compulsion, what then is the nature of the reluctance? Whatever the cause of their reluctance, it is not the neglect of their business affairs that renders Plato's philosophers reluctant rulers, for they have no such affairs to attend to. For Plato, the ideal ruler would much rather practice philosophy than rule; she would rather stay in the world of Forms.

Ruling may thus be a burden, but it is not too onerous: because philosopher-kings will only rule on a part-time basis, Socrates (*Rep.* 520df., trans. Grube/Reeve) expects that they will willingly shoulder that burden:

Then do you think that those we've nurtured will disobey us and refuse to share the labors of the city, each in turn, while living the greater part of their time with one another in the pure realm?

It isn't possible, for we'll be giving just orders to just people. Each of them will certainly go to rule as to something compulsory, however, which is exactly the opposite of what's done by those who now rule in each city.

This is in fact one of the leading guarantees which Plato gives against the abuse of political power. Similar ideas have resonated through history. Ruskin (1865: § 43, 101) claims that true kings 'rule quietly, if at all, and hate ruling; too many of them make "il gran rifiuto" [the great refusal]'. Mill (1861: 56; 1910: 203) puts it this way: 'the good despot ... can hardly be imagined as consenting to undertake it, unless as a refuge from intolerable evils'. Plato's rulers are represented as reluctant to desert the life of contemplation for the cares of office. Good men require to be compelled to rule, and that is why it is accounted a disgrace to enter on office desirously.

Evidently for Plato, a corollary of the advisability of reluctant and dutiful rulers is the existence of a preferential form of life for them. There must be something that they would prefer to be doing if we are to avoid a pursuit of rule for its own sake or for the sake of appetite and honour. In Plato's system, of course, this is provided by philosophy, the activity that, because of character and upbringing, philosopher-kings would much prefer be engaged in. Notice that the philosopher-kings are not engaging in philosophy as they rule. Philosophical contemplation is an alternative activity to ruling (cf. *Rep.* 517c). Socrates continues (*Rep.* 520ef., trans. Grube/Reeve):

> If you can find a way of life that's better than ruling for the prospective rulers, your well-governed city will become a possibility, for only in it will the truly rich rule – not those who are rich in gold but those who are rich in the wealth that the happy must have, namely, a good and rational life. But if beggars hungry for private goods go into public life, thinking that the good is there for the seizing, then the well-governed city is impossible, for then ruling is something fought over, and this civil and domestic war destroys these people and the rest of the city as well.

Having discounted ignorant democrats, who might indeed prefer to attend to their own commercial interests, Glaucon (ibid. 521b) is unable to 'name any life that despises political rule besides that of the true philosopher,' and agrees with Socrates that, 'surely it is those who are not lovers of ruling who must rule, for if they don't, the lovers of it, who are rivals, will fight over it.' It is important to note at this point that Plato advances reluctance as a necessary, not sufficient, condition of good rulership. The philosopher-king is not qualified to rule simply because she is reluctant. Rather her qualification to rule is her possession of philosophical wisdom. Reluctance to rule is – in a philosopher-king, but not in others – a sign of this possession.

If Plato is right about this, then a key to decent political leadership is the provision of alternative and preferable career paths for political leaders: things other than working as a fund-raiser and party functionary before they reach the political spotlight, writing memoirs and haunting the corners of celebrity after they leave it. Political careers must be an interruption of some other life.

Contemporary leadership and the limits of reluctance

How are we to understand the virtues of reluctant leadership in a contemporary context? There are several relevant sorts of circumstances: those in which either rotation or sortition of leadership positions makes sense and those in which it does not. Similarly, there are circumstances of leadership that require the dedicated development of leadership expertise, and these circumstances appear to make trouble for the core Platonic idea that leadership be an interruption of a preferred activity. In Plato's republic, philosopher-kings would prefer to be doing philosophy, but happily – so thinks Plato – philosophy just is the relevant sort of expertise for political leadership. The study of philosophy furnishes political leaders with knowledge of the Forms, and the wisdom this entails constitutes the sort of knowledge and power of judgement needed to make good and beneficial political decisions. Thus, by doing what they prefer, philosopher-kings make themselves fit for leadership without ever developing a preference for leadership as such. Plato is discussing political leadership, but what of leadership of other kinds, undertaken in other circumstances? It's not clear what Plato would think, but it nonetheless seems highly unlikely that the study of philosophy would generate qualified and well-motivated, if reluctant, leaders in all circumstances of leadership.

There are three different ways in which reluctance to lead impacts leadership, more broadly conceived. First, there are circumstances in which, much like Plato's ideal city, reluctance to lead best demonstrates non-vicious motivations to lead. Second, there are circumstances in which reluctance to lead is superfluous because we can find other ways of identifying good motivations to lead. Third, there are circumstances in which the motivation of leaders doesn't matter. These are circumstances in which poorly motivated leaders can still be good leaders. We consider each of these cases in turn.

Consider cases in which a direct application of the principles of reluctant leadership is possible. Cases of this kind share a particular structural feature with Plato's ideal city. In them, leadership can be shared around between a group of roughly equivalent expertise and suitability. In Plato's ideal city, this occurs because a group – the Guardians – is trained from childhood for leadership, but the situation might also occur because the demands of leadership do not require specialization and long years of training and preparation. A broad range of people would thus be equipped with the basic knowledge and skills (if not temperament and motivation) required for leadership. Academic leadership is a case in point. Alternatively, direct application of the principles of reluctant leadership might be apt because there exists a pool of potential leaders sharing the requisite training and preparation for leadership. Military leadership might furnish examples of this second sort. In cases like these it seems to us that the virtues of reluctant leadership generally outweigh the risks of reluctant leadership. Recall that reluctance is a necessary, not sufficient condition of good leadership. When all else is equal, the reluctant, but still strongly motivated, leader is a better choice than the person who longs for leadership, who is grasping for it.

The argument for this is quite straightforward and somewhat parallel to Plato's argument. Motivations to lead are generally speaking quite obscure. It is all too easy to fake an interest in, for example, the general good or shared military goals and to hide one's actual vicious motivation – appetitive, vainglorious or sadistic – even from oneself (or particularly from oneself). What we need, then, is a reliable test for the absence of a vicious motivation to lead. Reluctance – genuine reluctance, not the mere appearance of reluctance – is this test. (Of course it is only one test of fitness for leadership; there will be others, particularly those centring on competence and temperament.) Reluctant leaders are not immune from the sorts of personality traits that generate vicious motivations to lead, but they are much less likely to suffer from them. This is because personality traits of this kind (for example, narcissism, psychopathology, prejudicial hatred) are powerful initiators of desire and action and an absence of a strong desire to lead is good *prima facie* evidence of a lack of them. Narcissistic striving, for example, whether avowed or disavowed, is a powerful source of motivation. It drives the narcissist to seek out opportunities for self-satisfying display. Reluctance to lead is a fairly reliable indicator of a lack of such motivation; perhaps it is the most reliable indicator we have to hand.

Reluctant leadership requires an inducement to lead. Plato's suggestion is a plausible one. The fundamental inducement to lead for the reluctant leader is a fear of being subjected to another's worse leadership. Other inducements – career advancement, monetary rewards, privileges, honours, gratitude – are the very things that tend to attract viciously motivated leaders. For example, it is generally a bad idea to establish very generous compensations for leadership of an academic department. The worst, most ill-motivated, departmental heads are usually those that are after rewards. Perhaps the only decent reason a person could ever have to lead an academic department is that every other option is worse. Of course, where leadership positions can be rotated, issues of fairness may predominate. It may be tempting to leave an academic department in the hands of a skilful but reluctant incumbent, but fairness sometimes dictates that burdens like these be shared.

Heads of academic departments, and many others in like positions, might be thought of as mere managers rather than leaders. But it is misleading to draw too determinate a distinction between leadership and management positions. Leaders are those who decide upon goals and succeed in obtaining a co-operative effort towards their realization. People in managerial positions sometimes lead, sometimes follow the lead of others and sometimes manage according to long-established precedent and procedure. Leadership, of course, is something that extends beyond explicitly defined leadership positions.

Let us next consider cases in which reluctance to lead seems like an unreasonable imposition on potential leaders. If it takes many years of effort to become qualified to lead and if the effort to become qualified to lead qualifies you for little else but leadership, then it is hard to see how one might conscript reluctant leaders. We noted above that there are two kinds of cases: those in which good motivation matters, but can be assured by means other than reluctance to lead; and those in which good motivation doesn't matter. Here is an example where good motivation does matter. It takes many years of practice and study to become qualified to conduct a symphony orchestra. Learning to be an orchestral conductor is not incompatible with other musical attainments (for example, composition) but years of learning to conduct would be largely wasted if one did not conduct. It matters whether conductors are motivated by a love of the music they produce or whether they are motivated by less admirable things such as greed or narcissistic self-satisfaction. What is needed in circumstances like this is an alternative way of winkling out such poor motivations to lead. But it is not hard to see how this can be done, because if music-making suffers because of a conductor's poor motivation, this will soon become apparent. A conductor who only conducts for narcissistic self-satisfaction or for the money is likely to perform badly and be shown up as a phony. This is not to deny the narcissism of conductors. (Herbert Von Karajan, responding to a New York taxi driver who asked him for a destination, is reported, perhaps apocryphally, to have said 'No matter; I am in demand everywhere.') Herbert Von Karajan had his narcissistic side, but at his best, it seems that he was driven by the need to bring a piece of music fully to life. Of course, this isn't invariably the case with artistic endeavours. But the point stands whenever good motivation is necessary for success. In such cases, there is no need to insist on reluctance to lead because poorly motivated leadership will become apparent soon enough.

We turn now to the third of our categories: the category in which good motivations are superfluous. Our example is corporate leadership. It might be argued that the burdens and demands of corporate leadership make it a specialized affair, requiring long years of an apprenticeship that supplies its recipients with nothing but the skills of a corporate leader (building teams, making deals, lobbying governments, devising strategy papers, downsizing a workforce, negotiating a handy remuneration, and so on). In this case, it makes little sense to insist on reluctant corporate leaders. It is also unlikely that reluctant corporate leaders would flourish in the competitive environment of late capitalism. Nonetheless, amongst a frenzy of self-delivered bonuses and privileges it is hard to see how fully non-vicious motivations to lead are all that common in the corporate sector. In the case of the orchestra conductor, the peculiar nature of artistic competition ensured (to a degree) that only the well-motivated succeed. (The poorly-motivated are likely to produce humdrum or phony performances.) In the corporate sector, competition seems to work differently. Here, competition substitutes for good motivation. If competitive success in business is the only thing that matters from a corporation's point of view, and if this success is insensitive to the quality of a corporate leader's motivation, then it won't matter how badly motivated corporate leaders are. They may be motivated by greed and a lust for control, but this needn't matter. All that matters, within the confines of the game being played, is that skilful and effective leaders get to lead. That they are viciously motivated is an inconvenient and unwelcome truth, but not invariably a damaging one, at least by the standards of corporate success. The company thrives; it is productive and useful; its share-holders get rich. What does it matter that the CEO is a greedy psychopath as long as he is a greedy psychopath willing to play by the rules? Of course, such a line of reasoning assumes that the game of late capitalism is in good order. It assumes that corporate competition, and competition between corporate leaders in particular, fully delivers the social benefits it promises. This is an unlikely assumption. It represents competition among corporate leaders as a way of ensuring the most effective leaders win out in fierce competition for leadership roles. The grave danger here, of course, is that competition between corporate leaders becomes distorted by a relentless and co-operative pursuit of economic rents. It is also unlikely that the motivations of corporate leaders are always, or even usually, a matter of complete indifference. At least sometimes, the motivation of corporate leaders is of urgent moral concern and at these times it will not suffice to take comfort in the mere fact that corporate leaders work in a fiercely competitive environment or that results and only results matter in the corporate world.

Democratic leadership and Plato's paradox

The fundamental challenge of contemporary democracy, we believe, is to reinvigorate the quality of political leadership – not simply, or primarily, its competence and focus, but its motivation. To adapt an argument of Kant's (*Groundwork* 4: 393), competence and focus are very good and desirable things in many respects, but these things may also become extremely bad and mischievous if the motivation with which they are employed is not good. So what conceptual tools do we have available to describe the transformation of motives to rule in contemporary democracy? How can we adapt Plato's idea of the virtues of reluctant rulership to a contemporary democratic setting?

We have described three different kinds of circumstances: those in which reluctance to rule best demonstrates non-vicious motivations to rule; those in which reluctance is superfluous because a substitute for reluctance, such as artistic competition, encourages and reveals non-vicious motivations to lead anyway; and those in which non-vicious motivations to lead are themselves superfluous. Where on this list should democratic political leadership reside? First, it is obvious that the corporate competitive model – in which competitive pressures substitute for the very necessity of non-vicious motivation – does not apply. This is hardly surprising. We offered some general considerations as to why the corporate competitive model may not generally apply even in the corporate world. In the political world this fact is a great deal clearer still. Viciously motivated politicians are extremely dangerous and this may go some way to explaining why corporate leaders so rarely make a happy transition into politics.

In a well-functioning democracy one might hope that politicians would be like orchestral conductors, where the poorly motivated are exposed and dispensed with on grounds that are apparent in the very performance of their offices. The main trouble with this suggestion is that political life has pressures unmatched by artistic life. Artistic communities have their own (fallible) ways of winkling out phonies. In contemporary democratic politics, however, almost everybody is a phony, at least some of the time. This is a product of democratic politics itself; it is not a product of contingent character flaws. Politicians need to work in teams to be at all effective. They need to balance commitments to a political team with the commitments to the well-being of their constituents; and they need to balance a duty to act as trustee of their constituents' interests with a duty to represent their constituents' voice – to be forward thinking and popularist at the same time. They have to balance their own conscience and their desire for a career with all the other demands placed upon them. They need to both control their message and contrive a message worth controlling. Clashes between these various obligations and desires abound. Under the close attention of a curious and sometimes hostile or obtuse press, and in the face of the rhetorical game-playing of opponents, there are many occasions when a politician has no real choice but to phony-up (i.e. to advance arguments they do not believe, to distort opponent's statements for rhetorical effect, to support measures they strongly disagree with, to make promises they know they may have to abandon, and so on). In the midst of all this it is hardly surprising that typical electoral judgements are so very mediocre. It is hard to spot the phony when most politicians are acting the phony so much of the time.

The upshot of this argument is that political leadership falls into neither of the non-reluctant categories we have described. It does not fall into the category of the orchestra conductor or that of the corporate warrior. We are left in Plato's predicament: making sense of reluctant leadership in political life. The trouble with this, of course, is that a reluctant leader generally makes for a very poor spectacle in contemporary democracy – even a flourishing one. What we need, then, is a contemporary correlate of Plato's key insight. We need a substitute for reluctance: something that will do the work of reluctance without making the political class literally reluctant to rule. The idea that a political career should be an interruption of another career is a good start, but we need more than this.

Our suggestion is that we focus on the underlying logic of Plato's appeal to reluctance. Reluctance to rule is a test of the absence of vicious motivation. It eliminates vicious motivation to rule by ensuring that the qualities required for leadership not include an eagerness to lead and it does this because an eagerness to lead is, very often, an indication of vicious motivation. Generalizing on this thought, we arrive at a response to what we earlier called Plato's paradox of leadership. The paradox is encountered when the qualities required to obtain a leadership role are also qualities that undermine performance of that role. When applied to the specific issue of motivation to political leadership, the paradox is that motivations to seek political leadership are at the same time bad motivations to exercise or satisfy in leadership. A counter to this paradox – a way of avoiding the trap of it – would be to ensure that available or sensible motivations to lead are also benign motivations to exercise or satisfy in leadership. But how might this be done in a contemporary democratic setting?

The answer is to seek out bad motivations to rule and systematically deprive rulers of the satisfaction of them. If riches are the lure, then we must ensure that participation in democratic politics will not make a person rich. If a lust for control is a motivation to lead, then a necessarily collaborative political environment will deprive the lustful of their longing for absolute control. For example, a political environment that more often than not produces minority government would discourage the autocratically motivated to seek power. Such an environment would, for example, have discouraged figures such as George W. Bush and Donald Rumsfeld from seeking power. Minority governments are often frustrating for a pliant and lazy constituency, and can even be hazardous in times of emergency, but they rarely produce the kind of moral catastrophe that so marked the Bush administration of 2001–9. It is hard to imagine someone like Rumsfeld taking any interest in the role of US Secretary of Defense (a position he held from 2001 to 2006) if that role was a genuinely collaborative one. Rumsfeld, it seems, was interested in autocratic power within his political domain, and exercised it without much restraint. The trouble for the US is that what is essentially autocratic control of foreign policy is ceded to the US president through the US constitution. At crucial points (2002–3 and the lead-up to the US invasion and subjugation of Iraq was one of them) autocratic power in the hands of the ill-motivated has led to moral catastrophe. This is, we think, one reason that the US – a nation with a relatively benign and unengaged population and with very little reason to aggressively display its military supremacy – has nonetheless managed to do so much harm in international affairs.

Some of the main motivators of political engagement in contemporary democracy are narcissistic in nature. The response here should be to deprive the political class of the attention they crave. If there were a way – we don't know what this way would be – of preventing politicians from strutting, then better politicians would result. A key to the transformation of democratic political leadership, therefore, is – perhaps surprisingly – to pay less (but sharper) attention to politicians and deprive them of their celebrity. Preferably, we should pay them no attention at all until they present substantial proposals and support them with real evidence and argument rather than rhetorical jibing. At the moment, in typical democratic polities, the job of publically explaining government policy falls mainly to those who have designed it or their supporters in the commentariat. A division of labour here would improve political leadership considerably, we think. The perpetual media spotlight on political leaders – their *ad hoc* contributions to national debates; their appearance at high-profile sporting events; President Barack Obama's appearance (brilliant though it was) on the internet comedy show *Between Two Ferns* in March 2014 – produces in the long term a suite of very bad motivations to lead.

If we do not wish the autocratic and narcissistic to rule us, we need to amend our democratic ways. Of course, this evocation of Plato's paradox does not amount to a solution to the problems that beset contemporary democracy. It simply represents a way of thinking about the problems we face.

Bibliography

Bury, Rev. R. G. (ed.) (1926), *Plato: Laws* (2 vols). Cambridge, MA: Harvard University Press.

Coleridge, E. P. (trans.) (1938), *Euripides: Phoenissae*, in W. J. Oates and E. E. O'Neill (eds), *The Complete Greek Drama* (2 vols). New York: Random House.

Crawley, R. (trans.) (1910), *Thucydides: History of the Peloponnesian War*. London: J. M. Dent; New York: E. P. Dutton.

Forster, E. S. (ed.) (1927), *Isaeus*. Cambridge, MA: Harvard University Press.

Gregor, M. (ed.) (1998), *Kant: Groundwork of the Metaphysics of Morals*. Cambridge: Cambridge University Press.

Grube, G. M. A. (trans.) and Reeve, C. D. C. (rev.) (1997), *Republic*, in J. M. Cooper (ed.), *Plato: Complete Works*. Indianapolis/Cambridge: Hackett.

Henderson, J. (ed.) (1998), *Aristophanes: Acharnians. Knights* (rev. edn). Cambridge, MA: Harvard University Press.

—(ed.) (2000), *Aristophanes: Birds. Lysistrata. Women at the Thesmophoria*. Cambridge, MA: Harvard University Press.

Hicks, H. D. (ed.) (1925), *Diogenes Laertius: Lives of Eminent Philosophers* (2 vols). Cambridge, MA: Harvard University Press.

Jebb, Sir R. (trans.) (1887), *The Oedipus Tyrannus of Sophocles*. Cambridge: Cambridge University Press.

—(trans.) (1891), *The Antigone of Sophocles*. Cambridge: Cambridge University Press.

Lamb, W. R. M. (ed.) (1924), *Plato: Laches, Protagoras, Meno, Euthydemus*. Cambridge, MA: Harvard University Press.

—(ed.) (1925), *Plato: Lysis. Symposium. Gorgias*. Cambridge, MA: Harvard University Press.

Marchant, E. C. and Todd, O. J. (trans.) (1923), *Xenophon: Memorabilia. Oeconomicus. Symposium. Apologia*. Cambridge, MA: Harvard University Press.

Marchant, E. C. and Bowerstock, G. W. (trans.) (1925), *Xenophon: Scripta Minora*. Cambridge, MA: Harvard University Press.

Mill, J. S. (1861), *Considerations on Representative Government*. London: Parker, Son, and Bourn. Reprinted in J. S. Mill (1910), *Utilitarianism, Liberty, and Representative Government*. London: J. M. Dent; New York: E. P. Dutton.

Popper, Sir K. R. (1966), *The Open Society and its Enemies*, vol. 1 (rev. edn). London: RKP.

Rackham, H. (trans.) (1934), *Aristotle: Nicomachean Ethics* (rev. edn). Cambridge, MA: Harvard University Press.

—(trans.) (1944), *Aristotle: Politics* (rev. edn). Cambridge, MA: Harvard University Press.

Ruskin, J. (1865), *Sesame and Lilies*. London: Smith, Elder & Co. Reprinted in E. T. Cook and A. Wedderburn (eds) (1905), *The Works of John Ruskin* (vol. 18). London: George Allen.

Shorey, P. (trans.) (1930), *Plato: Republic* (2 vols). Cambridge, MA: Harvard University Press.

6

The Ethics of Authentic Leadership

Jessica Flanigan
Jepson School

Many of the leaders we admire are distinguished by their authenticity. Leadership scholars emphasize the importance of authenticity on the grounds that authentic leaders are more ethical and effective than inauthentic leaders. Or, authentic leaders are at least perceived as more ethical and effective. Yet we can imagine leaders who are authentic, but ineffective or unethical. Other leaders are inauthentic, but very ethical and effective. What distinguishes an authentic leader is that the way she presents herself to others reflects her personal commitments and character. Authentic leaders are genuine and straightforward in their interactions with people. Is there anything to be said for authenticity for its own sake? In this chapter, I argue that authenticity is a virtue. By this I mean that all else being equal, it is morally better for a person to have an authentic disposition. I also will show that authenticity is an especially important virtue for leaders.

Moral philosophers who have addressed authentic leadership suggest that leaders should be judged by what they accomplish rather than by whether they are authentic (Price 2003). Social scientists suggest that authenticity, as a quality of leaders, is best understood as instrumentally valuable because people like leaders who they perceive as authentic. In this chapter I challenge these assertions. I argue that authenticity is an important moral virtue in its own right because being authentic is a way of treating people as moral equals. Authenticity is especially important for leaders, who are uniquely susceptible to the belief that they are subject to different moral norms than everyone else.

Authenticity is related to moral equality in two ways. First, authenticity is characterized by a lack of strategy. Authentic leaders do not deceive followers or treat them as means to the leader's ends, rather they are forthright about their goals and seek followers' consent rather than mere compliance. Second, authentic leaders hold themselves to the same moral standards they apply to everyone else and refrain from hypocritical blaming or excessive moralization.

I first discuss recent scholarship that addresses authentic leadership, showing that the value of authenticity *for its own sake* merits a stronger defense. In the following section, I argue that there are moral reasons in favour of authentic leadership as a distinctive moral virtue. Namely, treating people with respect, rather than strategically, is a way of affirming one's moral equality with them and recognizing them as people who are entitled to make their own decisions. I then consider and respond to the objection that authenticity is incompatible with leaders' legitimate interest in crafting how they present themselves. Following this, I show that another moral consideration in favour of authenticity is that authentic leaders hold themselves to the same moral standards that they apply to others. Contrary to Machiavelli, I will argue that leaders are not exempt from the moral requirements that apply to everyone else. Finally, I discuss the implications of this argument for other leadership theories. This argument in favor of authenticity also explains why leaders are especially vulnerable to inauthenticity and why scholars are right to focus on authentic leadership.

Authentic leadership

Leadership scholars define authentic leaders as people who display self-awareness and present themselves and their motives as genuinely as possible (Gardner et al. 2011). For example, Malcolm X not only crusaded for black empowerment and independence; in his autobiography he emphasizes that he lived by those values as well (X and Haley 1987). Pope Francis, who exhorts Catholics to live simply and aid the poor, has declined the papal apartment, pope mobile and vestments in favour of a simple guesthouse and plain black shoes. Warren Buffet advocates for a safe long-term investment strategy and lives in a modest home in Omaha that he purchased in 1958. Buffet also supports more progressive taxation and has pledged to donate 99 per cent of his wealth when he dies. Joe Biden campaigned to assist working families and the middle class and also rode the Amtrak train from Delaware to Washington DC throughout his career as a senator. All these people are distinguished by the consistency of their public personas and their private conduct.

On the other hand, leaders who seem inconsistent or disingenuous are criticized for their lack of authenticity. Candidate Mitt Romney's 2012 US Presidential campaign was hampered by his 'flip-flopping' stance on healthcare reform, and speculation about which health plan he *really* supported. General Motors CEO Jack Welsh and Ford CEO Mark Fields were both sharply criticized for accepting large salaries and bonuses while implementing pay cuts, layoffs and benefit decreases for workers ostensibly for the sake of the company and shareholders. Franz-Peter Tebartz-van Elst, the bishop of Limburg, recently resigned from his position in the Catholic Church amid revelations that he commissioned a multimillion dollar renovation of his private residence despite the Church's commitment to serving the poor.

To date, most of the criticism of inauthentic leaders like Romney, Welsh or Tebartz-van Eltz has focused on the fact that their inauthenticity either masked immoral conduct or undermined their effectiveness as leaders. Leadership scholars in the social sciences focus on authenticity because they are interested in the empirical hypothesis that authentic leaders are more successful at prompting followers to achieve their ends and are perceived as more ethical. Perceptions of authenticity (in contrast to genuine authenticity) can potentially enhance a leader's effectiveness as well. Perhaps the most influential studies of authentic leadership involve surveys of leaders and followers that are designed to measure perceptions of leaders' self-awareness, openness, transparency, moral standards and consistency. For example, Bruce Avolio and others have developed the Authentic Leader Questionnaire (ALQ) to measure perceptions of authenticity and effectiveness (Walumbwa et al. 2008) in Kenya and the United States. Confirmatory factor analyses supported a higher order, multidimensional model of the authentic leadership construct (the Authentic Leadership Questionnaire [ALQ]). The ALQ asks respondents to rate leaders' commitment to values and consistency. Perceptions of authenticity, as measured by the ALQ, correlate with followers' task engagement, commitment, trust, satisfaction and sense of empowerment.

Other prominent leadership scholars also emphasize authenticity as an ideal element of a leader–follower relationship. Robert Greenleaf's theory of servant leadership stresses that a good leader should be genuinely dedicated to serving others, because otherwise followers will be reluctant to dedicate themselves to his cause (Greenleaf 1977). Transformational leadership theory also emphasizes the importance of authenticity because transformational leaders motivate people by presenting themselves as role models or mentors in an effort to change followers' values. (Bass and Riggio 2005) According to this theory, a leader who presents himself as an ideal ought to genuinely adhere to the values he promotes in his own life, otherwise followers are likely to question the legitimacy of the leader's goals (Landy and Conte 2010: 564) Yet despite leadership scholars' emphasis on authenticity, few have considered the ethics of authentic leadership. Instead, the value of authenticity is typically assumed but not argued

for. Or, leadership scholars assume that authentic leadership is mainly instrumentally valuable as a way of securing followers' commitment and obedience
without considering whether this management strategy is morally justified (see
e.g. Hartog and Belschak 2012).

It is not obvious that authenticity is a virtue for its own sake either. In one
of the few discussions of this topic Terry Price argues that authenticity is only
an ideal insofar as an authentic leader's behaviour aligns with what is morally
right. Price is sceptical that an appeal to authenticity will resolve the question
of whether a leader is ethical. Moreover, Price suggests that emphasizing
authenticity could paradoxically lead to less ethical leadership insofar as leaders
who are genuinely committed to their own values or the values of authentic
leadership may be blind to the larger social and moral norms (Price 2003). Price
is right to emphasize the importance of moral justification for a leader. Surely
an inauthentic leader who adopts morally justified goals is nevertheless more
ethical than an authentic leader whose goals are seriously immoral. Yet our
moral assessments of leaders should not exclusively attend to a leader's purpose
but to his methods as well. Even if a morally justified cause necessitates immoral
conduct in some cases, it is still morally worse to use immoral tactics to achieve
a just cause especially if a more ethical path was available. Moreover, in some
cases the ends do not justify the means. By failing to address the ethics of *how*
one leads in addition to where one leads, leadership scholars risk overlooking
an important component of ethical leadership.

For these reasons, even if more general ethical requirements should always
take priority over the ideal of authenticity in our overall assessments of leaders'
conduct, we should also assess the ethics of authenticity itself. It is striking
that for all the measures of authenticity and advocates for authentic leadership
in leadership studies, a direct explanation of why authentic leadership is a
praiseworthy trait is lacking. Price worries that authenticity may blind leaders
to moral requirements, but even this is an instrumental consideration against
authentic leadership. To know whether authenticity itself is a virtue of leaders,
we must ask if it is better for a leader to be authentic, holding fixed the leader's
other ethical commitments. That is, if two leaders were identical in all respects,
but one was authentic, would the authentic leader be morally better than the
inauthentic leader? If so, then authenticity is a moral virtue and it is *pro tanto*
better for a leader to be authentic.

Deception and inauthenticity

My central thesis is that while authenticity cannot guarantee that a leader is ethical, and inauthenticity is not an all things considered ethical indictment, there are moral reasons in favour of authentic behavior *for its own sake*. All else equal, it is morally better for a leader to behave authentically because an authentic relationship affirms the moral equality of leaders and followers.

By moral equality, I am referring to the equal moral standing that all mentally competent people have just in virtue of being persons.[1] This sense of moral equality is widely affirmed – it represents the idea that despite our differences in ability, wealth or social status, everyone has the same standing to demand moral consideration from others (Darwall 2009). Moral equality means that it is wrong for a person to make moral exceptions for himself, either by privileging his own interests over others' or by violating people's rights. Another way to think of moral equality is in terms of authority – everyone has the same authority to make his or her own choices, and is subject to the same moral requirement that they respect others' authority to do the same. Even if a person is a leader, though he may have more power or prestige than other people, leaders do not have greater moral authority than others. Formal positions of authority do not entitle leaders to disrespect the normative authority of other members of the moral community.

Paradigmatic forms of wrongdoing therefore consist in denying people's equal moral standing to make their own choices. These kinds of wrongdoing include acts of force, coercion and deception. Force deprives people of their ability to choose by physically restraining or interfering with someone's choice. Coercion uses threats of force to achieve the same result. Similarly, deception is wrong because victims of deception cannot consent to be lied to (otherwise the lie would not be effective) and in this way they cannot make voluntary choices when they are deceived (Korsgaard 1986: 333). For example, consider a deceptive borrower who has no intention of repaying a loan. If the lender had known that the borrower would not repay, he would not have made the loan (presumably), so the lender did not consent to the transaction.[2] Consent is a fundamental moral constraint on everyone's conduct. When a person consents, he changes the moral landscape between himself and others, authorizing treatment that would otherwise be impermissible (Pallikkathayil 2011). Consent is especially important for leaders, who are uniquely capable of using force, coercion or deception to achieve their goals.

This gloss on the wrongness of deception also illustrates what it is about deception that is wrong, and what counts as deception. It is not necessarily wrong to say something that is false. Rather, the problem with deception is that deceptive speech fails to acknowledge that the follower is a person who has the right to freely make up his own mind. Deception shapes a person's judgement about what to do in ways he could not consent to.[3] One way to understand the relationship between moral equality and deception is through the metaphor of objectification. Each person is equally entitled to be treated like a person and not as an object. When one person deceives another, he treats the deceived person strategically, as an object in his own plans rather than as a person with plans of her own (Langton 1992). This is not to say it is never permissible to enlist another person to accomplish a project, but rather that one must always treat them as a willing co-participant in those projects. Securing voluntary participation requires honesty, but it does not forbid transactions that are mutually agreed to.

On this account of deception, paradigm cases of inauthenticity, where the disconnection between an inauthentic person's private self and public persona is a strategic misrepresentation, are also cases of deception. Even if someone never says anything false, he may still wrongfully deceive people if he strategically misleads them. Lying per se isn't what is morally problematic; even saying things that are true can be deliberately misleading (e.g. when the Devil quotes scripture) (Langton 1992). What is morally significant is whether a person's speech is intended to communicate whatever information is necessary to secure the listener's consent, or if one's speech is intended to ensure that the listener does what the speaker wants. The distinction between strategic speech and persuasion may illuminate this point. A person who persuasively communicates treats the listener as an agent, and presents her with arguments and reasons that seek to secure her voluntary consent or agreement. A person who strategically communicates does not aim to convince the listener to voluntarily change her intentions or belief. Rather, strategic communicators treat their listeners as means to the speaker's ends. In other words, *strategic communication* is wrong because it objectifies the listener and violates the listener's entitlement to make her own choices.

Inauthentic leadership is therefore wrong because it is a form of strategic behaviour, which treats other people as means to the leader's ends rather than treating them with respect. Inauthentic leaders mask their true selves because they worry that being forthright would make them less effective at achieving their goals. In some cases, inauthentic leaders may be right that presenting themselves honestly would undermine their goals. Yet even if an inauthentic leader acts on behalf of a good cause, and even if he is more effective in virtue of his inauthentic self-presentation, it is still at least *pro tanto* wrong to adopt a strategic stance towards followers that is intended to secure their loyalty or obedience rather than their consent. This explanation for why authenticity is wrong also can explain the scope of authenticity requirements. Because leaders are obligated to refrain from strategic communication that denies people's ability to consent, they must therefore disclose whatever information a reasonable person would require to consent to a leader's decision.

The example of Nelson Mandela, an inauthentic leader who worked effectively for a morally justified cause, may help to illustrate this point. By any credible normative standards of leadership, Mandela was an exemplar. He effectively led the anti-apartheid movement, and later, South Africa. Yet Joanne Ciulla shows in a recent case study of Mandela's leadership that he also saw himself as a man of history, and to attain that role he constructed a narrative about his life and continually refined his public story (Ciulla 2013). Mandela's autobiography was intentionally written as a political document. His presentation of his personal history was crafted to gloss over potentially unflattering details (such as his divorce or his father's corrupt leadership) and to identify with the struggles of potential constituents. Mandela was aware that to some extent being an iconic leader came at the price of authenticity: he wrote once that he was worried that he presented a false image to the world while he was in prison. Insofar as Mandela manufactured a misleading narrative about himself to secure followers' loyalty and consent to his leadership, his actions treated followers as a means to his overall goals.

This is not to say that Mandela was not justified *all things considered* in presenting himself strategically, only that his calculated self-presentation was disrespectful to followers. If Mandela's persona was necessary to compel people who would otherwise act in a way that was not morally justified, then his strategic image may have been justified on balance. Yet it would have been morally better if those who followed Mandela knew who he really was and followed him voluntarily and not because they were under false impressions. Ciulla writes, 'Mandela is not a moral leader because he is authentic, nor is he an authentic leader because he is moral' (Ciulla 2013). This statement is correct, in that authenticity is neither necessary nor sufficient for a person to qualify as a 'moral leader', but it obscures the fact that authenticity does carry independent moral weight. On balance, Mandela was a moral leader because he made South Africa a more just society. If a strategic self-presentation was necessary for this end, then Mandela was right to act inauthentically, especially in light of the extraordinary injustices he sought to remedy. But, insofar as he could have advanced his cause without inauthenticity, Mandela would have been even more praiseworthy had he presented himself to his people more honestly.

Mandela's example illustrates how inauthentic conduct that is *pro tanto* impermissible can be justified in the service of a morally justified cause if it is necessary. There is also some evidence to suggest that inauthenticity may be necessary for political success in some cases because certain narratives are more likely to win support from followers. Political scientists find that low information voters tend to assess candidates on the basis of personal narratives rather than their voting records or policy record (Popkin 1994: 78). In these cases, a likeable persona may be more important to a leader's electoral chances than advocating for a just cause. Yet even if inauthenticity is necessary, authenticity is still a moral virtue. Consider an analogy to just war theory. In some cases, combatants for a just cause must use lethal force against unjust combatants and they are justified in doing so. Nevertheless, killing is still *pro tanto* wrong. If lethal force is not necessary for advancing a just cause, then combatants ought not kill. Even if lethal force is necessary, there is still something lost, morally, when soldiers kill. This is why combatants who carry out proportionate killings that are necessary for a just cause might still reasonably wish that circumstances did not necessitate killing, even if they were justified. Similarly, inauthenticity may be justified if it is necessary and proportionate and in the service of a justified goal, but it is still *pro tanto* wrong.

Kant's famous example of the murderer at the door illustrates how inauthenticity, such as Mandela's strategic self-presentation, can be a justified response to injustice, even though this kind of strategy is generally wrong. Imagine a murderer knocks on your door, axe in hand, asking about the location of a potential victim who is hiding in the attic. Though Kant argues that it is impermissible to lie even to a would-be killer, most would agree that deception in these circumstances is permissible. The interesting question is why it is permissible to deceive a murderer but not others. Some argue that lying is permissible because we are not required to make ourselves instruments of evil (Korsgaard 1986). Others add that the murderer is not entitled to know the whereabouts of his potential victim, and has forfeited his entitlement to know the truth by intending to do something evil (Langton 1992).

Rae Langton calls this justification of lying 'strategy for kingdom's sake', referring to Kant's ideal of a kingdom of ends where everyone is treated with respect. This idea of strategy for the sake of a moral ideal is especially relevant to leaders, who confront injustices like apartheid and in the face of either committed opposition or rigid bureaucracy must think of respect as a moral ideal to strive for, not as a guide to action in all circumstances (Langton 1992). For this reason, Mandela's strategic political presentation of his personal narrative may have been justified if those who were mislead by it would otherwise have failed to support Mandela's efforts to end apartheid. Those who supported and tolerated injustice were acting unjustly. Even if they were not like the murderer at the door, they were at least like people who tolerate murderers in the neighbourhood. Still, strategy for kingdom's sake is still in some sense disrespectful to the deceived even if it is ultimately excused because strategy consists in treating people instrumentally, as means to one's own goals. Were it not necessary to lie, it would be morally better to avoid doing so, just as it is morally better to refrain from using force against agents of injustice whenever it is possible.

In contrast, authentic leaders are not strategic in how they present themselves to others, though may be strategic in how they manage a business or wage a political campaign. By being honest and forthright, authentic leaders do not use employees or followers as objects of strategy. Rather, they allow others to decide freely whether to co-operate or follow. For example, when Alan Mulally was appointed as CEO of Ford Motor Company he told reporters that he drove a Lexus because it was 'the finest car in the world' (Vijayenthiran 2006). Strategically, Mulally's endorsement of Lexus cars was not the best way to motivate employees, and he was criticized for disparaging the Ford brand. Yet Mulally persisted at Ford with an honest leadership style that did not endear himself to longstanding employees at the company (Kiley 2007; Reed 2012).

Despite employees' strong initial disapproval, Mulally proved himself as an extremely effective CEO. He maintained the company throughout the recession when other automakers required government bailouts, streamlined the Ford brand and made the company profitable again. Yet even if his tenure at Ford had not been successful, a virtue of Mulally's leadership style is that by emphasizing the importance of realistic and honest assessments, admitting mistakes and sharing information even when it is unflattering to the Ford brand, Mulally treated his employees with respect even when doing so made them unhappy, and their co-operation and commitment was honestly won.

Mulally's example demonstrates why authenticity is a virtue even when it makes a leader less effective. My claim that authenticity is *pro tanto* praiseworthy also implies that even an authentic person who advances an unjust cause is in some sense praiseworthy. All else equal, it is better even for agents of injustice to be authentic because authenticity is morally good even for a person who is seriously immoral. For example, an authentic Nazi is in some sense morally better than an inauthentic Nazi, assuming they are both equally effective at advancing an unjust cause. Of course, the virtue of a person's authenticity is clearly outweighed by his commitments to Nazism, so authentic Nazis were obviously not virtuous people.[4] But in one small sense, by refraining from strategic speech authentic agents of injustice do treat people with more respect than they would if they were inauthentic, even if their behaviour is fundamentally immoral in all other respects.

One may object to this claim as follows. Imagine two people who publically endorse and advance an unjust cause, such as slavery. If one slaveholder is inauthentic, in that he privately does not believe that slavery is permissible, while the other slaveholder is authentic and he privately endorses the justice of the cause as well, it does seem that in some sense the inauthentic slaveholder is morally better because at least some of his attitudes are morally praiseworthy (his private condemnation of slavery). In that sense, I concede that an inauthentic slaveholder is in a sense morally better, but he is also morally worse in a sense because he strategically misrepresents his private commitments. Indeed, perhaps if he were motivated to be authentic he would bring his public commitments in line with his private condemnation of slavery. In contrast, the authentic slaverholder presents his moral commitments straightforwardly to others, and in this way he deals with people more honestly. This is not to say that the authentic slaveholder should have resisted revising his public or private commitments for fear of being inauthentic. As the example of Nelson Mandela illustrated, even though authenticity is a moral virtue, the value of authenticity can be outweighed by other moral considerations such as the moral worth of condemning slavery or opposing apartheid.

In sum, authentic leadership is neither necessary nor sufficient for ethical leadership, but it is a moral virtue of leaders because inauthenticity consists in a strategic posture that denies the moral equality of leaders and followers. Inauthenticity is a form of deception, and like other forms of lying it may be excused or justified, such as in circumstances of extreme injustice, but there is always a kind of moral loss because deception is a fundamentally disrespectful way to treat people.

Objection – privacy and autonomy

One objection to a moral defence of authentic leadership is that authenticity is so demanding we should not think of it as a moral virtue. One may argue, for example, that leaders are entitled to a measure of privacy, and so some degree of inauthenticity is permissible. I have argued that authenticity is important because it enables people to freely choose whether to follow a leader, but perhaps a leader's own freedom may be unduly burdened by the demands of authenticity. Of course leaders are not generally entitled to lie to people, but other forms of strategic communication such as crafting a persona or concealing one's true motives may be difficult to distinguish from permissible and ordinary behaviours such as trying to be friendly or simply maintaining a private life.

On the one hand, part of being an autonomous, free person does consist in having the discretion to develop one's own self-presentation (Velleman 2001). Autonomy requires at least some privacy because living a life that one chooses includes living with the freedom to choose what to conceal and what to expose. This is why unwarranted searches or surveillance are rights violations. On the other hand, deception and strategic communication violate other people's ability to make their own autonomous choices. A society that respects the value of autonomy should discourage strategic speech, yet it cannot require that everyone reveal everything about himself or herself.

In ordinary cases these considerations do not pose a dilemma. Simply developing a self-presentation is not dishonest, since it is generally understood that we all present a particular version of ourselves to others and others all understand that the version they see just is the socially visible face we have decided to present (Velleman 2001; Nagel 1998). No one can claim to be misled by a person who tries to present herself as especially intelligent, interesting or beautiful, because we all understand that everyone manages his or her public exposure in these ways. Similarly, if it was truly understood by both parties that a loan would not be paid back, then the lender cannot object to the borrower who takes money with no intention of returning it. Deception requires a mismatch between the truth and the deceived person's beliefs. So for example, if people know that a persona is a persona then it is not deceptive. This is why actors and comedians behave permissibly when they perform, because the audience is in on the joke. Even a persona that is recognized as such can be deceptive though, if the development and presentation of that persona is part of a ploy to manipulate people.

So one might think that just as leaders have privacy rights, they also have rights to be strategic in what they conceal and what they reveal to followers as long as they do not deliberately mislead people into thinking that their public persona is indicative of their private selves. Yet unlike actors and comedians, leaders are not generally forthright about the phoniness of their self-presentations. Rather, leaders cultivate the expectation that they are being honest even when they are not. Appearing authentic amounts to its own kind of inauthenticity, such as when millionaire politicians try to seem folksy or relatable by emphasizing their humble origins (Dickerson 2014). In these cases, it is difficult to determine which parts of a leader's persona are fact or fiction. Therefore, the fact that people expect leaders to be authentic, and that leaders may even cultivate that expectation, explains why leaders have obligations to be authentic and why inauthentic leadership is morally deficient.

One may reply that expectations of leader's honesty are not justified, because leaders have the same interests in developing a self-presentation and maintaining some privacy as everyone else. If our expectations of leaders' authenticity are unreasonable then they should not be morally authoritative even if those expectations are pervasive. Yet expectations of authenticity are justified because people can consent to be leaders, but followers cannot consent to be lied to. For this reason, a leader's interest in privacy and autonomy does not license inauthenticity, because leaders could protect those interests by simply declining to assume a leadership role.

One of the few philosophers to address how leaders in particular should balance their interests in privacy with moral requirements like authenticity is Terry Price. In a recent discussion of privacy and leadership, Price grants that privacy rights are justified by an appeal to the value of autonomy, but concludes that leaders have weaker claims to privacy than others (Price 2014). Leaders incur special obligations to followers when they voluntarily accept a leadership position, including the obligation to maintain a private life that does not interfere with their public role. Followers are therefore entitled to know about a leader's private self in those cases that the private life of a leader is relevant to securing the followers' consent. For example, while most people have an entitlement that their tax returns remain private, public officials may be legitimately asked to release their tax returns insofar as voters rightly think that compliance with tax laws and fiscal responsibility are qualifications for office.

Price's account of privacy effectively responds to the objection that the expectation of authentic leadership may be unduly burdensome to leaders' autonomy. If a person wishes to shield himself from legitimate expectations of forthrightness, then he should not volunteer for a position that exposes him to heightened obligations to be authentic. A lack of control over one's self-presentation and privacy is only one of the ways that leaders voluntarily sacrifice their autonomy for the privileges of leadership. Followers cannot consent to be lied to, however, which explains why the expectation of authenticity is typically more morally urgent than a leader's expectation of control or privacy.

In some cases, however, other autonomy-based rights may conflict with the expectation that a leader act authentically, and I do not mean to suggest that authenticity for leaders is always more urgent than a leader's other rights. For example, Martin Luther King was a vocal advocate of non-violent resistance. He even went so far as to say that the best defence for civil rights advocates was to refuse to hit back so that members of the oppressive white majority would be forced to confront their own brutality (King 1987). Yet in his personal life, one of King's advisors described his home as an arsenal and he kept a loaded pistol for self-defence (Cobb 2014). Even if there was something *pro tanto* morally problematic about the inconsistency between King's public commitments and private endorsement of using violence for self-defence, his conduct was justified on balance because his advocacy for non-violence was in the service of a just cause and King also had an especially weighty autonomy-based reason (his right of self-defence) to be prepared to use violence if threatened.

Nevertheless, we should not entirely discount the demands of authenticity and the ways that authenticity requirements can threaten a leader's autonomy and privacy rights. As the foregoing discussions of Martin Luther King and Nelson Mandela illustrated, constituents are not always entitled to full authenticity even if it is always morally better for leaders to present themselves in a straightforward manner. One reason to tolerate a leader's or anyone else's inauthentic self-presentation is that inauthenticity may not always rise to the level of deception or strategic communication such that it deprives followers of the ability to consent. Another reason to tolerate some inauthenticity is that strategy for the sake of justified ends may be permissible. Yet even when inauthenticity is not very burdensome to followers, moral reasons in favour of treating people in a straightforward manner are still relevant because authenticity affirms our moral equality. In these cases inauthenticity is a kind of morally permissible moral mistake.

Like other moral virtues, moral importance of authenticity must be balanced against other moral reasons and there is not a single principle that can inform this balance in all cases. There are some general considerations that should inform how we understand the moral importance of authenticity, such as the principle that authenticity is even more morally weighty for leaders because legitimate leadership requires people's consent. Depending on the circumstances, being authentic is sometimes morally required (as a form of honesty), but sometimes it is only supererogatory. Inauthenticity can be impermissible, but even when it is permissible it is still morally bad. In describing this category of action, Elizabeth Harman writes,

Our own moral lives include a substantial realm of moral permissibility. Each of us has her own projects and her own interests as well as her own loved ones, and we have agent-relative permissions to privilege our projects and our interests in substantial ways. Nevertheless, we often have reasons regarding others which tell in the other direction .... our other regarding reasons continue to exert a force on us even though they do not in these cases render the behavior they favor morally required. (Harman 2014)

Harman focuses on failures of beneficence as examples of morally permissible moral mistakes, but failures of authenticity qualify as well. Even in those cases where inauthenticity does not rise to the level of deception and renders followers incapable of consent, it is morally worse to present oneself to others inauthentically because doing so also consists in treating people as means to one's own ends and this kind of strategic disposition denies our moral equality.

Hypocrisy and inauthenticity

Inauthenticity can also be wrong for other reasons relating to our moral equality. In particular, inauthentic leaders may in some cases craft personas that blame followers for moral mistakes that the leader makes as well. In these cases of inauthenticity, which I am calling hypocrisy, a leader's ethical commitments in public are at odds with his private conduct. The case against hypocrisy is similar to the case against deception because in both cases inauthenticity undermines a relationship of equal moral standing. Whether by deception or hypocrisy, inauthentic people apply different moral standards to themselves that they do not extend to others.

In leadership studies, the classic case of Bathsheba syndrome illustrates how leaders are especially susceptible to hypocrisy. Bathsheba syndrome is named after the biblical story of King David, who impregnated a soldier's wife (Bathsheba) and then assigned the soldier to be killed on the front lines of battle in an attempt to mask his unethical conduct. David then suffered a series of military losses and other indignities, and the story is meant to show that no one is so powerful that he can escape God's judgement. Yet the story is also an example of hypocritical leadership. At one point in the story the prophet Nathan tells David a story about a rich man who stole a poor man's prized possession. David morally disapproves of the rich man in the story and proclaims that the rich man deserves to die. Nathan then points out that David's conduct is the same as the rich man's (Price 2000).

Leadership scholars focus on David as an archetype of leaders who become immoral after they encounter professional success. Some argue that David's success gave him privileges and control over resources that tempted him to behave immorally, as well as an inflated sense of control over outcomes (Ludwig and Longenecker 1993). On this account, leaders hold themselves to lower moral standards because they are weak-willed and because they think they can get away with publically endorsing one set of principles while privately living by another.

Other leadership scholars argue that David's success led him to believe that moral norms did not apply to him. Since David was exceptional in other ways perhaps David came to believe that he was morally exceptional as well (Price 2000). On this account, leaders hold themselves to lower moral standards because they genuinely believe that their private conduct is not subject to the same standards as others, and they only present themselves as immoral because they acknowledge that other people may fail to recognize their exceptional moral status.

On either account, one of David's moral mistakes was that he was inauthentic. David's stated moral commitments were at odds with his private behaviour, either because he thought he could get away with it or because he thought the rules did not apply to him. By endorsing standards of blame he did not privately apply to himself, David made a moral exception for himself. As R. Jay Wallace argues, this kind of hypocrisy is morally problematic because it consists in privileging one's own interests over others in the practice of blaming (Wallace 2010). If people are genuinely morally equal, then the same moral standards will apply to everyone. In this way, hypocrisy denies the foundational assumption of moral equality that is the basis of practices of praise and blame.

Just as it could be justified on balance for a leader to strategically develop an inauthentic persona, some hypocrisy could be justified as well. If the most effective leader for a just cause is someone who does not live by the standards of that cause, it may nevertheless be permissible for him to lead while espousing principles he cannot meet. But there is still something morally deficient about a hypocritical leader. For example, imagine a president who condemns a rebel militia for waging an unjust war in one territory, while simultaneously waging his own unjust war in another. With his considerable influence and resources, the president may be the best placed person to stand on the global stage and condemn an unjust army. But in addition to his own immoral conduct (waging his own unjust war) he is also criticizable for his hypocrisy. Publically presenting himself and his country as exceptional or exempt from the moral requirements that bind everyone else denies a presumption of moral equality, even if condemnation of the unjust militia is nevertheless justified.

As this example shows, another good reason to discourage leaders from publically endorsing moral principles that they do not privately accept is that holding leaders' conduct to their public commitments may encourage them to behave more morally. On the other hand, norms against hypocrisy could risk a kind of indifference to immoral conduct if people become reluctant to judge others' hypocritical conduct for fear that they are hypocritical as well. But even in these cases, attentiveness to authenticity could at least prompt more introspection by leaders who encounter others' immoral behaviour.

Transformational leadership, charisma and moral ambition

The arguments in favour of authentic leadership also have surprising implications for other leadership styles. First, authentic leadership is sometimes discussed as if authenticity is a component of transformational and charismatic leadership (Bass and Bass 2009: 232). Yet this characterization is a mistake, and the foregoing discussion of authenticity and moral equality explains why. Inauthentic leadership is disrespectful to followers because it deprives followers of the opportunity to consent to a leader and inauthentic leaders hold followers to different moral standards. Second, morally ambitious leaders – those who hold themselves to a higher moral standard, also act wrongly in some sense because they too offend against a presumption of moral equality between themselves and their followers.

Transformational leaders are so named because they change followers' goals from self-oriented to morally justified or collectively beneficial projects. They therefore focus on acting in ways that get followers to change in these ways, and in this way transformational leadership potentially encourages a kind of strategic disposition that risks violating followers' entitlement to choose for themselves. One may try to justify transformational leadership on the grounds that some goals are in the followers' objective interests, or that transformational leaders only seek to motivate people to do what they ought to want to do anyhow. However, deceptive leaders act wrongly even when they lie in an effort to advance the well-being of their followers. If a transformational leader's cause were justified, it would be morally better if followers fully understood the leader's goals and consented to adopt them. Advocates of transformational leadership should therefore take care to focus on whether followers have an opportunity to freely and knowingly consent to adopting the leader's proposed goals.

Consider for example a transformational leadership relationship, where the leader of a non-profit gives motivational speeches and crafts an inspiring narrative in an effort to encourage employees to work harder and longer for the cause. The leader may genuinely believe that the employees morally ought to work harder and longer. Assume that the leader is altruistic: he does not deceive to promote his own interests and his cause is genuinely a good one. Nevertheless he acts wrongly insofar as he has strategically cultivated a leadership style that treats employees as means to the non-profit's goals rather than as people with their own plans and projects. This kind of manipulation is different from persuasion, which consists in presenting the reasons in favour of working harder and longer to employees so that they can make a well-informed decision in light of all relevant considerations. Strategic speech may also alert people to the relevant considerations, but promoting a well-informed decision is not the main purpose of strategic speech.

In contrast, authentic leadership respects the followers' right to decide by ensuring they are not treated strategically or used as a means to the leader's or group's goals. When a transformational leader crafts a strategic persona in an effort to change people's values, he substitutes his own judgement for the judgement of the deceived followers. By doing so, he is implicitly saying either that his judgement is better than those of the followers or that his or the group's interests are more important or urgent than those of the followers. In either case, a transformational leader acts inauthentically, and in doing so he discounts followers' entitlement to freely make up their own minds. Of course, not all transformational leaders are inauthentic. It is possible to change people's hearts and minds without any strategic posturing at all. Based on the foregoing defence of authenticity, transformational leadership is only morally problematic when followers only change their goals because of their leader's strategic presentation and communication. Yet proponents of transformational leadership tend to disparagingly characterize instances of leadership that lack strategy as mere transactional exchanges, where leaders simply show followers that a course of action is mutually beneficial given their interests (Burns 1998). In light of the foregoing arguments, I contend that transformational leadership scholars should perhaps rethink transactional exchanges as an ethical ideal, *because* they are characterized by consent and a lack of strategy.

Authenticity should also be distinguished from charismatic leadership. People may find honesty refreshing and genuine authenticity can be attractive and even a kind of charisma, but not all charismatic leaders are authentic. One way to be charismatic is to appear authentic, which is itself a kind of strategy. Authenticity is the opposite of this cynical strategy. When thinking of authentic leadership, it is important to bear in mind that a respectful relationship to followers consists in *actually being* authentic with them rather than merely appearing authentic. Another concern about charisma is that charismatic leadership is effective because it bypasses a follower's ability to reason and consent to a leader's plans by exploiting the follower's cognitive biases and emotional vulnerabilities (Flanigan 2013). In these cases, charismatic leadership styles also might not respect people's entitlement to freely consent to a leader's goals insofar as charisma undermines people's ability to make informed choices. In contrast, authentic leadership enables followers to reason in light of all relevant considerations and decide for themselves.

Finally, the link between authentic leadership and hypocrisy has surprising implications for morally ambitious leaders. One trope that is sometimes repeated in descriptions of leaders is that they hold themselves to higher moral standards. This is almost always described as a virtue, yet as Joanne Ciulla writes, when people praise leaders who subscribe to higher moral standards, it seems to suggest that it is acceptable for everyone else to live by lower moral standards (Ciulla 2004).

Moral ambition, at least when it includes excessive moralizing, is a species of hypocrisy. Above, I argued that it is wrong for leaders to exempt themselves from moral standards they endorse for others. Yet the same reasons against hypocritical blaming are also considerations against moral ambition. It is wrong for a leader to refrain from blaming others for conduct he would judge blameworthy for himself because respect requires holding people to equal moral standards by blaming them in some cases. As Stephen Darwall argues, equal treatment also requires that we hold people accountable for their actions (Darwall 2009). Refusing to blame people for conduct that is blameworthy is not only infantilizing, it is tantamount to a refusal to include them as responsible, accountable members of the moral community.

Consider for example a politician who privately maintains that divorce is immoral and would judge himself or people in his family for divorcing, but publically refuses to criticize divorced families. On one hand, it is laudable that he displays tolerance towards his constituents. Yet insofar as he genuinely thinks it is morally wrong to be divorced he should hold others accountable to that conduct. This example also shows that moral ambition is often just a species of excessive moralizing in one's personal life. Though a leader may appear virtuous for living by a strict moral code, if he cannot in good conscience extend that code to others then he should consider revising his principles instead. The case of moral ambition also serves as a warning against unnecessary sanctimony. Whether a leader holds himself to a higher or lower moral standard, his differential application of moral judgements is a way of denying moral equality. In both cases, a leader should either refrain from making moral judgements or apply them equally to himself and others.[5] In some cases, such as the case of King David, a leader should extend his moral standards to apply to his own conduct. Yet in other cases, such as the upstanding politician, leaders should perhaps simply refrain from excessive moralizing even when it applies solely to their own conduct.

A closer look at the value of authenticity therefore has surprising implications for our assessments of other leadership styles. Transformational leaders are not necessarily praiseworthy insofar as their transformative influence can be credited to strategic interactions with followers. Similarly, though charisma may make leaders more effective, leaders should not strive to seem more charismatic if it requires that they develop a misleading persona. Morally ambitious leadership is also overrated. Leaders should apply the same moral standards to themselves and others and refrain from unwarranted moralizing.

Conclusion

I have defended authenticity as a moral virtue for leaders on the grounds that inauthenticity is often wrong for the same reasons that deception and hypocrisy are wrong. Both considerations in favour of authenticity are related to the importance of moral equality. When inauthentic leaders adopt a strategic attitude towards followers they violate followers' entitlement to consent to a leader's plans and thereby fail to respect followers as moral equals. In contrast, loyalty to an authentic leader is justly won because followers are not under any illusions when they consent. When inauthentic leaders hypocritically blame they also deny their moral equality with followers by holding themselves to different moral standards.

Even if an inauthentic leader has altruistic motives, inauthenticity is still *pro tanto* wrong because it is disrespectful. This is not to say that inauthenticity is never justified. Often inauthenticity is simply a morally permissible moral mistake, when it does not rise to the level of deception. In other cases, inauthenticity is necessary for a leader to effectively accomplish a just goal, even if it is morally non-ideal. This essay is not intended as a sweeping incitement of all inauthentic leaders. Rather, I have sought to explain why even morally justified inauthentic leaders are in some sense worse than they would be were they to abandon strategic posturing and hypocritical blaming.

It is especially important for leaders to recognize the value of authenticity because leaders are especially prone to lose sight of the fact that we are all moral equals. By their very nature leaders are exceptional in all the ways that distinguish them as leaders. But leaders are not morally exceptional. Leadership does not license deception or any other immoral conduct. Inauthentic leaders lose sight of that fundamental truth. When followers demand authenticity from leaders they are not asking that leaders act folksy, or seem genuine, or that a leader be the kind of guy you'd like to have a beer with. Rather, calls for authenticity are best understood as calls for leaders to treat everyone with equal respect.

Notes

1　My argument rests on a non-consequentialist (broadly Kantian) moral framework. Consequentialists may also agree that authenticity is a moral virtue, but only insofar as an authentic disposition would tend to promote morally better states of affairs.

2　In discussing this case, Japa Pallakithayal points out that the lender does in *some sense* consent to handing over the money, just as in some sense the victim of a robbery consents to hand the mugger her wallet, but it's not really an action that she voluntarily performs because 'consent requires not just that [the lender] choose to act in a way that furthers [the borrower's] true ends but that [the lender] choose this action under a description that makes some reference to [the borrower's] true ends'.

3　On this account, it is wrong to treat people in ways they cannot consent to even if doing so promotes their well-being. For example, paternalistic deception, such as a physician withholding a bad diagnosis, is wrong even if the patient would have been happier not knowing. This principle justifies practices like the doctrine of informed consent (Buchanan 1978).

4　I am grateful to Michael Levine for prompting me to qualify this point. Michael raised the objection that there seems to be nothing morally good about an authentic Nazi.

5　Jacqueline Boaks suggests that leaders may appear to be holding themselves to higher standards when they are in fact simply giving others the benefit of the doubt. Insofar as a leader is applying different moral standards to himself for epistemic reasons, and not because he thinks that stricter moral standards apply uniquely to him, the leader does not offend against a commitment to moral equality. I am grateful to Jacqueline for prompting me to clarify this point.

Bibliography

Bass, B. M. and Riggio, R. E. (2005), *Transformational Leadership*. Psychology Press. Available at http://books.google.com/books?hl=en&lr=&id=2WsJSw6wa6cC&oi=fnd&pg=PT6&dq=Bass+and+Riggio+transformational+leadership&ots=I53YkZIIEE&sig=lveKmhvKeZHpo2QBvGj3DUtqGlA

Bass, B. M. and Bass, R. (2009), *The Bass Handbook of Leadership: Theory, Research, and Managerial Applications*. Simon and Schuster. New York, New York: USA.

Buchanan, A. (1978), 'Medical paternalism', *Philosophy & Public Affairs*, 7 (4): 370–90.

Burns, J. M. (1998), 'Transactional and Transforming Leadership', in G. R. Hickman (ed.), *Leading Organizations: Perspectives for a New Era*. Thousand Oaks, CA: USA.

Ciulla, J. B. (2004), 'Ethics and Leadership Effectiveness', in J. Antonakis, A. T. Cianciolo, and R. J. Sternberg (eds), *The Nature of Leadership*. Thousand Oaks, CA: Sage Publications, pp. 302–7.

—(2013), 'Searching for Mandela: The Saint as a Sinner Who Keeps on Trying', in D. Ladkin and C. Spiller (eds), *Authentic Leadership: Clashes, Convergences and Coalescences*. Edward Elgar Publishing, Cheltenham, England, pp. 152–71. Available at http://books.google.com/books?hl=en&lr=&id=uebDAQAAQBAJ&oi=fnd&pg=PA152&ots=YQTOto-hpE&sig=c0rRPwW9ZC79ft5X1Dz7LG52kw8

Cobb Jr, C. E. (2014), *This Nonviolent Stuff'll Get You Killed: How Guns Made the Civil Rights Movement Possible*. New York: Basic Books.

Darwall, S. (2009), *The Second-Person Standpoint: Morality, Respect, and Accountability*. Cambridge, MA: Harvard University Press.

Dickerson, J. (2014), 'Crying poor'. *Slate*, 23 June 2014. Available at http://www.slate.com/articles/news_and_politics/politics/2014/06/joe_biden_says_he_doesn_t_own_stocks_or_bonds_why_politicians_pretend_to.html

Flanigan, J. (2013), 'Charisma and moral reasoning', *Religions*, 4 (2): 216–29. doi:10.3390/rel4020216.

Gardner, W. L., Cogliser, C., Davis, K. M. and Dickens, M. P. (2011), 'Authentic leadership: A review of the literature and research agenda'. *The Leadership Quarterly*, 22 (6): 1120–45. doi:10.1016/j.leaqua.2011.09.007.

Greenleaf, R. K. (1977), *Servant Leadership*, vol. 7. New York: Paulist Press. Available at http://www.trainingabc.com/product_files/P/ServantLeadershipLG.pdf

Harman, E. (2014), 'Morally permissible moral mistakes'. *Working Paper*. Available at
   http://www.princeton.edu/~eharman/ (February).

Hartog, D. N. and Belschak, F. D. (2012), 'Work engagement and Machiavellianism
   in the ethical leadership process'. *Journal of Business Ethics*, 107 (1): 35–47.
   doi:10.1007/s10551-012-1296-4.

Kiley, D. (2007), 'The new heat on Ford'. *BusinessWeek: Magazine*, 3 June
   2007. Available at http://www.businessweek.com/stories/2007-06-03/
   the-new-heat-on-ford

King Jr, M. L. (1987), *Stride Toward Freedom: The Montgomery Story*. HarperCollins
   Childrens Books. New York, New York: USA

Korsgaard, C. M. (1986), 'The right to lie: Kant on dealing with evil'. *Philosophy &
   Public Affairs*, 15 (4): 325–49.

Landy, F. J. and Conte J. M. (2010), *Work in the 21st Century: An Introduction to
   Industrial and Organizational Psychology*. John Wiley & Sons. Hoboken New Jersey:
   USA.

Langton, R. (1992), 'Duty and Desolation'. *Philosophy*, 67 (262): 481–505.

Ludwig, D. C. and Longenecker C. O. (1993), 'The Bathsheba Syndrome: The ethical
   failure of successful leaders'. *Journal of Business Ethics*, 12 (4): 265–73.

Nagel, T. (1998), 'Concealment and exposure'. *Philosophy & Public Affairs*, 27 (1): 3–30.
   doi:10.1111/j.1088-4963.1998.tb00057.x.

Pallikkathayil, J. (2011), 'The possibility of choice: three accounts of the problem with
   coercion'. Available at http://philpapers.org/rec/PALTPO-7.

Popkin, S. L. (1994), *The Reasoning Voter: Communication and Persuasion in
   Presidential Campaigns* (1st edn). Chicago: University of Chicago Press.

Price, T. (2000), 'Explaining ethical failures of leadership'. *Leadership & Organization
   Development Journal*, 21 (4): 177–84. doi:10.1108/01437730010335418.

—(2003), 'The ethics of authentic transformational leadership'. *The Leadership
   Quarterly*, 14 (1): 67–81. doi:10.1016/S1048-9843(02)00187-X.

—(2014), 'Judgmental privacy and the special obligations of leadership'. *Leadership and
   the Humanities*, 2 (2): 120–8.

Reed, J. (2012), 'How Alan Mulally rescued Ford'. *Los Angeles Times*, 15
   April 2012. Available at http://articles.latimes.com/2012/apr/15/business/
   la-fi-books-20120415

Velleman, J. D. (2001), 'The genesis of shame'. *Philosophy & Public Affairs*, 30 (1):
   27–52. doi:10.1111/j.1088-4963.2001.00027.x.

Vijayenthiran, V. (2006), 'New Ford CEO admits to driving a Lexus LS430'. *Motor
   Authority*, 11 September 2006. Available at http://www.motorauthority.com/
   news/1029165_new-ford-ceo-admits-to-driving-a-lexus-ls430.

Wallace, R. J. (2010), 'Hypocrisy, moral address, and the equal standing of
   persons'. *Philosophy & Public Affairs*, 38 (4): 307–41. doi:10.1111/
   j.1088-4963.2010.01195.x

Walumbwa, F. O., Avolio, B. J., Gardner, W. L., Wernsing, T. S. and Peterson,

S. J. (2008), 'Authentic leadership: Development and validation of
a theory-based measure'. *Journal of Management*, 34 (1): 89–126.
doi:10.1177/0149206307308913

X, M. and Haley, A. (1987), *The Autobiography of Malcolm X: As Told to Alex Haley.*
Reissue edn. Ballantine Books. New York, New York: USA.

7

Leadership and Gender: Women's Mandate to Lead

Fiona Jenkins
ANU

Gender and the mandate for leadership

Gender equality has not so far meant equal power for women but something more like the equal right to participate, and in supporting rather than in leading roles. Although the most obvious and explicit formal barriers to participation have generally been removed in liberal democracies, and the last bastions of exclusion in the church or military appear to their critics to identify such institutions as simply anachronistic, it remains the case that the proportion of women occupying elite leadership positions is today still absurdly low. Women have formal political equality, but few govern; and although they have entered the workforce in large numbers, it is still on terms of inferiority – lower paid, lower ranking, less secure in their employment.[1] The so-called 'glass ceiling' – or what others term the 'sticky floor' – reflects what many find to be a surprisingly recalcitrant problem of stalled career advancement and of deep residual obstacles for women entering conventional leadership roles. If we equate leadership with power exercised at the national and world level, in state and economic organizations, these clearly overwhelmingly remain the preserve of men.

Indeed, the equation of leadership with power is presumed in most of the discussions of women's continuing exclusion from high-ranking positions such as that of company director or in the membership of boards, roles in government cabinets or in the top tiers of the public service. There are many reasons to care about the so far limited success of feminism in enabling women to access positions of power. Some would turn on the evidence this gives of the remaining lack of equal opportunities available to individual women; while others would give consideration to how more equal distributions of power and influence in communities and workplaces both represent the means of realizing gender equality and reflect the aims of this project of social transformation. Yet aligning leadership rather with ethics, as the discussion of this volume proposes, might allow a somewhat different light to shine on these familiar problems, or at least to suggest a different emphasis in taking them up. If leadership stands not only for access to or the exercise of power, but also for an acceptance of the proper authority of the leader based in ethical considerations, then it is worth thinking about how gender operates in the field of perceptions of ethical aptness for leadership, and affects how trust is lodged in a leader such that authority is transferred to him or to her. It is this broad set of considerations I intend to capture by speaking of a 'mandate' to lead – a term I shall discuss in further detail in due course.

Gender stereotypes have a tenacious grip when it comes to determining the meaning, character and entitlements of leadership and this poses questions about how a theoretical approach to the ethics of leadership might critically engage with gender roles and assumptions – as two of the leading theorists of gender and leadership write, illustrating some of the issues here:

> Men, unlike women, do not bear the burden of having to be especially likeable to be influential, or to be accepted as leaders, nor do they have to establish themselves as clearly superior in ability. People presume that men are agentically competent, even for behavior that might be seen as not so competent if it were exhibited by a woman. Dominance is accepted in men – allowing them with little, if any, penalty – to be relatively non-communal and self-serving in their interactions with others. Because men generally receive the benefit of the doubt, they are relatively less affected by how much they establish themselves as communal or competent. They enjoy considerable leeway in how they lead and influence others. Thus their path to leadership is relatively clear and direct.
>
> Women are not so fortunate. For them the path to leadership wends through a labyrinth. (Eagly and Carli 2007: 117)

These authors, who substitute the figure of the 'labyrinth' for the 'glass ceiling' in explaining the paucity of women in elite leadership roles, in order to emphasize the multiple blockages women face, also note that in certain 'culturally feminine' spheres broadly associated with care – such as social services and education – women's path to and occupation of positions of leadership is less tortuous and meets less resistance (2007: 118). Congruence between presumptive feminine concerns with caring for others and a public role can facilitate women's path to leadership along a somewhat smoother track.

One direct way in which ethical leadership has been aligned with questions of gender difference is through taking account of the diverse value that typically masculine and feminine virtues are thought to bring to leadership. As in the example of care work, stereotypically feminine qualities are in certain contexts able to function as a mandate for leadership in specific roles. Sexual difference arguments might in this way support women's progress into leadership, but I argue in what follows that perceived 'feminine' virtues supply a mandate for leadership that remains unduly restrictive for women. My attention then shifts to considering what follows from the fact that leadership *is* mandated, and on terms that typically express an ethical relationship between leaders and their constituencies. Yet despite the relationship of accountability and trust implied by a mandate, the terms of approval for leadership are often quite subtly bound up with discriminatory practices, including what I shall argue is an important discrepancy between the generally accepted terms on which women's equality is recognized and the terms on which a mandate for leadership is conferred. My prime example of this, following the discussion of virtue, will be how we think about 'merit', a notion that foregrounds qualification for a position in ways we might think of as both gender-neutral and as offering a sound ethical basis for mandating individuals to positions of authority, accountability and trust. Yet the invocation of merit, I argue, tends to be far from gender neutral; and although merit functions as a criterion to support women's rights of *participation* it may well be inhibiting their assumption of *leadership* roles.

Indeed, both 'merit' and 'virtue' function to ethically mandate women's leadership in equivocal ways, as I shall try to show. My aim here will be to critically open up a space in which those limitations can be acknowledged, as well as the possibility canvassed that the more ethically stringent limits so imposed on women in leadership might in some cases be good limits. One assumes in such cases it would be desirable to see these kinds of ethical mandate extended as norms to men (so that they too must be 'likeable, communal and altruistic', as well as held accountable to others in an ongoing way, in order to gain a mandate to lead). Conversely, however, an important question to consider is what the right balance might be to strike between imposing restrictive mandates on leaders, as opposed to allowing them more free rein and relatively independent decision-making powers. The person who is regularly required to account for themselves, for instance, may be less capable of leading others in unanticipated or novel directions – and sometimes those may be good directions to explore or pursue. Thus this critique also suggests the importance of considering broader conceptions of leadership – embracing dimensions such as the capacity to represent or include others, transformational capabilities, vision and the renegotiation of shared values – in ways that take us beyond the presently strong influence of gender binaries in our thinking and our practices of leadership, where one sex tends to be trusted and the other called into question. Not only do we need to shift gendered assumptions about what leaders normally look like, and what they normally do, we also need to develop an understanding of ethical leadership that foregrounds the role of mandate, thus embedding leadership in a set of social relations. These are too often ignored within the presumptive norm of 'masculine' leadership described by Eagly and Carli above.

Feminine virtue and leadership

The very notion of 'leadership' readily connotes the most iconic masculine qualities of strength and authority, technical competence and emotional control; and since women's access to leadership roles across a wide range of sectors is today still so very limited, the few women who become leaders in these spheres of power do so in contexts where role expectations have been derived from a masculine norm.

However, as this section explores, ideas about feminine 'virtues' can situate women as potentially superior leaders where representative or co-operative leadership is stressed. By the same token, the stereotypical associations of feminine virtues can mark their leadership as implicitly weak.

The disparities between ideas of femininity and ideas of leadership have long been argued to create double-binds for women, who are judged to fail against masculine norms when they show 'feminine' traits, such as caring for others, but are equally harshly judged for betraying their femininity if 'masculine' toughness and cool or calculated decision making is displayed.[2] When placed in leadership roles a woman can often act as a 'social man'.[3] Yet in most conventional contexts dominated by masculine norms she will be required, in one way or another, to negotiate the dissonance between perceptions of her leadership and perceptions of her femininity. This might, indeed, play out as a particularly pronounced display of 'toughness' – for given gender stereotyping, a woman will often be simply assumed to not be tough enough, even where no such charge would be levelled at a man taking equivalent decisions; and such a woman must trade this perception against the likelihood she will therefore be seen as '*un*womanly'.[4]

There are, however, certain contexts in which women seem to be mandated to act as leaders not because they are 'honorary men', but rather because they are held to exercise an especially virtuous or 'good' power, exhibiting greater social responsibility or concern for the well-being of others. This mandate can intersect in important ways with at least part of a commonly assumed ethical mandate for progressing gender equality as such, linked to the idea that women's influence on social life is typically beneficent. Alongside the basic human rights arguments that underpin women's entitlement to full social and political participation, and thus their implied equal right to access leadership roles, we regularly find arguments that make the case for women's empowerment on the basis of the special feminine values that women bring to the table, and most paradigmatically as carers and as helpers to others, or as willing collaborators with co-operative, non-competitive styles.

Sexual difference is invoked here in ways that simultaneously advantage and disadvantage women. The advantages could have to do with how this mandate puts a value on qualities women have developed in contexts of gender roles that have hitherto been undervalued, despite their clear ethical importance. But because such ethical concerns for and with others seem less than necessary to invoke when men's leadership is in question, this also risks making women subject to a much more stringent and context-limited mandate than that applied to men.[5] Moreover, they reflect specific assumptions about gender identity that ignore the contexts of unequal power and differential role expectations that work to shape men's and women's moral attitudes, characteristics and behaviour.[6]

If appeals to feminine virtues legitimize female leadership in a context characterized by the persistence of gendered demarcations of appropriate roles for women – notably nursing, teaching, social work and other caring professions – they risk entrenching the social understanding of these roles as informed by gender stereotypical associations of women with other-directed attributes of compassion, intuition, flexibility, selflessness and empathy. The sphere of care has historically been that of unpaid labour; and arguably it remains a place of massive economic and social exploitation of women's unrecognized contributions. When women's leadership gains the narrow social legitimacy that it does have on what we might think of as broadly ethical grounds, but ones that nonetheless can have a problematic reliance on gendered role differences, some suspicion about how that plays out seems apt. How will forms of women's leadership, qualified by an ideal of displaying feminine 'care', gain recognition in spheres of power that more broadly retain adherence to a highly traditional set of gender relations? If the virtues that are taken to mark women's femininity and difference from men are also taken to demonstrate where women may be socially useful or contribute appropriately for their gender, then this works to simply reconfirm a gender binary – and probably also the relatively lowly status of such work. Yet in assuming the mandate for change that is linked to gender equality we should surely avoid tying the virtues requisite for its realization too closely to qualities that we can imagine might themselves be transformed as the traditional gender hierarchy shifts.

This set of problems might be illustrated by the current global focus on women's empowerment in a wide range of local leadership contexts. Here the project of gender equality centrally involves an account of women's superior ethicality, in particular ascribing a beneficent role for women in development that owes its health and education focus in their roles as mothers.[7] There is much that is of great merit in pursuing a range of measures to improve women's access to education and capacity for economic and political participation. Nonetheless, there is some irony in the extent to which the *rationale* for this emphasis on gender equality in the articulation of development goals reflects gender-stereotypical expectations: for instance, that as women emerge from social subordination, they will continue to prioritize family commitments and concerns for the common good over the private self-interest that seems to be taken to characterize men in these schemas.[8] This line of thinking, attractive as it is in many respects, could also be said to rhetorically align an idea of economic development as beneficial for purportedly 'backward' nations, with the beneficent role of empowered women. Certainly it seems to function as a persuasive supplement to the basic human rights case for gender equality, and perhaps with mixed results, since here a mandate for profound social change seems tethered to maintaining what are in certain key respects fairly stable gender roles, despite the potentially radical and even unforeseeable outcomes of women's economic and political empowerment.

Moreover, we might reasonably ask how gender differences play out in the implementation of such plans. Ironically, the international agencies facilitating women's leadership and empowerment in the developing world all too often retain all the signs of a gendered hierarchy in their own organizations. Although many women lead NGOs, as the budget of the organization grows, the numbers of influential women thin out.[9] Being caring or showing social responsibility is rarely enough, apparently, to qualify a woman in the eyes of others for the responsibilities – fiscal and strategic – of running a large organization. As scale grows, the masculine norm of 'tough' leadership reasserts itself – or perhaps simply the assumption that it is natural for men to be taking certain types of decisions, and unnatural for women, who risk being perceived as aggressive or threatening when they do so.

Here it is clearly a problem that 'masculine' and 'feminine' qualities are typically thought of as exclusionary of each other, posing a seeming either/or dilemma for virtues of care and concern or of toughness and sound reasoning. The mandate provided by certain gendered qualities, moreover, is presumptively present or lacking – for instance, as noted above, 'toughness' as a quality that a feminine woman will be held to lack becomes a quality she has to prove; while it is not necessarily a quality men will have to *prove* they possess, since it is instead taken as a natural part of 'masculinity'. There is no easy alignment of these features with ethical considerations either. 'Toughness' in taking decisions can be part of ethical virtue, emerging in a range of moral contexts: for example, doing what is necessary, even though it may be unpleasant for some people; or taking the broad public view rather than concerning oneself with private individuals. Taking a utilitarian, or a rule-governed approach to impartial judgement may form part of this image of 'toughness' and as such it may be pursued by men and women alike. Yet the *interpretation* of the meaning of a 'tough' decision may also reflect a gendered segregation between acting in the (masculine) public sphere, or conversely having concerns proper to the (feminine) private sphere of the family and particular others. Just such 'tough-mindedness' as readily seems vitally important for public life can be viewed with horror when applied in the private sphere. Women's ethical association with the responsibilities of the private sphere, on the basis of traditional gender roles, thus might again function as a powerful restriction on the forms of leadership they are able – or considered mandated – to exercise, given these gendered constructions of ethical appropriateness in public and private life.

Men no doubt also have to negotiate with masculine norms in cultivating an acceptable leadership style, and the way in which individuals do this may vary widely. For both men and women, an implicit reference to gender stabilizes the meaning and propriety of leadership roles, and these ways of understanding the 'mandate to lead' may lag well behind wider processes of social change. For instance, a 'collaborative' style of leadership may reflect the need for women to seek a mandate from others repeatedly, rather than being able to assume they have the power to decide; yet it is interpreted as a specific 'feminine' difference, thereby essentializing a behaviour that rightly demands much more careful contextual interpretation, one taking account of how power is being negotiated and is shifting as women take up their still limited leadership mandate.

This is not to say that a collaborative or a caring style is a bad thing, only that we need to give critical consideration of the social circumstances in which such styles arise, as well as the actions and values they may enable or thwart, recognizing that in certain contexts these could be aspects of *perceptions* and *practices* that continue to disable women in leadership roles and reflects the limited access they have to decision-making power. As women enter spaces of leadership where their mandate is qualified and often fragile, it is vital to resist the power of gender essentialism to offer ready accounts of inherent differences that may seem to acknowledge differences but risk serving to disable women further from having a mandate to lead that embraces social change at its core. Indeed, the 'stabilizing' function of upholding regulatory gender norms can be intensified in times of social change, as Judith Butler has argued.[10]

Today there are a growing number of voices questioning gender-stereotypical assumptions, and demanding that women's present lack of access to leadership positions be remedied. The sense of anachronism conveyed by figures like that of the mere 3.5 per cent of women who are CEOs in an 'advanced' nation like Australia is palpable.[11] There is also a growing recognition of the value of bringing different perspectives to problems, as well as concerns about what 'testosterone-fuelled' decision making can be like, for example in the context of high-risk behaviour among leaders in the banking sector in the period prior to the global financial collapse of 2007–8. Yet these are themselves not unproblematic arguments in the terms I have outlined above, and in certain iterations are illustrative of the problem that the popular image of women's leadership when not thoroughly 'feminized' as a kind of 'good' maternal power is too often conceived as a subtractive notion – that is to say, as leadership minus certain problematic *aspects* of a dominant masculinity. In both these cases, I suggest, the concept of leadership itself remains profoundly beholden to a masculine norm, which women's participation is imagined to either complement or moderate. If women are today widely deemed to be an advantage to company boards because they bring diversity (in relation to the norm), a moderating influence (upon the norm) or a greater sense of social responsibility (improving the ethical orientation of the norm), it remains to be seen how far these 'feminine' virtues can come to be recognized as reflecting complex social relationships, and thus start to be translated back into a reconceptualization of leadership itself, as that is questioned and thrown open by losing some of the gendered underpinnings that make it appear as a given quantity. As Ronit Kark (2004; see Note 5) points out, the current conception of transformational leadership, with its emphasis on follower empowerment, is both in line with contemporary organizational changes and management theorizing – stressing the need for organizations to become less hierarchical, more flexible, team-oriented, participative, etc. – and is also all too readily associated with stereotypes of women. Here we need to tread a careful path between valuing the emergence of new forms of leadership and relying on gendered ideas of the virtues appropriate to them.

The problems posed by invoking feminine virtues as an aspect of women's mandate to lead are easily concealed by a tacit acceptance of gender essentialist beliefs about the 'nature' of men and of women, and perhaps just as importantly about the complementary paternal and maternal functions proper to them. Such beliefs strongly shape moral judgements and expectations of individuals along gender lines – thus, in a neat slogan, women 'take care' while men 'take charge'. They also shape vital questions about how the moral or political entitlement to exercise leadership takes on a form that facilitates the access some have to it, while depriving others.

In gender-specific mandates for leadership, it is almost as though women's legitimacy as leaders is predicated upon a curious non-power, contrasting with a masculine assumption of power and the right to be a decisive 'head' that accompanies it. Yet ethical leaders should today be setting agendas that reflect women's and men's changing social circumstances and gender relations, rather than reinvesting in tired notions of masculinity and femininity. By explicitly considering the idea that leadership is 'mandated', a transformational notion of ethical leadership might be articulated that would be less vulnerable to these difficulties.

Mandate and constituency

When we speak of a 'mandate' it is often in the context of an ongoing relationship that someone in power has with a constituency. A mandate expresses approval of that person taking charge of some agreed project. To speak of a 'mandate for change' is a common usage, and while such mandate would leave significant latitude in terms of the means for bringing about the change, some common agreement about the ends to be achieved would be presumed. Mandates, however, can be more or less specific, and more or less determined by an ongoing process of consultation with the preferences or wishes of those who form the constituency. A prime minister may be assumed to have a mandate to take a nation into war, without having a referendum on the question, but not to introduce some other controversial agenda that has not been approved by a majority through a democratic process. Thus a mandate may be more or less focused on placing trust in a leader, in ways that entail transferring authority to him or her; or more or less focused on the leader's role in bringing about some desired result, though elements of both these will always be present. Moreover, mandates may differ with respect to the need to renew them regularly, through consultation or engagement with a community that may offer or withdraw its support.

Adapting the language of 'mandate' emphasizes the range of relationships that are at stake in all leadership, as well as the forms of accountability and of degrees of trust, or of authority implied by them. Leadership, I assume here, always has ethical, social and political dimensions, arising from the necessity to leadership of a high degree of acceptance of a person's capacity and entitlement to lead, that is, the presupposition of at least some kind of mandate. The 'mandate to lead' is the tacit or explicit rationale for the willingness to accept a leader as such, indicating the sense of the appropriateness or rectitude of the leader's authority. This might include considerations of qualification for the task, the capacity for representation of others, shared values, virtues of the leader or the belief that the leader has a direction or a vision worth following. An important aspect of this mandate, however, is that it contains what one might think of as a natural limit constituted by an important tension between the leader's autonomy and their responsiveness to a constituency. Insofar as authority is transferred to the leader, the transition to leadership in certain respects moves an individual from being one who 'qualifies' for the role in the eyes of others, to being one who sets the agenda, bringing about change in ways that cannot be fully anticipated and which impact the constituency itself. Both the mandate and the 'excess' over what can be mandated are important for leadership, and both may be important for realizing social transformation. By 'excess' I mean that there is more to transformational leadership than can be mandated in advance. A classic consideration of a related issue in Rousseau's considerations of democracy may perhaps illustrate its importance.

In general, it seems more democratic for a leader to demonstrate trustworthiness to a constituency in an ongoing way. Yet the extra-mandated dimension of leadership may also be ethically important, particularly where the current ethical limitations of a constituency are well-recognized. Rousseau speaks of a paradox of democracy, whereby a people are both authors and subjects of the law they authorize – in order for there to be a people or constituency well-formed enough to choose good leadership, there must already be good leaders, for how else will the constituency itself be well-formed? The problem that Rousseau poses is, where would good leaders come from without an already well-formed and virtuous constituency mandating them?[12] And how will this depend in turn on the leadership that influences the constituency? Regarded in this light, two conclusions relevant to our discussion, but in tension with one another, might deserve consideration. The first is that extending the type of mandate that requires ongoing answerability to a constituency may often be important for realizing gender equality, both so that women's voices are heard as constituents by leaders, and also generally working in favour of a greater democratic and ethical accountability, and applied more equally to both men and women in leadership roles. But the second conclusion might pull in a rather different direction, to suggest that the 'excess' over every mandate in leadership – which is not only its autocratic and traditionally conservative authority, but also potentially its creativity and transformative power – might well come more strongly into focus as both an aspiration and an entitlement for women.

If women tend to be held more stringently accountable for their leadership and are thus less able to access both the kind of decision making that is not readily explicitly mandated, and are also thereby more inhibited in their attempts to influence a constituency to undergo change, then they may be excluded from accessing a dimension of ethical leadership vital for realizing gender equality – insofar as that requires *overcoming* existing constituencies which are themselves full of gender biases. Put otherwise, the transformation of existing constituencies, which at present tend overwhelmingly to mandate male leadership, is part of the change we need to see if more women are to access leadership positions. However, I am arguing that the current forms of mandate for women in leadership tend to foreclose transformational capabilities that are more readily allowed to men.

As we have seen, the gendering of leadership works in specific ways that tend to deprive women of legitimacy and authority in leadership roles, while predisposing us to see men as more appropriate leaders, entitled to 'head' (act as decision-makers in) hierarchically structured organizations. I have already argued that a woman whose *entitlement* to lead is based on ideas about what is feminine may find herself hampered in her *capacity* to lead, including being penalized for transgressing the tacit 'mandate' provided by received ideas about the ends and means proper to women.[13] Moreover, if, as I have suggested, exceeding a mandate is sometimes an essential aspect of leadership, then women whose claim to exercise leadership rests on 'qualification' alone will suffer for lacking the symbolic authority that would license doing *more* than others grant her.[14] Less obviously, perhaps, some apparent vehicles of women's advancement may backfire on them when it comes to leadership positions: for instance, as I explore in what follows, in the context of the legitimation provided by ideas of equal opportunity and by the seemingly gender-transcending focus of the notion of merit. Ideas about merit are not as free from gender bias as we might like to think; but even more fundamentally, I shall argue, merit-based entitlement tends to secure women their rights to equal participation at lower levels of a hierarchy – more so than it secures rights to leadership roles. That is in part because leadership is not secured by sheer 'qualification' in quite the way that merit tends to model, but also because notions of merit impose a special burden upon women to demonstrate they possess it – one that is not equivalently imposed upon men. Putting these issues in conjunction, the problem for gender equality in leadership roles is not simply that there are biased judgements of merit – though there certainly are these. Rather the problem is that 'qualification' as such becomes an overriding criterion of selection for women in a way that it is not for men, and further, that it is *not* for 'leadership' either – especially when we consider aspects of that leadership to go out 'beyond' explicit mandate. Merit, in other words, does not establish the element of superiority – or of the excess over qualification – that is required for a form of leadership capable of going out beyond a determinate and specific mandate.

The lack of gender equality in conventional leadership roles tells us something about broad societal biases at work in the relevant constituencies. But it should also give rise to a consideration of women's own relations with the 'mandate to lead'. In addition, it is worth considering in a gendered analysis of leadership the nature of the 'excess' over an explicit mandate, or approved project, that we might associate equally with decision making, agenda setting or trans-formational powers of leadership – powers that potentially change the very social space in which the leader became mandated as such. It is probably fairly uncontroversial to say that conventional conceptions of the mandate to lead are highly gendered in ways that help to explain some of the barriers women face in assuming leadership, and this can be tracked across ethical, social and political registers that link leadership to masculine traits and images, and tend to confer extra authority on men. More specifically, however, and I suspect more controversially, I am proposing we should try to identify how some of the more common ways in which certain virtues or qualities that secure for women a mandate to take on public roles or to lead in certain fields might have equivocal effects in progressing gender equality. Indeed, one of the multiple double binds women find themselves in when leadership is in question flows from the difference between being symbolically entitled or mandated to participate or contribute to defined roles and being symbolically entitled to lead, in this stronger sense of extra-mandated authority.

On my hypothesis, women continue to be substantially barred from leadership roles not only because the attributes associated with leadership remain highly masculinized, but more subtly because the restrictive terms on which women receive recognition for their useful or important social contributions under conventional rubrics for advancing gender equality, do not fit them well for receiving a higher level of personal mandate – that of authoritative leadership – which involves not only qualification, but a certain excess over that qualification (or 'merit') for fulfilling pre-determined roles. What happens for men and for women, at that internal limit where a relatively limited mandate to carry out an agreed agenda becomes a relatively unlimited authority to act, and where are the constituencies located that lend such authority? I have briefly discussed a restricted mandate that turns on ideas of women's particular virtues. I now want to consider how ideas that have been important for securing women's rights in terms of workforce participation – notably meritocratic ideals – might limit the mandate necessary for women to readily access roles as leaders.

Gendering merit as a qualification

Consider an indicative illustration of how women themselves experience some of the phenomena I have been describing thus far. Research conducted by Ruth Sealy with a number of women who had been, in an objective sense, highly successful in the male-dominated field of investment banking showed how these women nonetheless often felt insecure and discontented, even considering leaving the profession in which their careers had been made. Sealy's study found that these women's adherence to the notion of meritocracy had diminished over time, as merit appeared to be less defined by human capital (ability and experience) and more by social capital (seen as political behaviour).[15] They experienced this with considerable disillusionment. Particularly at the most senior levels of the organization, political factors perceived as contrary to the meritocratic ideal became pronounced, as ability and experience became less valuable than contacts, influence and other aspects of politically cultivated social capital. Sealy reports that the women 'spoke of their belief that their competence should speak for itself, and that they wanted to be judged on the merit of their work not their political skills' (Sealy 2010: 189). In part this desire reflected not only the sense of conditions of fairness being in place, but a need for self-assurance about their own worth and value. Whereas for men in the organization a mandate to lead took an overtly political form, requiring the cultivation of a constituency impressed by their clever manoeuvres, women sought a more ethical and apolitical grounding in ideas of merit.

Although in many respects clearly reasonable, was this perhaps an unrealistic desire on the women's part that leadership roles should be 'apolitical'? What assumptions does it reflect about how those rising to leadership should be related to the constituency supporting them – by seeking approval granted by that constituency, or by actively shaping it into a supportive group? How far did the women's discomfort with that political situation itself reflect the very minimal conditions of entitlement for women's participation in this field: conditions that are constituted in terms of merit for women, but perhaps less so for men, who more readily access an actively political sphere of seizing leadership roles?

The women's strong desire to place confidence in meritocratic processes was undercut in other ways too. Where women had been promoted to very high levels in their organization, they nonetheless felt unconfident about their means of access to it and consequently, perhaps again, their *entitlement* to assume leadership roles:

> Even at their very senior level, with an impressive list of achievements behind them, they worried about being "a token promotion" – meaning that they were only being promoted for their sex, as some kind of company policy, rather than for their genuine ability and being truly deserving of the grade. A number referred to quotas or some sort of affirmative action, initially rejecting the policy as a violation of merit … Despite so much evidence of others being promoted outside of meritocratic ideals, for most of these women there was still a clear need to prove their worthiness. However, about a quarter of the women in discussing the notion of quotas further appeared to reduce their opposition, not because they liked the idea but out of a desire to reduce the discrimination occurring in what was obviously an unmeritocratic system. (Sealy 2010: 186)

Further, Sealy found that more than half of the women had 'struggled throughout their career with finding the right balance of "toughness" and "softness"'. As one woman commented:

> Working in a male environment … I've had to toughen myself up … You can't be soft … but if you come across too sort of forceful on things, they say 'Oh she's being very aggressive', whereas a man would be passionate. (ibid.: 190)

Many of the women had the sense that their own 'natural' way of working was not valued; and if early in their career they conformed to a norm that modelled a form of gender equality in terms of competitive performance indicators, in later stages they wrestled with the politics that determined seniority on bases that seemed clearly to differ from merit alone. The constituency that promoted them to positions of leadership was not one they wholly trusted or indeed felt was much under their influence.

While the example has its own particularities – and the experience of women in male-dominated industries differs from those where the reverse is true – it illustrates a central set of issues as they play out in what I take to be a highly typical subjective experience. The question of how leadership roles find a social mandate offers a valuable point of reflection here. Thus as is well attested in the literature, women need to 'qualify' and keep qualifying in ways that are objectively and subjectively more demanding than equivalently placed men, precisely because their merit is all that 'entitles' them to position.[16] Yet they face the further problem that 'merit' is insufficient to either cultivate or demonstrate the socially mandated entitlement to lead. They may *participate* in the body of an organization on the basis of their merit, but if acting as the 'head' or leader is still only rarely mandated for women, we need to inquire what this has to do with how roles and practices of decision-making power are themselves socially mandated on terms that *exceed* those of demonstrating straightforward 'merit' for the job. Moreover, the women's anxiety that they were 'token' appointments reflects a concern that might well arise from the social perception that women's entitlement to play a role in public life still needs such a rationale as that of 'representing gender equality' to support it, one that is entirely invisible or irrelevant for men who have traditionally always held such positions.

The rules comprising meritocratic frameworks of 'qualification' enter into a complex relation with gender, perhaps with the consequence that institutional structures that we are inclined to think of as being conducive to equality or equal treatment are not simply imperfectly realized under present-day conditions, but also contain profound tensions, making them liable to backfire on those they appear to benefit.

Merit is invoked as a vital consideration in uneven ways. As legal scholar Margaret Thornton has wryly commented, the headline 'Woman of Merit Elected to the Bench' would look ridiculous in the reverse gender.[17] To say 'Man of Merit Elected …' would draw attention to something odd going on about the appointment itself through the very redundancy of the attribution of merit. Indeed, one would likely wonder what was being communicated by the statement exactly – as if all the others who were not appointed somehow *lack* merit, an odd consideration in a generally well-qualified field. Something revealing about the role of high-level constituencies, those charged with electing fellow leaders, may also be detected here. Do those authorities appointing men to the bench claim fairness and objectivity to be the vital element in their choice, as they do when a woman is so elected? Or is it rather the subtly different idea at work, that this is the person whom the good, just and powerful have chosen because he is someone 'distinguished' (like themselves) and thus eligible for a weighty decision-making role? In the latter case the constituency proposes a relation of trust and affinity with the leader they elect, comprising a mutual authority and influence that seems blocked in the former case. Moreover, the example suggests that in a woman's case, her merit is displayed as the criterion of choice in order to offset the question that might otherwise hang over her appointment – and typically, that question *is* as to whether it was merely 'token'. A woman's mandate for an authoritative senior role is thus constructed as one of merit or the absence of merit; and this is an ethical consideration for mandating her authority that seems curiously bypassed in the very many cases where merit finds no particular mention. Non-qualification thus haunts the affirmation of a woman's 'merit', as the ever-present alternative; and paradoxically the *reassurance* that 'merit' is indeed the key for a woman in fact shadows the appointment with a *doubt* that is lacking in the case of a man. A man's mandate is constructed from a much more richly drawn up picture of qualities, and in no way shadowed by the alternative that he *may* be simply appointed to represent 'men in general'.

One of the paradoxes of meritocracy is that those whom the system has rewarded with power and influence become the judges and arbiters of what should be allocated to the next generation – these are leaders who are also 'gate-keepers'. We may imagine that social followers regulate these leaders' power of judgement, and negate its tendency toward simply favouring others 'like themselves', by reference to impartial standards such as those of merit-based systems; and no doubt in part they do. But another possibility is that the appearance of following neutral procedures for measuring talent hides something that is always open-ended in the moment of decision making. It hides, indeed, the moment of judgement when we decide in effect to what kind of people we want to lend power like ours, or whom we will allow to wield authority over others in our institutions. Such moments are not only unavoidable; they are also full of potential for transformation, and deserve to be brought into focus, and especially perhaps when we try to elect leaders who will be socially progressive. Yet they are moments that meritocratic ideology makes it hard for us to own up to, because they open on to questions of *vision* that exceed rule-governed or calculative processes.

Perhaps it is this aspiration to vision that women need to be guided by in pursuing leadership, and that may involve leaving behind some of the attachment to a notion of 'qualification' that derives from a limited social mandate provided by an idea of merit, albeit that this aims to track the possession of qualities that are indeed important. Committing to the redistributive transitions that are needed and engaging with the social changes that women's participation in the workforce have brought does not mean throwing out all competition-based indicators of promise and performance, but it does mean recalibrating them in light of revisiting some substantive judgements and decisions about the ends we are pursuing, both in terms of genuine excellence and in terms of genuine equality. This is ethical work, and requires leadership of the first order.

Yet what faith in meritocracy too often expresses is the desire that there should be an 'objective' way of determining a person's capacity and value, and that this information should be fed into the institutional systems we rely upon to deliver competitive and effective, as well as fair, institutions. It is a desire likely to be passionately felt by those who have found themselves dependent upon such measurements in order to be allowed in at the door at all – hence many women's profound hostility to the idea connoted by affirmative action or by quotas, on the grounds that these would undercut all their hard-earned personal merit. The diverse investments of a range of parties are thus at stake in the idea of correcting merit-based judgements case by case, and making them operative at all levels of social hierarchy. Consequently, and despite all the flaws evident in our systems, we tend to maintain confidence even against the evidence. The *promise* of achieving the *right* results about social hierarchy through determining merit too often protects the system from critical scrutiny on the results it has *actually* delivered over many years. Meritocratic systems, moreover, protect themselves from critical scrutiny being directed at their own workings by placing blame on those who 'fail' – thus women are charged with being bad at competition, self-promotion or entrepreneurship, with not wanting to succeed or prioritizing a private life over their careers, judgements that again draw upon and consolidate gender stereotypes.

Yet it is notable that globally women's access to leadership positions, at least in the sphere of political life, has been most successfully realized by establishing quotas, which introduce into the schema of leadership the quasi-mechanical mandate of aspiration to representative numbers, and de-mystify the notion of leadership based upon special individual qualities.[18] Quotas for women in board-rooms or in public office reflect a certain impatience as well as a commitment to bring about change by whatever means necessary. Not only do they bypass routes to leadership roles that depend upon judgements susceptible to the types of bias outlined so far, but they also invoke a democratic conception, by including the capacity to represent others like oneself as being critical to what would entitle a person to leadership, but crucially indexing this to a project of social change. The disadvantages of taking this approach in the context of other selective systems are evident to all, insofar as the method will appear insufficiently individualized or discriminating. Yet in being driven by deep concern about the slow pace of progress toward gender equality, the turn to gender-based quotas has the advantage of clearly recognizing and acting to deal with the weight of the social and structural conditions that prevent women from advancing under normal ('malestream') mechanisms of competition and appointment. Moreover, accepting the legitimacy of a process for attaining power that authorizes female participation on the basis of a 'group-representation mandate' foregrounds the role of leaders precisely as those who are able to speak on behalf of a group.

More often, however, women's formal equality as citizens has been translated in institutional contexts into highly regulated modes of making appointments and offering promotions on 'merit'. It is from this perspective that quota systems are most harshly criticized, being viewed as 'undercutting' women's proper claims to merit-based equality. However, we might turn the criticism around to ask why merit-based systems, despite being well-established culturally, through policy and regulation, have failed to deliver gender equality in senior leadership roles. Although designed to generate equal opportunities, I have canvassed the idea that these policy and procedure based modes of selection and promotion are a source of ambivalent results for many women, shaping and constraining the forms of authority they are mandated to exercise, and effectively limiting the pursuit of the kinds of transformational leadership by which gender equality might begin to be realized, as a serious reshaping of the constituencies supporting leaders. Meritocracy risks both political and ethical under-determination insofar as it affirms simply that we should choose the 'best' for the job.[19]

Socially, we can aspire for good reason to have forms of leadership that are highly dependent upon a regularly renewed mandate of approval – as is generally the case for political leadership in liberal democracies. But I have argued that we also want leaders to play a role in shaping the constituencies that support them, taking them beyond what they already are and thus playing a transformational role. The idea of the leader as representative of a group, and speaking on their behalf, is an important one here, but needs to allow for the ways in which the nature of the group is itself a contested one, requiring regular critical review to examine whom and what it includes and excludes, who it supports or thwarts. The further lesson to draw from this might be that we should think about where mandates need to be more limited and accountable, but also where more authority should rightly be transferred and invested in a person by a mandate. I have argued that, in approaching this question, a critical analysis of gender will be important. The present consensus seems to be that we should make institutions more truly meritocratic, removing some of the politics that works against women. A countervailing view might be that we should be more explicit, reflective and responsible about the kinds of choices that are made in allocating or mandating the power of leaders, thus developing more complex ethical understandings of how entitlement is secured than can be conveyed in the notion of 'merit' as such.

Notes

1   An authoritative and regularly updated source of data is the World Bank's Gender Statistics: http://data.worldbank.org/data-catalog/gender-statistics
2   Eagly and Karau 2002: 573–98. See also Ritter and Yoder 2004: 187–93.
3   Acker 1990: 139.
4   'While research suggests that women tend to receive positive evaluations when their leadership roles are defined in feminine terms, on traditional, masculine measures of leadership women's leadership effectiveness is often perceived to be lower than that of men' (ibid.: 82). See also Ryan and Haslam 2005: 81–90.
5   Kark 2004: 160–76. See also Due Billing and Alvesson 2012: 144–57.
6   See examples in Kark 2004.
7   Consider the NGO CARE's statement: 'girls and women aren't just the faces of the poverty; they're also the key to overcoming it. CARE's nearly seven decades of experience makes clear that when you empower a girl or a woman, she becomes a catalyst for positive change whose success benefits everyone around her' – and see their promotional video 'The Girl Effect', which shows the educated girl helping her family and community, empowering other girls to do the same and thereby changing the whole world: see http://www.care.org/work/womens-empowerment/women
8   International Needs Australia, to give an example, is one of many NGOs proposing the role of gender equality in eradicating poverty by pointing out that: 'When you invest in a woman, she invests 90% back into the health, nutrition and education of her family. Contrast with men who invest only 30–40% back into their families': see https://internationalneeds.org.au/Women.aspx
9   Ama Marston reports that women head just 12 per cent of the largest NGOs in

the US and 27 per cent in the UK, and of the UK's top influential development
NGOs, which are collectively known as the British Overseas Aid Group,
only *one* is currently headed by a woman. Women leaders in development
NGOs in Kenya and South Africa estimate that women hold only 15–20 per
cent of director positions. Women are concentrated in administrative and
support roles in the development sector, with rare exceptions. 'Women in
leadership: "It's not going to work the way we're doing it."' See http://www.
theguardian.com/global-development-professionals-network/2013/aug/01/
women-in-leadership-international-ngos

10   Butler 2004: 40–56.
11   See, for example, the figures and statements of the Committee for
     Economic Development in Australia, or CEDA: http://www.ceda.com.au/
     research-and-policy/other-research/women-in-leadership
12   Rousseau 1987: 164. See also Honig 2001: 20.
13   Fitzgerald explores how this plays out in the lives of senior female academic
     leaders (Fitzgerald 2013).
14   Margaret Thatcher could be said to have demonstrated a consummate
     understanding of the rigours of this dilemma. In response she successfully
     mobilized a set of feminine virtues apt for managing the economy by aligning the
     task with the responsibilties of thrifty housewifery, while simultaneously assuming
     the transgressive mandate of militaristic leader. This did not secure her against
     criticism of course, which often invoked her monstrousness as a woman. What is
     interesting, however, is that while her morality was often questioned, her capacity
     and right to leadership were very rarely in doubt. Julia Gillard, coming to power
     as prime minister in another advanced economy decades later, was regularly
     denied legitimacy (in part due to her use of sheer political tactics in achieving
     the ousting of Kevin Rudd as prime minister) and her leadership as such was
     perpetually in question in popular discourse.
15   Sealy 2010: 184–97.
16   Eagly and Carli 2007.
17   Thornton 2007: 391–413.
18   See Pande and Ford 2011.
19   See my more detailed argument in Jenkins 2013: 81–102.

Bibliography

Acker, J. (1990), 'Hierarchies, jobs, bodies: A theory of gendered organizations'. *Gender and Society*, 4 (2): 139–58.
Butler, J. (2004), 'Gender Regulations', in *Undoing Gender*. New York and Abingdon: Routledge, pp. 40–56.

Due Billing, Y. and Alvesson, M. (2012), 'Questioning the notion of feminine leadership: A critical perspective on the gender labelling of leadership'. *Gender, Work and Organization*, 7 (3): 144–57.

Eagly, A. H. and Carli, L. L. (2007), *Through the Labyrinth: The Truth about How Women Become Leaders*. Boston, MA: Havard Business School Press.

Eagly. A. H. and Karau, S. J. (2002), 'Role congruity theory of prejudice toward female leaders'. *Psychological Review*, 109: 573–98.

Fitzgerald, T. (2013), *Women Leaders in Higher Education: Shattering the Myths*. Routledge.

Honig, B. (2001), *Democracy and the Foreigner*. Princeton and Oxford: Princeton University Press, p. 20.

Jenkins, F. (2013), 'Singing the Post-discrimination Blues: Note for a Critique of Academic Meritocracy', in K. Hutchison and F. Jenkins (eds), *Women in Philosophy: What Needs to Change?* New York: Oxford University Press, pp. 81–102.

Kark, R. (2004), 'The transformational leader: Who is (s)he?: A feminist perspective'. *Journal of Organizational Change Management*, 17 (2): 160–76.

Pande, R. and Ford, D. (2011), 'Gender quotas and female leadership: A review'. Background paper for the World Development Report on Gender. Available at http://scholar.harvard.edu/files/rpande/files/gender_quotas_-_april_2011.pdf

Ritter, B. A. and Yoder, J. D. (2004), 'Gender differences in leader emergence persist even for dominant women: An updated confirmation of role congruity theory'. *Psychology of Women Quarterly*, 28: 187–93.

Rousseau, J-J. (1987), *On the Social Contract* (trans. and ed. Donald A. Cress). Indianapolis: Hackett, p. 164.

Ryan, M. K. and Haslam, S. A. (2005), 'The glass cliff: Evidence that women are over-represented in precarious leadership positions'. *British Journal of Management*, 16: 81–90.

Sealy, R. (2010), 'Changing perceptions of meritocracy in senior women's careers'. *Gender in Management: An International Journal*, 25 (3): 184–97. Available at https://dspace.lib.cranfield.ac.uk/bitstream/1826/7786/1/Changing_perceptions_of_meritocracy.pdf

Thornton, M. (2007), '"Otherness" on the bench: How merit is gendered'. *Sydney Law Review*, 29: 391–413.

Part Three

Leadership – Applications and Examples

8

Leadership and Stakeholding

Thom Brooks
Durham University

Introduction

What is the nature of *leadership*? This question has perhaps never had more importance than in recent days. While there are a great many self-professed 'leaders' working in industry, politics and other areas, there might appear to be a growing disconnection between our common expectations from leaders and the varieties of alleged leadership on display. The recent global banking crisis is one of many examples where there were plenty of leaders, but arguably too little leadership. Virtually everyone was affected, but yet there was little accountability. This has helped contribute to eroding public confidence in our institutions and in the ability of our elected governments to regulate them satisfactorily.

There is a need to clarify the concept of leadership in light of these crises, exposing three key elements: leadership as *sustainable* providing stability, leadership as *accountable* to enable transparency and leadership as *ethical* to set normative limits for what is permissible. I examine in this chapter these elements as built around an important principle of *stakeholding*. This can be stated briefly as the claim that those with a stake should have a say about outcomes affecting them. I argue below that stakeholding is central to leadership because it helps identify how it can be sustainable, accountable and ethical. Each of these three key elements is examined in turn. It has been argued before that stakeholding theory can offer a persuasive view about business ethics.

My account here is distinctive because I transform a concept found in that literature and develop it as a principle of justice, and a principle that confirms sound leadership. Stakeholding is not merely about the good management of others or a process, but an important part of leadership – and being a leader – as well. The idea of leadership needs to be reconfigured to some extent, or rather reconceptualized to better track the qualities that leadership should possess. My argument is that stakeholding is useful for bringing out these qualities – leadership as sustainable, accountable and ethical – in a powerful restatement.

Leadership as sustainable

So how does *stakeholding* inform a compelling understanding about *leadership*? The first step is to consider the roots of stakeholding in stakeholder theory. These roots are closely associated with the still growing literature on business ethics and corporate governance (Freeman et al. 2010; Kaler 2002; Plender 1997). This research originated with R. Edward Freeman's *Strategic Management: A Stakeholder Approach* published in 1984 and later popularized further by Will Hutton's defence of 'the stakeholder economy' (Freeman 1984; Hutton 1995). These early accounts of stakeholder theory argued for a new alternative to the orthodox views about business and its management.

One orthodox view is that firms exist purely for profit creation to benefit their shareholders. According to Hutton, this view of firms is that they adopt the mindset that 'they eat what they can kill', where every penny of income generated is considered to be theirs and theirs alone.[1] The firm as profit creator attempts to eat everything it can in its path and is never fully satisfied.

The orthodox view suffers from several problems. One is that it does not aim for sustainability. The firm's attempts at profitable growth are measured in the short term. Firms engorge themselves today without much thought for tomorrow. Firms do not aim primarily at self-perpetuation, but profitability. A second problem is a lack of accountability: if the firm aims to increase profits, then it is thought this helps drive us towards greater efficiencies. These often include a more 'efficient' leadership structure – or, in other words, a top-down structure where decisions are made at the top by a few and distributed to the many below. Such a structure prioritizes swift decision making over transparent, collective decision making. A final problem is the lack of ethics: there seem few normative constraints on a firm's activity beyond that which makes it possible. But can such problems be addressed without sacrificing enterprise and entrepreneurial activities?

Stakeholder theory arises as an alternative meant to provide answers to problems faced by the orthodox view. It defends a new model for firms that provides for stability, enables transparency and sets normative limits on their activities. This theory puts *stakeholders*, not profits, at its heart. Stakeholders are defined simply as those who have a stake in outcomes: each is a partner engaged in a shared project actively promoting some shared conception of the good. Instead of understanding the firm then as about generating profits (and so focusing on how profits can be maximized), stakeholder theory views the firm as the collective activity of stakeholders and so focuses on their relevant relationships to each other. The idea of the stakeholder economy sets out a new alternative for more than the management of any single firm, but a perspective on how a centre-left view of economic justice might be forged (Freeman et al. 2007; Hutton 1999; Hutton 2010).

One central idea motivating stakeholding is sustainability. Stakeholding is only opposed to profit maximization when it is pursued for its own sake – and not for its stakeholders. A wide variety of people have a stake in the success of a firm. These include those who work for it, but also their dependents and the firms that do business with it. The state also has a stake in the success of its firms as a means to secure economic growth as well as tax revenues. For stakeholder theory, shareholders are not the only ones who count. This is because shareholders do not exclusively have a stake in the success of a firm.

So stakeholding rejects the idea that the firm should aim to accumulate as much as it can for those in the firm, instead defending the view that firms should benefit stakeholders. This shift from the focus on benefitting shareholders to stakeholders is a move away from short-termism to sustainability. Why? Consider the Profit-Only Firm. Its focus – and identity – is bound up in its profit creation. If market conditions brought this to an end, then supporters of the orthodox view might exclaim, 'So what?' Where firms fail to be profitable, they die and this is how markets develop over time. Now consider the Stakeholder Firm. Its focus is on its stakeholders. Many of those with larger stakes will work directly for the firm, but not all stakeholders do. This leads to a very different outcome whereby if its future became threatened this *would* become a problem. This is not because stakeholder theory claims what exists today must or should exist in future. Instead, the failure of firms to remain sustainable is a problem where they fail to benefit stakeholders. If Profit-Only Firms die, there are other firms to turn to. When Stakeholder Firms are under threat, the problem is not only one for those in the firm, but rather all those with a stake in its continuation. Sustainability matters and has an importance for the firm as a firm organized by stakeholders.

This has clear relevance for leadership. The Profit-Only Firm view of leadership is built around a (too) narrow consequentialism where managerial decisions are legitimated and supported by their ability to contribute to profitability. If this firm were to fail at securing profits, then this structure could not be sustained nor might the firm continue to exist. This form of leadership is maximizing and future-oriented, but short term.

The Stakeholder Firm view of leadership is inclusive and long term, accounting for backward-looking and forward-looking considerations. If leadership is about stakeholding, then it must be inclusive to bring together relevant stakeholders. Decision making cannot also be solely focused on *this* firm and *its* promotion either. This is because there are stakeholders outside the firm, persons with a stake in the firm's outcomes. The stakeholder model of leadership is not a view of how one should decide matters for all, but how all who have a stake can feed into a sustainable, decision-making process.

Those who have a stake should have a say. The issue is then how best to enable such a structure to ensure it is workable and delivers sustainability. We turn to this in the next section.

Leadership as accountable

Stakeholder leadership is about more than ensuring sustainability; it is about securing accountability. Consider again the orthodox view of the Profit-Only Firm. Accountability in that sphere is about an accountability to shareholders to deliver on short-term profit creation. Those in executive positions benefit most because they are accountable to shareholders for the decisions made. Of course, executives cannot claim the greatest rewards for taking the biggest risks, as the burdens of profitability can often take the form of restructuring and efficiency-savings leading to most job losses endured by those not on the executive team. To be accountable is not so much to be held to account in general – otherwise, more might share in the success (or failure) of the firm rather than benefits moving only to the top and not the bottom of the managerial structure.

Notice that this view of accountability is largely *post facto*, or 'after the fact'. We hold executives to account for the decisions reached after we witness their outcomes. Accountability is about examining the outcomes of decisions already made. To be held to account is to be judged for actions already performed.

Compare this with the view of the Stakeholder Firm. Accountability here is diffused and spread out across all stakeholders. This view rejects the idea that the executive is accountable only to its shareholders because they are not the only persons with a stake in the future success of the firm. Stakeholders include a wider range of people than firm employees and shareholders alone. Likewise, the stakeholder view of leadership is a more expansive view about the leader's decision making and its outcomes.

But what does it mean to be 'accountable' in this way? One central idea is the importance of *transparency*. If those who have a stake should have a say in outcomes that may affect them, this requires these stakeholders to possess sufficient information. Each must have access to information about available and likely outcomes. So it is not enough that information is 'out there'; it must also be accessible to persons as stakeholders. Transparency is necessary for accountability because all potentially relevant information must be made available *and accessible.*

This point can be clarified by an example. In his *Philosophy of Right*, G. W. F. Hegel defends the right to trial by jury on distinctive grounds, namely, transparency (Brooks 2013: 94–5). He argues that juries are required because without them:

> knowledge [*Kenntnis*] of right and of the course of court proceedings, as well as the ability to pursue one's rights, may become the property of a class [*Stand*] which makes itself exclusive … by the terminology it uses, inasmuch as this terminology is a foreign language for those whose rights are *at stake.* (Hegel 1990: §228)

The difference between a judge-only trial versus a jury trial is not the amount of information available, but its accessibility. Each might present the same evidence and raise the same legal issues. However, genuine accountability is not achieved through mere exposure to information. The judge-only trial is problematic because it risks becoming an event where only the legally trained can access the reasons supporting trial outcomes. The jury trial better guarantees the trial's procedures and outcomes will be accessible to the defendant because his or her peers are similarly situated (insofar as all lack full legal knowledge) and so the decisions reached by a group of twelve such citizens can serve as a good barometer for what we can and should expect most defendants to understand (Brooks 2004). In other words, we require *accessibility* to secure *accountability.*

This impacts on our understanding of leadership because it cannot be about accountability where those who have a stake in outcomes are unable to access the relevant information to support their decision making. Consider one illustration of what is often thought to be political leadership: the ready availability of information online about government-related activities. This has certainly had a welcome effect of exposing political decision making to greater scrutiny, but there remains the possibility of the general public becoming overwhelmed by the sheer volume of available information. The problem is much of this matter may be relatively inaccessible: we all might have opportunities to consider such material, but many of us might lack sufficient knowledge to engage with others. Leadership should view the availability of information as undermined by any lack of accessibility: the two go hand-in-hand. Stakeholding is not only about bringing together people who *are* stakeholders, but engaging with them *as* stakeholders.

This speaks to a particular form of relationship between stakeholders. This is complex and part of the criticism faced by stakeholder theory (Prabhakar 2004). The main worry is simple: Who are the stakeholders? (Kaler 2002). For example, it is not obvious that corporate partners of any single firm form an exclusive stakeholder group. This is because these partners are not alone in sharing a stake in that firm's future performance. The problem about who to include is then also a problem about numbers: How many stakeholders are there? Stakeholder theory's defenders, such as Will Hutton, claim we're *all* stakeholders: 'companies should be run and managed balancing the interests of shareholders, customers, employees and wider society, rather than prioritising shareholders' (2010: 151). We are all stakeholders in the firm's future success occupying various different roles, such as the workforce, the senior management, customers, supply firms, the families of each and the wider economy.

But if we're all stakeholders, how can firms make any decisions? The answer lies in variable power distribution. To say many, if not all, have some stake in outcomes potentially affecting them is not to say that every person has an equal share or that the outcome effects from decisions will be shared equally. Some will have more of a stake than others. Some might have different stakes depending upon other factors. So perhaps persons running a firm have a largest stake and even the largest say about outcomes. This does not mean they can or should avoid consulting with all other stakeholders.

Restorative justice conferencing is a useful illustration of stakeholding in practice (Brooks 2012: 65–8, 71–3, 77–84). Restorative justice is an alternative to the formal trial procedure for determining sentencing outcomes for criminal offenders.[2] Instead of a trial, restorative justice aims to provide a context for healing between offenders and their victims as well as others. This is done by bringing together the offender, victim and their support networks (often a spouse or close friend), as well as individuals from the local community conducted by a trained facilitator. The victim speaks first to express the impact of a crime on him or her. Others speak with the offending going last. The meeting is predicated on the offender accepting guilt for the crime and often the offender will apologize to the victim. The benefits of restorative justice have been impressive: it delivers higher participant satisfaction for all participants, can lead to up to 25 per cent less recidivism and can save £1 for every £9 spent (Brooks 2012: 83).

Restorative justice conferencing is a form of stakeholding. It brings together persons who have a stake in the outcome. This includes the victim, the offender, their close family and friends, but also the general public. Yet, it is clear that some have greater stakes than others. For instance, victims and offenders might each be thought to have the largest stakes: the victim as someone subjected to a public wrong and the offender as a person that will be punished. It is admittedly difficult to come to any clear view about the number of other potential stakeholders – including 'the public' of you and me – who may be affected by the criminal justice system's outcomes beyond ensuring the conference's workability.

Crucially, all participants to a restorative justice conference have a say on its outcome: namely, the punishment of the offender. These stakeholders have a stake and so can engage with other stakeholders about outcomes. This renders restorative justice unique: instead of top-down decision making by judges and magistrates in court, restorative justice is a more collaborative enterprise whereby stakeholders engage each other to create outcomes that can be shaped by this engagement. Each is also accountable to each other through practical reasoning about outcomes.[3]

Stakeholding brings out the dimension of accountability that is an important part of leadership. Stakeholder accountability requires transparency, but also engagement that is effective without requiring a hierarchical structure. Restorative justice is not a mere analogy, but an example of stakeholder accountability in practice. It illustrates a model whereby persons with stakes in outcomes should – and do – have a say about them engaging with others as fellow stakeholders. The restorative justice model is one example of how both the process and its outcomes can benefit from a stakeholder model.

Leadership as ethical

There is also an *ethical* dimension to the kind of accountability that stakeholding supports. This is aimed at setting normative limits for what is permissible. Leadership is not merely occupying a privileged position and maintaining it (e.g. sustainability). Nor is leadership only providing decisions that are publically accessible in a transparent process (e.g. accountability). Leadership requires that sustainability and accountability work in certain ways that bring out normative implications.

The ethics of the Profit-Only Firm are simple: rightness and wrongness are not central; profit creation is all that counts. So corners can be cut and perhaps long-term sustainability sacrificed in the blind pursuit of maximizing profitability for today. Pursuing profits lacks sufficient normative constraints. Any such constraints that are used might endorse different goals. For example, market regulations may undermine profit creation for a firm in the short term in the name of securing other goods, such as a more sustainable market.

The Stakeholder Firm view is starkly different. Effective leadership is not only about ensuring the firm can continue to benefit its stakeholders, but is undertaken as an exercise in stakeholding. So it is not only important to identify the relevant persons: we must also ensure a certain relationship between them. This is described by Hutton as fundamentally about inclusion where this is 'not a one-way street' and demands reciprocal obligations (1999: 74; see Fassin 2012).

Stakeholders must engage one another as stakeholders. What is its importance? Consider Philip Pettit's groundbreaking work on republicanism (2001). Pettit argues that citizens must engage each other with 'discursive control' through shared, deliberative interaction where each has the ability and opportunity to contribute (2001: 70). Each person 'must be able to see their own signature' in their attitudes and actions (Pettit 2001: 79). To enjoy discursive control, our freedom is secured by satisfying an ideal of non-domination and not subjected to arbitrary interference (Pettit 2001: 138).

Stakeholding is compatible with republican freedom. Citizens exercising discursive control free from domination engage others as free and equal stakeholders. Each has a stake in outcomes and so each should be able to enter deliberations about how these outcomes are decided. A stakeholder is a citizen who enjoys freedom as non-domination.

However, stakeholding further develops republican freedom. Republicans, such as Pettit, claim that there is not one political discourse, but several with different memberships. No one might be a member in all, but some may have memberships across more than one (Pettit 2001: 72). But which public discourses are there and who ought to be recognized as participants? Stakeholding offers an answer. Different areas of public life may include various memberships that reflect the multiple stakes citizens might have in each. Public affairs – to be 'public' – affect us all and so we each have some stake in their outcomes. Some stakes may be greater than others.

For example, public funding for the arts concerns everyone, but some, such as artists and musicians, might have a greater stake than others. Criminal justice is of public concern, but some, such as defendants and victims, may also possess a greater stake than others. Precise determinations about relative stakes in every case might be difficult and hotly contested. Nonetheless, stakeholding can offer some insight into distinguishing between different discursive groups and their members more clearly than republicanism. This is because stakeholding claims that those who have a stake should have a say and so provides a principled view on group membership.[4]

Stakeholding further develops republican theories in another respect. Republicanism claims non-domination is secured through discursive control: citizens enjoy republican freedom where they can exercise an opportunity for dialogue without arbitrary interference. Republicans mistake the opportunities to exercise discursive control for non-domination. The idea is that citizens should be held accountable and lack the right to complain should they fail to exercise available opportunities. But my having opportunities is insufficient. Citizens must see themselves as stakeholders. If they fail to believe that they have a stake, then they may be insufficiently motivated to contribute even where opportunities for public deliberation are widely available. Citizens must have an interest as stakeholders to incentivize their public deliberation.

This raises a special problem for stakeholding. I have argued that providing opportunities for stakeholding is insufficient: individuals must possess a conviction about their being stakeholders. The problem is whether it is more tolerable to have opportunities for the exercise of stakeholding where many citizens fail to acquire this belief, or instead a polity where many share the conviction that they are stakeholders, but where opportunities are more limited. The criticism directed at republicanism is that it can be satisfied by the former without regard for the latter: what matters most is the existence *in fact* of opportunities. This does not deny the importance for ensuring citizens are aware of these opportunities, but convictions about stakeholding are much less important. However, both elements are necessary for stakeholding to become manifest: citizens should understand themselves as stakeholders with sufficient opportunities to exercise stakeholding. Nonetheless, beliefs are important for stakeholding in a way in which they are not for republicanism. If citizens are to enjoy freedom as non-domination, then they must see themselves as non-dominated, which stakeholding can help secure.

Alienation is perhaps the greatest concern for stakeholding. Someone who is alienated lacks the sense of self as connected and engaged with others. But this can only be a problem if our social and political world is worth having. For stakeholding, it is not only important that people are seen as stakeholders, but that they see themselves in this light.[5]

Conclusion: Leadership as stakeholding?

I have argued for a new model of leadership from a different perspective. I have focused on stakeholding: this is the idea that those who have a stake should have a say about outcomes. This idea finds original expression in the business ethics and corporate governance literature, but it is an idea that has applications elsewhere. Stakeholding is about more than a compelling alternative to structuring the decision-making process of firms: it can also provide us with significant insights for leadership.

The first claim is that leadership is about sustainability. When we consider what leadership means, many of us will think of someone who held a position of leadership that was maintained. Stakeholding highlights a new way of thinking about sustainability in which it is one of several goals, and not to be considered in isolation from them.

The second claim is that leadership is about accountability. This is often thought to mean those who decide are held to account after decisions have been made. We effectively reward and punish when speaking about 'accountability' for decisions already made in the past. Stakeholding argues that accountability must include accessibility and that the process can be as important as its outcome. Leadership is not only about effective decision making, but follows an interactive engagement with others who have a stake in outcomes, too. Crucially, stakeholders must not only be able to access available information, but it must be accessible for them to truly engage with others as stakeholders.

Finally, the third claim is sustainability and accountability are exercised within clear normative boundaries. It is important that not only should stakeholders have opportunities to exercise stakeholding, but they must be able to view themselves as stakeholders. This rests on a larger question about whether our social and political world is a world worth having a stake in. This larger, background issue is highly relevant, but beyond the confines of my discussion here.

Nonetheless, I have argued for a new view of leadership and ethics.[6] Stakeholding is more than a metaphor imported from a different literature, but has clear relevance for how we think about leadership and related issues of justice. Leadership is best conceived as a form of stakeholding. This chapter has tried to explain this case.

Notes

1   See http://www.totalpolitics.com/print/5558/its-not-big-but-fair-will-hutton.thtml
2   Restorative justice has other applications, but I will focus only on its use in the criminal justice system for this example.
3   Restorative justice is also interesting because of its ability to address 'penal pluralism' in a new way. Penal pluralism is the idea that punishment can and should possess multiple penal purposes (Brooks 2014a). So instead of having to select *either* retributivist desert, deterrence or rehabilitation, penal pluralism seeks to integrate them together into a 'unified theory of punishment' (Brooks 2012: 123–48). Restorative justice can have a unified character by supporting multiple penal purposes, such as desert (ensuring punishment to only those confirming their guilt), deterrence (providing penalties sufficiently strong to dissuade others from engaging in similar activities), rehabilitation (focusing on tackling factors linked with reoffending) and others (Brooks 2014b).
4   My account of stakeholding is normative. As such, it is meant to apply across multiple areas – and I do not believe it is limited to leadership alone. I have already noted the relevance of stakeholding for business ethics and discussed its relation to political and economic justice. But should associations and non-public forms of community and organization adopt some kind of stakeholder model? Possibly yes, if it can be agreed that it is sufficiently valuable to engage others as stakeholders in these domains.
5   A critic might respond that what I refer to is merely 'consultation', but this is not the case. To be consulted does not require that I provide feedback, or that my feedback is taken seriously or that I am engaged as someone with a stake. Instead, my standing may be nothing more than the receiver of a mass distributed *communique*. Stakeholding refers to something much deeper regarding the relational engagement between participating individuals and their self-identities as stakeholders who reciprocally recognize each other as stakeholders.
6   Should leadership depend on 'success'? I do not think so. My stakeholder account defends a principled normative approach. While consequences matter, I'm unpersuaded they should be the sole metric for determining success. This is, in part, because consequences may be *shaped* by effective and justifiable leadership without being *determined* by it. So normatively 'good' leadership cannot be judged

on outcomes alone, but how these are pursued. The stakeholder account attempts to deliver satisfactory results, but focusing first and foremost on the processes that produce them.

Bibliography

Brooks, T. (2004), 'The right to trial by jury', *Journal of Applied Philosophy*, 21: 197–212.

—(2012), *Punishment*. London: Routledge.

—(2013), *Hegel's Political Philosophy: A Systematic Reading of the Philosophy of Right* (2nd edn). Edinburgh: Edinburgh University Press.

—(2014a), 'F. H. Bradley's penal pluralism: On "some remarks on punishment"', *Ethics*, 125 (2014): 223–5.

—(2014b), 'On punitive restoration', *Demos Quarterly*, 2: 41–4.

Fassin, Y. (2012), 'Stakeholder management, reciprocity and stakeholder responsibility', *Journal of Business Ethics*, 109: 83–96.

Freeman, R. E. (1984), *Strategic Management: A Stakeholder Approach*. Boston: Pitman.

Freeman, R. E., Harrison, J. S. and Wicks, A. C. (2007), *Managing for Stakeholders: Survival, Reputation, and Success*. New Haven: Yale University Press.

Freeman, R. E., Harrison, J. S.,Wicks, A. C., Parmar, B. L. and Colle, S. de (2010), *Stakeholder Theory: The State of the Art*. Cambridge: Cambridge University Press.

Hegel, G. W. F. (1990), *Elements of the Philosophy of Right* (A. W. Wood (ed.)). Cambridge: Cambridge University Press.

Hutton, W. (1995), *The State We're In*. London: Jonathan Cape.

—(1999), *The Stakeholder Society: Writings on Politics and Economics* (ed. D. Goldblatt). Cambridge: Polity.

—(2010), *Them and Us: Changing Britain – Why We Need a Fair Society*. London: Little, Brown.

Kaler, J. (2002), 'Morality and strategy in stakeholder identification', *Journal of Business Ethics*, 39: 91–9.

Pettit, P. (2001), *A Theory of Freedom: From the Psychology to the Politics of Agency*. Cambridge: Polity.

Plender, J. (1997), *A Stake in the Future: The Stakeholding Solution*. London: Nicholas Brealey.

Prabhakar, R. (2004), 'Whatever happened to stakeholding?' *Public Administration*, 82: 567–84.

9

Parents, Children and Good Leadership: Is Parental Authority Compatible with Children's Freedom?

Allyn Fives
Galway

Leadership involves the exercise of power, as leaders make decisions, and act, on behalf of their followers. It is the case that an exercise of power need not also be an act of leadership. It is not an instance of leadership when my exercise of power concerns those who are merely affected by my actions as opposed to those who follow me. Also, power is not the only issue relevant to a full understanding of leadership. Other important considerations include the qualities required by a good leader, and how leadership itself changes depending on the institutional context and the specific social roles involved. Nonetheless, as the exercise of power is an integral part of leadership, whenever we wish to make a normative judgement of any instance of leadership, we are led to ask whether this exercise of power is morally justifiable. This chapter analyses the normative justification of the power exercised by leaders and it does so by examining the relationship between parents and children in the context of the family. Parents, like other leaders, are expected to guide, care for and take charge of others who are less powerful. Parents are in a position of leadership, and in judging parental authority we are led to ask whether the exercise of power over children is morally justifiable.

This chapter will explore the relationship between power and freedom and it will do so in two ways. Republicans and others believe that the most important issue is the extent to which some individuals or groups have the *capacity to interfere* with the freedom of choice of others and therefore coerce others, for example, when husbands have such a capacity with respect to the choices of their wives. Liberals and others believe that what needs to be addressed is whether or not those in authority *in fact do interfere* with the freedom of choice of others and therefore coerce others: for instance, when husbands do in fact interfere with the choices of their wives. It follows, for republicans, to diminish coercion requires 'regulating' the power of those in authority and 'protecting' and 'empowering' those subject to authority, what Philip Pettit (1996) terms 'anti-power', while for liberals, as Isaiah Berlin (1958) argued, to diminish coercion requires reducing actual instances of interference within each individual's realm of freedom. If parents are entitled and required to exercise power over children, it would seem logical to ask when, or under what conditions, is parental authority normatively justified and when, in contrast, is it coercive?

However, political theorists have tended to treat childhood as exceptional, as they have assumed that the concept of coercion cannot be applied to the situation of children, and that parental authority is to be evaluated instead on the basis of its impact on children's development and progression to adulthood (Brighouse 1998; Noggle 2002). This essay attempts both to reverse the tendency to see childhood as exceptional and also to apply the concept of coercion to the analysis of parental authority. What this chapter argues is that it is possible to expand what liberals define as freedom (i.e. children's freedom from interference) even when we have not ended what republicans consider to be coercion (i.e. parents' capacity to interfere). Indeed, as empirical data from parenting studies suggest, in particular, behaviourist strategies that parents are trained to implement with their children (Fives et al. 2014), what republicans consider to be (parental) coercion can in fact be used to help expand what liberals call (children's) freedom.

The argument in this chapter has implications for our understanding of the normative evaluation of leadership more generally. The aim of so-called 'transformative' leadership is to empower followers, whereas in contrast the aim of 'transactional' leadership is merely to retain control over the input of followers and to maintain the organization over time (Burns 1978). This chapter provides qualified support for the transformative leadership model, as it argues that a leader's capacity to interfere can be used to increase freedom from interference among followers. That is, power can be positive-sum and not only negative-sum, as power can be exercised so as to empower others (Haugaard 2012). However, this chapter goes further in acknowledging that both republican and liberal accounts of coercion are valuable. It therefore accepts that republican anti-power measures can and should limit and restrict coercive power relations. It also argues that, as the republican and liberal conceptions of freedom are two distinct moral values, there can be instances of genuine conflict between them, and therefore moral judgement is required about the appropriate balance of republican and liberal anti-coercion measures.

Leadership, parents and power

Power is a central consideration in the normative evaluation of leaders. In conceptualizing the relationship between leaders and followers, a distinction is made between transformational (or transformative) leadership on the one hand and transactional leadership on the other hand (Burns 1978; Bass and Steidlmeier 1999). In the transactional model, followers 'exchange … services … for various kinds of rewards … that the leader controls' (Leithwood 1992: 9). In the education environment, for instance, such a relationship could exist between a school principal and the teachers in his/her school (ibid.). In this model of leadership the focus is on the leader ensuring day-to-day routines are carried out so as to maintain the organization over time. In the transformational model, in contrast, the leader moves ahead of his/her followers and seeks to produce revolutionary changes not only to structures of power, but also to the attitudes, beliefs and values of the community of followers. Nelson Mandela's decision to enter into negotiations with the Apartheid government in South Africa is represented as an example of transformative leadership in part because his followers in the ANC were opposed to such a strategy at this time, and also because of the intended consequences of his approach (Reid 2010).

The aim of transformational leadership is to empower followers. The transformational leader strives to help followers become autonomous and competent, to reach 'self-actualization' and also higher levels of 'morality' (Popper and Mayseless 2003). Again this model of leadership has been applied to the education setting, and here the role of the transformative leader is to build a shared vision, improve communication and develop collaborative decision making (Leithwood 1992). Therefore, a good leader is one who hands over power to his/her followers. The concept of servant leadership (Greenleaf 1969) is very similar, as its stated aim is to allow 'extraordinary freedom' for followers to exercise their own abilities (Stone, Russel and Patterson 2003: 4). In contrast, the aim of the transactional leader is not to empower followers. Rather, transactional leaders must retain power over their followers' exchange of services for rewards if they are to realize their aims, namely to ensure the organization is maintained over time.

It has also been argued that the relationship between followers and leaders is analogous to that between children and parents. Both leaders and parents are expected to guide, direct, take charge of and care for others who are less powerful, and to help the follower/child to grow into a functioning and autonomous adult (Popper and Mayseless 2003). Therefore, the argument that parenting is a form of leadership does not presume any one conception of the power relation between leaders and followers, and in particular it does not imply that followers lack all capacity for autonomous self-direction. On the contrary, the argument of Popper and Mayseless is that *good* parenting is analogous to *transformational* leadership. In particular, good parents and transformative leaders must be 'sensitive and responsive', and show individual consideration for their 'protégés'; they must 'reinforce the protégés' autonomy' in a supportive, non-judgmental way; they must 'set limitations and rules which are flexible'; and finally they should be 'positive examples to identify with and look up to' (ibid.: 44). Therefore, the argument is that good parenting provides criteria of judgement for the normative evaluation of leadership more generally.

Children's moral agency

In the literature on leadership, it is argued that good parenting is analogous to good leadership. However, we have said that political theorists have tended to treat childhood as exceptional, as they have assumed that the concept of coercion cannot be applied to the situation of children, and that parental authority is to be evaluated instead on the basis of its impact on children's development and progression to adulthood. This approach in political theory must be addressed if parenting is to provide insights into leadership and, therefore, power, more generally.

The argument from simple agency

One line of argument is that power relations in the family in the main are justified because children do not have full or complete moral agency. This will be called the argument from simple agency. Robert Noggle has categorized children as 'moral patients' (Noggle 2002: 100). Their moral standing entitles them to moral concern and consideration by adults. Children do have the rudiments of moral agency as well, what he refers to as 'simple agency', for they are capable of the deliberate, intentional and rational pursuit of goals. However, unlike adults, they do not have fully developed moral agency. Children lack stable preferences, a sense of moral decency, the ability to take into account their own long-term interests and also their own conception of the good (ibid.: 101). This state of simple agency requires 'parental authority' as an 'interface' between the child and the moral community, as, it is assumed, the community cannot assume that without parental authority children will be motivated to act in 'morally decent' ways (ibid.: 110). Therefore, the wider community is right to expect that children obey their parents, but also to expect that parents raise their children so as one day to become morally decent individuals who then may gain 'entrance into the moral community' (ibid.: 111). What also follows is that parents are permitted to 'share a way of life' with their children. It is assumed that children do not have a value system, a set of fundamental moral commitments, and that the family must supply the 'default value system' for the child. Noggle stresses that parents do not have an unconditional right to propagate their beliefs, and the right to share a way of life with their children does not apply to intolerant and indecent world views (ibid.: 114). However, according to this argument, parents would be entitled to expect that their children share their values, for example traditional or religious values, and take steps to promote the acceptance of those values by their children. Such measures could include choosing to educate children using a curriculum shaped by traditional or religious values and/or requiring that their children attend ceremonies and perform rites associated with those value commitments. While there is no guarantee that such efforts will be *successful*, and that children will come to adopt the values in question, at issue is the parents' *right* to pursue such a course of action.

According to this line of thought, parents are entitled and required to make decisions for their children that their children should obey, including decisions about their children's values. However, this assumes parents may rightly possess a capacity to interfere in their children's choices and also to decide when to interfere with choices their children would otherwise have freely made. To express this in the terms of political theory, parents may rightly exercise authority over their children that, were it to arise in relations between adults, would be considered instances of coercion by both republicans (as it grants parents the capacity to interfere with the freedom of choice of their children) and liberals (as parents may in fact interfere with the freedom of choice of their children). Therefore, political theorists are happy to view certain relations between parents and children as normatively justified even though the power of parents would be considered unjustifiably coercive by both republicans and liberals were it to arise in relations between adults.

The argument for autonomy-facilitating education

Two reasons are given to justify this exceptional status of childhood. The first is that, as we have seen, parents may only exercise their power over children because children are unique in lacking full moral agency. The second consideration is that this exercise of power is justified as a means to bring about the best outcomes for children, namely to safeguard the interests of children. Some have argued that this fundamental duty of parents is a duty of care (Archard 2010: 43) while others have argued that it is a duty to help the child to mature into a fully autonomous adult (Brighouse 1998: 740). The latter will be called the argument for autonomy-facilitating education. Harry Brighouse's position is that, if parents have legitimate claims to be guardians, it is only because in this way children's interests are better protected. Brighouse gives the interests of children priority over those of their parents in particular when there is a conflict of interests concerning the teaching of autonomy. Therefore, if for instance civic education classes are available to children whose purpose is to facilitate the development of children's autonomy, parents are not entitled to prevent their children from taking part in those classes. Crucially, however, it is assumed in Brighouse's argument that children are not autonomous *qua* children, and so the argument is directed towards the interests of the adult the child will grow up to be. Brighouse contends that a 'truly liberal' position accepts that 'children have powerful interests in *becoming* autonomous', and takes the interests of children (i.e. the interests in becoming autonomous adults) to be paramount in determining the institutional distribution of authority (ibid.: 740; emphasis added).

I have argued that political theorists have treated childhood as exceptional, as they have assumed that the concept of coercion cannot be applied to the situation of children, and that parental authority is to be evaluated instead on the basis of its impact on children's development and progression to adulthood. This can be seen by contrasting what political theorists have said about parental authority with what they say about other power relations. While republicans believe that relations between spouses are coercive if one spouse has the capacity to interfere with the freedom of choice of the other, liberals believe they are coercive if one spouse does in fact interfere with the freedom of choice of the other. Childhood is thought to be different either because parental authority is required when children cannot be relied upon to act in morally decent ways (the argument from simple agency) or because the exercise of such authority is in the best interests of the child and ultimately results in the child gaining their autonomy (the argument for autonomy-facilitating education). That is why it is fair to say political theorists have treated childhood as exceptional, and this can be seen most clearly when their understanding of parental authority is contrasted with power relations that are considered uncontroversially unjust by political theorists, in particular slavery.

In his autobiography of a life of slavery in nineteenth-century Maryland, Fredrick Douglas noted that slavery became truly unbearable for him once he himself had developed the skills and strengths required for autonomy. Once that point had been reached he then became uncomfortably aware of what slavery was denying him:

> I would at times feel that learning to read had been a curse rather than a blessing. It had given me a view of my wretched condition, without the remedy … In moments of agony, I envied my fellow-slaves for their stupidity. I have often wished myself a beast … The silver trump of freedom had roused my soul to eternal wakefulness. Freedom now appeared, to disappear no more forever. It was heard in every sound, and seen in everything. It was ever present to torment me with a sense of my wretched condition. (Douglas 1845: 63–4)

Political theorists think that slavery is uncontroversially unjust for a particular reason. Not only is slavery not motivated by the best interests of the slave, slavery itself can be said to be designed to prevent or stunt the development of autonomy. The same criteria are appealed to by political theorists in justifying the authority of parents, as the power of parents over children is justified when it is motivated by the best interests of the child and also when it is a necessary means for the child's development of autonomy. In turn the power of parents over children becomes unjustifiable coercion when the latter are no longer children, that is, when (all things being equal) they are capable of autonomy.

According to the view being ascribed to political theory in this chapter there is a transition from childhood, where the individual is thought to lack the full capacity for moral autonomy, to adulthood where the full capacity for moral autonomy is assumed. Such a transition has been represented in science fiction, in Isaac Asimov's *The Bicentennial Man*. Although the eponymous hero begins life as a robot, and therefore as a being without any entitlement to or capacity for freedom, the Bicentennial Man develops the wish to be human and therefore to be free. As with Fredrick Douglas's own desire to no longer be treated like and thought of as a slave, Asimov's fictional robot wishes to be accepted as a human and therefore as a being whose freedom should be respected. Unlike Douglas, however, the robot's wish to be free is recognized by those with authority in his society. The enlightened judge hearing his case concludes: 'There is no right to deny freedom to any object with a mind advanced enough to grasp the concept and desire the state' (Asimov 1976: 646). Political theorists now take a similar position when it comes to children's progression into adulthood and autonomy. Children may be granted the respect owed to free and equal fellow humans, but only once they have passed through their formative period and have developed the capacity to grasp the concept and desire the state of autonomy.

When power is coercive

Earlier we introduced two separate views on coercion. One is associated with republicanism. It focuses on the power of those in authority and the empowerment of those subject to authority. The other is associated with liberalism. It concerns protections against actual interference in freedom of choice.

In the seminal contemporary account of republican freedom, Philip Pettit defines domination as the capacity to interfere, with impunity and at will, in certain choices of another. One agent dominates another if and only if he or she has a certain power over that other, in particular the power to interfere in the affairs of the other and to inflict a certain damage (Pettit 1996: 578). The interference must involve a more or less intentional attempt to worsen another agent's situation of choice (ibid.: 579): the 'with impunity' requirement means there is no penalty or loss for the person who interferes; while the 'at-will' condition requires that the person can initiate interference at his/her own pleasure (ibid.: 580). This amounts to an absolutely arbitrary power, something which, for example, may have been available to slave-holders (ibid.: 581). It can be 'approximated' in rule-governed societies: for example the husband who beats his wife, the employer who fires his/her employees on a whim, the prison warder who 'can make life hell for inmates' and, most relevant to our purposes here, the teacher who can chastise his/her pupils 'on the slightest excuse or pretense at excuse' (ibid.: 581).

Isaiah Berlin provides what we have referred to as the alternative liberal account of freedom and coercion. For Berlin, freedom is a matter of the following question: 'What is the area within which the subject – a person or group of persons – is or should be left to do or be what he is able to do or be, without interference by other persons?' (Berlin 1958: 169). What matters is how many paths or doors or options are open to me (ibid.: 177 n. 1). If freedom is defined as non-interference, then coercion 'implies the deliberative interference of other human beings within the area in which I could otherwise act' (ibid.: 169). While Pettit was concerned not only 'that the doors be open' but also that 'there is no doorkeeper on whose goodwill you depend for one or another of the doors remaining open' (Pettit 2011: 709), in contrast, according to Berlin, for coercion to be identifiable, there must be actual interference with an individual's freedom of choice. For instance, in the workplace, there may be a clear division between a class of managers who alone have authority to make decisions to change work practices, and a class of workers who cannot influence such decisions. According to Pettit's argument, because managers have the capacity to interfere, this counts as domination even if they never exercise this power. Pettit's argument against Berlin's approach is to contend that freedom as non-interference is consistent with a relationship of domination, provided the dominating party (in this case, the managers) does not actually interfere with the dominated (the workers) (Pettit 2001: 600). Pettit's position is that domination has come to an end only when 'the authority of just laws replaces the will of particular individuals' (Larmore 2001: 231).

Moreover, according to Pettit, social amelioration is necessary so as to neutralize the will of particular individuals, and in that way to ensure our freedom from interference is not determined by the goodwill of those in authority (Pettit 1996: 600). In contrast, Berlin does not accept that social amelioration is either necessary or sufficient for freedom. John Rawls would later argue that while poverty does not of itself infringe liberty it lessens the 'worth of liberty' (Rawls 1971: 204). For Berlin: 'It is argued, very plausibly, that if a man is too poor to afford something to which there is no legal ban … he is as little free to have it as he would be if it were forbidden him by law' (Berlin 1958: 170). Although Berlin accepts there are strong normative grounds to oppose such social and economic inequalities, in particular, in Rawls' terms, as they lessen the worth of liberty, nonetheless he believes such inequalities in and of themselves are not infringements of liberty: 'Mere incapacity to attain a goal is not lack of political freedom' (ibid.: 169). At the same time, the efforts we make to ameliorate social and economic inequalities may themselves infringe liberty, and to the extent that this happens, there will be a clash of values between liberty and social justice, a genuine moral dilemma: 'Nothing is gained by a confusion of terms … it is a confusion of values to say that although my "liberal", individual freedom may go to the board, some other kind of freedom – "social" or "economic" – is increased' (ibid.: 173).

Is the power of parents coercive?

The two conceptions of freedom can be employed now to address the issue of parental authority. It is widely accepted by political theorists that parents are entitled and required to make decisions for their children that their children should obey, including decisions about their children's values. Parents have the right to 'share a way of life' with their children. To test this view we shall look at some illustrative examples. The 'way of life' may involve traditional and/or religious commitments, and those commitments may place a high value on the acceptance of moral truths on the basis of respect for authority and orthodoxy. Also the way of life may place a high value on a traditional division of labour between males and females, which requires not only that young females stay in the private/domestic sphere but also that young males enter into a family profession (e.g. a trade, a family business, the family farm, and so on). If parents wish to 'share' this way of life with their children, and if parents also have the capacity to interfere with their children's choices and do in fact interfere with their choices, is this relation normatively objectionable, and if so, why or when?

As we have seen, Pettit believes that we are un-free so long as there is someone with the capacity to interfere, with impunity and at will, in some of our choices. However, parental authority by definition involves the capacity to interfere, with impunity and at will, in some of the choices of the parents' children. Not only are parents duty bound to interfere so as to promote the interests of their children, parents have the right to interfere so as to pursue their own interests as parents, although both duty and right come with qualifications, as we have seen (Brighouse 2002; Noggle 1998). Within Pettit's approach it is possible to make either an extreme or a moderate argument when interpreting parental authority. The 'extreme' argument is that, unless these parental rights and duties are removed, children will be un-free. That is, so long as parents retain the capacity to interfere in their children's choices, then children will continue to be dominated. This is an extreme argument as it implies that parental authority is coercive by definition.

It is also possible to make a 'moderate' argument within Pettit's approach. Pettit has noted that 'if institutions get rid of a certain amount of domination without putting any new forms of domination in their place ... then we may say they promote anti-power' (Pettit 1996: 588). Anti-power is not itself a form of domination and can include any of the following strategies: 'giving the powerless *protection* against the resources of the powerful ..., *regulating* the use that the powerful make of their resources, and ... giving the powerless new, *empowering* resources of their own' (ibid.: 589–90; emphasis added). Therefore, the 'moderate' argument in interpreting parental authority would read as follows: it is possible to diminish in a piecemeal fashion the domination of children, insofar as children are *protected* against some forms of parental interference, are provided with resources necessary for their own *empowerment* and the actions of parents are *regulated* by various forms of anti-power. Returning to our examples above, concerning parents who wish to share a way of life with their children, the 'moderate' argument allows that various measures may reduce parental domination by creating anti-power for children. Such measures may include compulsory formal schooling for children, and/or autonomy-facilitating education, including civic education (Brighouse 1998). These would count as anti-power to the extent that they empower and protect children in their relations with their parents, and also regulate parents in their exercise of parental authority.

We are asking the following question. If parents wish to 'share' this way of life with their children, and if parents also have the capacity to interfere with their children's choices and do in fact interfere with their choices, is this relation normatively objectionable, and if so, why or when? Berlin's conception of freedom provides another way to approach this issue. We have already seen that he defines freedom as non-interference. However, two further considerations are relevant to our discussion. First, Berlin sets out how to distinguish between greater and lesser degrees of freedom. He believes the extent of my freedom can be made greater or lesser depending on the following: (i) how many paths are open to me; (ii) how easy or difficult each of these possibilities is to actualize; (iii) how important these possibilities are in my plan of life; (iv) how far they are closed and opened by human acts; and (v) what value I and the general sentiment of society places on them (Berlin 1958: 177 n. 1). The second point is that, for Berlin, the scope of my freedom is broader than the specific paths I am disposed to choose. That is, he distinguishes non-interference from non-frustration, as freedom is not the 'absence of frustration … but the absence of obstacles to possible choices and activities' (Berlin 1969: 32). The distinction is important as one can overcome 'obstacles to the fulfillment of desire' simply by killing desire (Berlin 1988: 326) or by adapting one's preferences so as to desire whatever options happen to be available: 'There is a clear sense in which to teach a man that, if he cannot get what he wants, he must learn to want only what he can get, may contribute to his happiness or his security; but it will not increase his civil or political freedom' (Berlin 1969: 32).

Both of these considerations can be applied to the evaluation of parental authority. The power of parents can be said to be problematic, on Berlin's view, to the extent that it leads to the 'adaptation' of preferences by children to those that would find favour with their parents, and for that reason, the closing off of 'paths' or options that the children otherwise would have chosen. Coercion of this kind may occur when parents try to 'share' a religious/traditional way of life with their children. For instance, adolescent girls and boys may decide to give up their secret desire to pursue a career path or way of life radically different from that of their parents' expectations, and instead adopt a preference to work in the family profession or business or work within the home. Or they may decide to give up their secret desire to live a life free from any outward religious devotion and instead adopt a preference for a life lived in conformity with the religious values and rituals of their childhood. If the young people have adapted their preferences because they did not feel that the preferred ways of life or routes through life were options, doors that they were free to walk through, and if this adaptation occurred because of and in response to the opinions, practices or suggestions of their parents, then, following Berlin's argument, we can say their freedom of choice has been interfered with. The range of options to choose from was unjustifiably limited and as a result the young people had their freedom unjustifiably interfered with.

What are we to do about this type of situation? The republican answer, based on the 'moderate' argument above, is that freedom is protected and promoted simply and solely insofar as we limit parents' capacity to interfere. However, an alternative answer, based on what has been said in discussing Berlin, is that parents themselves can be the ones to protect and promote the freedom of their children, and they can do so because of their capacity to interfere. We look at the two different approaches now.

The republican response: To protect and empower children and regulate parents' power

There are various policies and services, laws and conventions, that we can describe as measures whose aim is to strengthen the anti-power of children. This is the case in particular concerning the UN Convention on the Rights of the Child (CRC) (United Nations 1989). The articles most relevant to the republican theory of freedom can be mentioned briefly. While acknowledging the rights and duties of parents in the rearing of children (Article 5), the CRC requires that signatory states guarantee certain basic rights of the child. The Convention includes rights that can be categorized as welfare rights and rights of liberty.

First, there are rights to basic resources required to achieve well-being: for example, the right to the highest attainable standard of health (Article 24), to a standard of living adequate for the child's physical, mental, spiritual, moral and social development (Article 27), to education (Articles 28, 29), the right to rest and leisure, to engage in play and recreational activities (Article 31) and 'the right ... to be protected from economic exploitation and from performing any work that is likely to be hazardous or to interfere with the child's education, or to be harmful to the child's health or physical, mental, spiritual, moral or social development' (Article 32.1). And independently of any specific area of children's welfare, Article 3 guarantees the best interests of the child principle. That is, it requires that in all decisions affecting children their interests must be given priority.

The convention also guarantees rights to liberty. These include the right to have one's say in decisions that affect one's interests as a child: States 'shall assure to the child who is capable of forming his or her own views the right to express those views freely in all matters affecting the child, the views of the child being given due weight in accordance with the age and maturity of the child' (Article 12). They also include rights to access information and material especially those aimed at the promotion of children's well-being and health (Article 17), 'to freedom of expression' including 'freedom to seek, receive and impart information and ideas of all kinds' (Article 13) and 'the right ... to freedom of thought, conscience and religion' (Article 14).

If the articles of the CRC are enforced, then the state will require parents to act in certain ways so as to guarantee their children's welfare rights and rights of liberty. To the extent that this happens, the power of parents will be regulated and children will be both empowered and protected: that is, children's anti-power will be strengthened. One specific way in which to promote children's rights of liberty is through civic education, and civic education can be described as a form of anti-power for children, as it is one way to regulate the power of parents and to protect and empower their children (Fives 2013a, 2013b). This is the case in particular concerning the power of parents to 'share a way of life' with their children and this is done by teaching the values and virtues needed for citizenship and for an autonomous way of life. For instance, in the case of *Mozert v. Hawkins County Board of Education*, fundamentalist Christian parents sought an exemption for their children from a reading curriculum the objective of which was to expose children to other ways of life and also to teach the values and virtues of citizenship (Gutmann 1995: 566). The parents argued that their children should not be exposed to knowledge about other, non-fundamentalist, ways of life as this would hamper the parents' efforts to 'share' their, fundamentalist, way of life with their children. The parents 'rejected the relevance of the distinction between exposure to knowledge and inculcation of belief' (ibid.: 571). However, in reaching its decision, the court found that the goal of the civic education curriculum was not to inculcate any one way of life but instead to teach children to make critical judgements, to use their imagination and to make choices.

While the goal of civic education of this sort is to help children understand and respect other unfamiliar ways of life, its goal is not to ensure they accept one particular way of life (ibid.: 572). Nonetheless, such a civic education programme is designed to make it more difficult for parents to share their way of life with their children. On the one hand, it requires that we as parents be 'asked to surrender some control over our own children for the sake of reasonable common efforts to insure that all future citizens learn the minimal prerequisites of citizenship' (Macedo 1995: 485–6). On the other hand, civic education teaches children about other ways of life and also it provides the skills and resources needed to be more autonomous in their choice of a way of life. Civic education can make people's choices 'meaningful' by 'equipping children with the intellectual skills necessary to evaluate ways of life different from that of their parents' (Gutmann 1999: 30). Therefore, civic education programmes that fit this description can be seen as an instance of anti-power, protecting and empowering children and regulating the power of parents. The freedom of children can be promoted by limiting what republicans see as the coercive power of parents.

The liberal response: Parenting strategies to extend children's liberty

We have looked at measures taken to promote what can be defined as a republican conception of freedom, freedom as anti-power. To promote children's freedom in this way requires that parental authority be diminished or restricted. Also we have seen that liberals provide a different conception of freedom, defining it as freedom from interference or the absence of obstacles to possible choices and activities. Pettit has argued that non-interference is not sufficient for freedom as it is compatible with what republicans define as domination: a benign despot or a Hobbesian ruler with absolute power could guarantee that their subjects enjoyed freedom from interference even while they continued to exercise absolute power over those subjects. Even if Hobbes' Leviathan guarantees 'the liberty to buy and sell, and otherwise contract with one another...' (Hobbes 1651: Ch. XXI, Section 6) the ruling individual or group retains absolute power and therefore their power is unjustifiable domination. However, this characteristic of Berlin's conception of freedom in fact gives a clue to its great strength when we want to consider the justification of parental authority. As we said earlier, the aim of many behaviourist parenting programmes is to train parents to employ certain strategies for the benefit of their children. Berlin's definition of freedom allows us to conceptualize how parents can use their power, a power considered freedom-denying by republicans, so as to enhance their children's freedom from interference.

So far we have seen that many of the articles of the CRC can be interpreted in such a way as to require the promotion of children's anti-power, that is, republican freedom. Nonetheless, the CRC acknowledges the role that parents can and should play in protecting their children's freedom. The CRC recognizes the 'rights and duties of the parents ... to provide direction to the child in the exercise of his or her right [to freedom of thought, conscience and religion] in a manner consistent with the evolving capacities of the child' (Article 14). Therefore, according to the CRC, parents have both a right and a duty to provide direction to the child in exercising his/her rights of liberty. Therefore, it is assumed that the capacity to interfere, which parental authority involves, need not be incompatible with children's freedom. The same assumption is evident in the design of various behaviourist parenting programmes. These programmes presuppose that parents have the power to help change their children's behaviour, but also such power can and should be used in the appropriate manner (O'Brien 2011). In addition, programmes like the *Triple P* Positive Parenting Programme aim to use the power of parents to promote children's agency among other outcomes.

Triple P aims to teach parents of young children (between 3 and 7 years old) how best 'to assist children learn to solve problems for themselves' (Sanders 1999: 76). This is part of a wider approach to create a positive learning environment for children, and to teach new skills and behaviours in developmentally appropriate ways. In teaching such self-care skills as brushing teeth, dressing, setting the table and tidying up, parents are encouraged to give as little or as much help as the child needs. While the parent does so by breaking the task in question up into smaller steps, crucially parents are told: 'you do not do it for them' (Turner et al. 2002: 108). The *Triple P* programme can be targeted at parents with poor parenting skills and parents of children with behavioural problems, but also, as a 'universal' programme it is for 'every family', and its principles of positive parenting are believed to be beneficial for all parents and children, including teenage children. Other parenting programmes also aim to promote the competencies of parents with the related aim of furthering their children's agency. This is the case with *The Incredible Years*, which focuses on 'personal self-control, communication skills, problem-solving skills, and strengthening social support and self-care' (O'Brien 2011: 9).

Evaluations of parenting programmes have sought to measure changes in parental and child outcomes that can be ascribed to the programmes. As we have seen, parents attending *Triple P* are asked to encourage greater independence and problem-solving behaviour in their children. One instrument that has been used in the evaluation of *Triple P* measures the child's hyperactivity, and this can be taken as a good indicator of the child's agency, defined as the capacity for the deliberate, intentional and rational pursuit of goals (Noggle 2002: 100). The items on the Hyperactivity sub-scale of the Strengths and Difficulties Questionnaire concern whether the child in question 'thinks things out before acting', 'sees tasks through to the end' or is 'easily distracted', 'restless' or 'constantly fidgeting'. Positive scores on this sub-scale indicate higher levels of agency. Evaluations of *Triple P* have found that children made statistically significant gains in hyperactivity scores between pretest (prior to the start of the programme) and posttest (after completion of the programme) (Sanders et al. 2005). What the results demonstrate is the effectiveness of a certain use of parental power in facilitating their children to develop from a condition of little or no agency to a much greater level of agency. To the extent one's agency is improved in these ways, what Berlin defines as one's freedom from interference is also expanded. In particular, having the capacity to think things out before acting can increase 'how many paths are open to me'; while having the capacity to see tasks through to the end and to not be easily distracted can increase 'how easy or difficult each of these possibilities is to actualize' (see Berlin 1958: 177 n. 1). These evaluations of the outcomes of behaviourist parenting interventions provide empirical evidence to support the hypothesis that parental authority can be used to promote children's agency and freedom from interference. Specifically, encouraging independence and problem-solving behaviour in children can improve children's capacity for the deliberate, intentional and rational pursuit of goals, which can increase children's options and decrease the difficulties they encounter in pursuing these options.

As we saw earlier, according to the 'argument from simple agency', while children are capable of the deliberate, intentional and rational pursuit of goals, they do not have full moral agency. Children lack stable preferences, a sense of moral decency, the ability to take into account their own long-term interests and also their own conception of the good (Noggle 2002). However, even if it is accepted that many children, in particular younger children, lack full moral agency, it is possible to make qualitative distinctions between greater and lesser degrees of freedom from interference and it is possible for parents to exert their power in such a way as to either increase or decrease their children's freedom from interference. Therefore, even before children reach adulthood, even before adulthood is (all things being equal) ascribed to the individual, children's freedom can be increased or decreased and done so through the exercise of parental power.

The moral point of view and two conceptions of freedom

What is good leadership? In what way should the power of those who are leaders be exercised? Pettit's argument is that the exercise of power is justified insofar as it is limited by various forms of anti-power. Therefore, leadership is better the more that its powers are diminished. This chapter has shown ways in which children's freedom as anti-power can be increased, in particular by defending children's welfare rights and rights of liberty, including rights associated with civic education. However, this chapter has also found that freedom from interference is a separate value and can be promoted independently of the promotion of anti-power. In contrast, for Pettit, freedom as anti-power is the ultimate moral value of democratic societies, and the exercise of power can be morally justified by appeal to this moral value. The liberal critique of republicanism has been that, in Charles Larmore's words, Pettit seems to think the republican conception of freedom serves all by itself as the basis of a cogent ideal of social justice, that it is the supreme political value (Larmore 2001: 234).

Berlin encourages us to take a different approach. He argues that, although 'some portion of human existence must remain independent of the sphere of social control', there has been disagreement over how large this area should be (Berlin 1958: 173). There has been disagreement between optimists who would grant a larger sphere and those like Hobbes who believe the sphere of freedom must be smaller. Crucially, Berlin accepts that this 'has been, and perhaps always will be, a matter of infinite debate': namely, 'That which a man cannot give up without offending against the essence of his human nature? What is this essence? What are the standards which it entails?' (ibid.: 173). If we have sufficient reason to follow Berlin here, we are led to the conclusion that the just exercise of power is a matter for moral deliberation and debate. In debating the just limitation of power and the proper scope of freedom we must therefore appeal to moral notions more fundamental than freedom itself. This of course makes sense if we have reason enough to accept there are various forms of freedom, a plurality of freedoms.

One way to approach the moral decisions required in political debate concerning the limits to be placed on power is to consider whether it is 'reasonable' to expect our moral equals to accept such proposals. The approach of John Rawls and Thomas Scanlon is to start from our equality as moral agents and then proceed to examine what we as moral equals could reasonably be expected to accept (Rawls 1997; Scanlon 1998). What limitations of power should be accepted as required of us by morality? The argument in this essay suggests the following proposals. It is reasonable to accept that children can be better protected, that the power of parents can be more regulated and that society should work to ensure children are empowered. At the same time, it is reasonable to accept that we cannot do away with parental authority as such, even when it has been regulated and diminished. What is more, it is reasonable to accept that parents can and should exercise their power in such a way as to expand their children's freedom from interference. This means that, in the relations between parents and children, good leadership is not only a matter of the extent to which parental power has been restricted by various forms of anti-power. Good leadership in addition involves the exercise of power in such a way as to promote freedom from interference for those subject to parental authority, including the children's freedom to resist interference by their parents.

Implications for leadership generally

What are the implications of these arguments for the normative evaluation of leadership more generally? Relationships among adults between leaders and followers are not in all senses analogous to the relations between parents and children. In relations among adults it is the exception rather than the rule that one party is legally responsible for another and that one party is assumed to be fully competent while the other is not. Nonetheless, in a liberal democratic society, there are power relations between those who lead and those who follow. Some of these relations are entered into on the basis of democratic elections, for instance, the election of governing parties. Other relations are entered into on the basis of meritocratic competition for positions, for instance, in hierarchically organized employment. In such instances, although it is assumed that the adults involved are legally independent and fully competent, nonetheless, there is an inequality in power between leaders and followers. The literature on leadership also assumes that such power relations between adult leaders and followers can be normatively evaluated, and arguments have been made for so-called transformative leadership, whose aim is to empower followers.

The conclusions from our discussion of parental authority therefore are highly relevant to the discussion of relations between adult leaders and followers. The idea of transformative leadership is tied to the notion that power is not always zero-sum but rather can be positive-sum (Reid 2010). That is, the exercise of power can empower those over whom it is exercised, namely followers, as it need not always be exercised in such a way as to take away power from followers (see Haugaard 2012). Our discussion of parental authority focused on how parents can and should promote their children's freedom from interference. In applying these ideas to the discussion of leadership more generally, we can say that good leadership involves promoting the power of followers to resist, and this ability to resist can be directed against those leaders as well as against others. In addition, this chapter acknowledges that both republican and liberal accounts of coercion are valuable. It therefore accepts that republican anti-power measures can and should limit and restrict coercive power relations. Therefore, there are grounds for considering that we should promote both republican and liberal principles of freedom in relations between adults. On the one hand there are grounds for protecting and empowering citizens and employees and for regulating the power of governing parties and management. However, in addition, there are grounds for using the power of the state and employers to extend the freedom from interference of citizens and employees.

Bibliography

Archard, D. (2010), *The Family: A Liberal Defence*. Houndmills: Palgrave.
Asimov, I. (1976, 1995), 'The Bicentennial Man', in *The Complete Robot*. London: Voyager, pp. 635–82.
Bass, B. M. and Steidlmeier, P. (1999), 'Ethics, character and authentic transformational leadership behavior'. *Leadership Quarterly*, 10: 181–217.

Berlin, I. (1958, 2004), 'Two Concepts of Liberty', in H. Hardy (ed.), *Liberty*. Oxford: Oxford University Press, pp. 166–217.

—(1969, 2004), 'Introduction', in H. Hardy (ed.), *Liberty*. Oxford: Oxford University Press, pp. 3–54.

—(1988), 'Final Retrospect', in H. Hardy (ed.), *Liberty*. Oxford: Oxford University Press, pp. 322–30.

Brighouse, H. (1998), 'Civic education and liberal legitimacy'. *Ethics*, 108 (4): 719–45.

Burns, J. M. (1978), *Leadership*. New York: Harper & Row.

Douglas, F. (1845, 2011), *Narrative of the Life of Frederick Douglas An American Slave* (ed. D. Mullan). Dublin: A Little Book Company.

Fives, A. (2013a), *Political Reason: Morality and the Public Sphere*. Houndmills: Palgrave.

—(2013b), 'Non-coercive promotion of values in civic education for democracy'. *Philosophy and Social Criticism*, 39 (6): 577–90.

Fives, A., Pursell, L., Heary, C., Nic Gabhainn, S. and Canavan, J. (2014), *Parenting Support for Every Parent: A Population-level Evaluation of Triple P in Longford Westmeath. Final Report*. Athlone: Longford Westmeath Parenting Partnership (LWPP).

Frick, D. M. and Spears, L. C. (eds) (1996), *On Becoming a Servant Leader*. San Francisco, CA: Jossey-Bass Publishers.

Greenleaf, R. K. (1969), 'Leadership and the Individual: The Dartmouth Lectures', in D. M. Frick and L. C. Spears (eds), *On Becoming a Servant Leader*. San Francisco, CA: Jossey-Bass Publishers, pp. 284–338.

Gutmann, A. (1995), 'Civic education and social diversity'. *Ethics*, 105 (3): 557–79.

Haugaard, M. (2012), 'Rethinking the four dimensions of power: Domination and empowerment'. *Journal of Political Power*, 5 (1): 33–54.

Hobbes, T. (1651, 1996), *Leviathan, or The Matter, Form, and Power of a Commonwealth Ecclesiastical and Civil* (ed. J. C. A. Gaskin). Oxford: Oxford University Press.

Larmore, C. (2001), 'A Critique of Philip Pettit's Republicanism', in E. Sosa and E. Villanueva (eds), *Social, Political, and Legal Philosophy: Philosophical Issues 11*. Boston and Oxford: Blackwell Publishing, pp. 229–43.

Leithwood, K. A. (1992), 'The move towards transformative leadership'. *Educational Leadership*, 49 (5): 8–10.

Lovett, F. (2012), 'What counts as arbitrary power?' *Journal of Political Power*, 5 (1): 137–52.

Macedo, S. (1995), 'Liberal civic education and religious fundamentalism: The case of God v. John Rawls'. *Ethics*, 105: 468–96.

MacLeod, C. M. (2003), 'Shaping children's convictions'. *Theory and Research in Education*, 1 (3), 315–30.

Macleod, C. M. (2004), 'A liberal theory of freedom of expression for children'. *Chicago-Kent Law Review*, 79: 55–82.

Noggle, R. (2002), 'Special Agents: Children's Autonomy and Parental Authority', in D. Archard and C. M. Macleod (eds), *The Moral and Political Status of Children*. Oxford: Oxford University Press, pp. 97–117.

O'Brien, K. M. (2011), *Evaluating the effectiveness of a parent training protocol based on an acceptance and commitment therapy philosophy of parenting*. PhD Dissertation. University of North Texas.

Pettit, P. (1996), 'Freedom as antipower'. *Ethics*, 106 (April): 576–604.

—(2004), 'The Common Good', in K. Dowling, R. E. Goodin and C. Pateman (eds), *Justice and Democracy: Essays for Brian Barry*. Cambridge: Cambridge University Press, pp. 150–69.

—(2011), 'The instability of freedom as non-interference: the case of Isaiah Berlin'. *Ethics*, 121 (July): 693–716.

Popper, M. and Mayseless, O. (2003), 'Back to basics: Applying a parenting perspective to transformational leadership'. *The Leadership Quarterly*, 14: 41–65.

Rawls, J. (1997, 2001), 'The Idea of Public Reason Revisited', in S. Freeman (ed.), *John Rawls. Collected Papers*. London: Harvard University Press, pp. 573–615.

Read, J. H. (2010), 'Leadership and power in Nelson Mandela's *Long Walk to Freedom*'. *Journal of Political Power*, 3 (3): 317–39.

Sanders, M. R. (1999), 'Triple P-Positive Parenting Program: Towards an empirically validated parenting and family support strategy for the prevention of behavior and emotional problems in children'. *Clinical Child and Family Psychology Review*, 2 (2): 71–90.

Sanders, M., Ralph, A., Thompson, R., Sofronoff, K., Gardiner, P., Bidwell, K. and Dwyer, S. (2005), *Every Family: A Public Health Approach to Promoting Children's Wellbeing*. The University of Queensland, Brisbane: Parenting and Family Support Centre.

Scanlon, T. M. (1998), *What We Owe to Each Other*. Cambridge, MA: Harvard University Press.

Scarre, G. (1977), 'Children and paternalism'. *Philosophy*, 52: 167–77.

Stone, A. G., Russell, R. F. and Patterson, K. (2003), 'Transformational versus servant leadership: A difference in leader focus'. Paper presented at Servant Leadership Research Roundtable. Regent University: School of Leadership Studies.

Turner, K. M. T., Markie-Dadds, C. and Sanders, M. R. (2002), *Facilitator's Manual for Group Triple P*. Milton: Triple P International.

United Nations (1989), *Convention on the Rights of the Child*. Geneva: United Nations Office of the High Commissioner for Human Rights. Available at www2.ohchr.org/english/law/crc.htm (accessed September 2010).

10

Leadership Ethics and Asymmetry

Constantine Sandis
Oxford Brookes

Nassim N. Taleb
New York Poly and Sorbonne

Asymmetry in ethics

To stick one's neck out: the more a person has to lose by saying or doing something, the greater the likelihood that those very same statements and actions will have integrity. In this respect, integrity increases in proportion to the degree in which one stakes his or her skin in the game. Those who (knowingly or otherwise) try to enhance their status without risking anything they value are deficient in integrity. Many academic papers, for example, take no risks in that the price which the author(s) would pay for being wrong is negligible. This is only acceptable if the cost that would be transferred to others (via any possible mistake) is equally small – as is arguably the case with much contemporary philosophy. To achieve integrity (a necessary but not sufficient mark of good leadership), the harm which our mistakes could inflict upon others must be matched by a cost to ourselves. Such *symmetrical constraints* place the agent in the same realm of liability as those affected by his or her actions. We shall unpack what we mean by 'same realm' in due course, in response to potential counter-examples.

This chapter argues that there are ethical and prudential grounds for a symmetrical constraint on all forms of leadership. In particular, we argue that leaders should have 'skin in the game', i.e. should expose themselves to the same amount of damage risk that they expose those which they are leading. This normative claim is not merely about what makes a leader 'good' but a claim about the very notion of leadership, ethical or otherwise. We demonstrate the prudential benefits of symmetrical leadership, arguing further that a person with insufficient skin in the game is not just a bad leader but really no leader at all. Insofar as alleged leaders are aware of the asymmetries in their decision-making behaviour they are frauds that need to be exposed. Our view is that 'skin in the game' can and ought to be applied across a range of ethical domains, including that of leadership. While we do not suppose that the skin in the game heuristic is the sole or even the central mark of an ethic of leadership, it is one that many contemporary 'leaders' have failed to meet. We begin, however, by introducing the constraint in general terms that make no particular reference to leadership

Around 1800 BC, Hammurabi's code specified that if a builder builds a house and the house collapses and causes the death of the owner of the house, that builder shall be put to death. This approach may seem a little excessive and we would not want it as an inviolable law. After all, houses fall down for all sorts of reasons that are not necessarily structural and liability always comes in degrees (perhaps the builder was instructed to use cheap materials). What the ancients understood well, however, was that any qualified builder knows more about the risks than the client, and is able to hide sources of fragility and improve his profitability by cutting corners. This is facilitated by the fact that the person hiding risk has a large informational advantage over the one who has to find it. While the punishment dished out by Hammurabi's code is excessive, it reveals that the ancients understood much better than us that absences of personal risk may motivate people to only appear to be doing good, rather than to actually do it, though their appeal here is restricted to motives of prudence. This is particularly true of people in the public realm, for whom appearances matter a great deal, be they popular celebrities or political leaders. If your career depends upon your being liked then it is fragile in a way which may tempt you to place your reputation above the very things upon which it should depend.[1]

In Taleb and Sandis (2014), we argued for such a skin in the game heuristic as a rule of thumb that places a pragmatic accountability constraint on all normative theories, including ethical ones. The rule tells us that we should look out for people or institutions who – blatantly or discreetly – pass the cost of their risk-taking to another party whilst keeping any potential benefits for themselves (the Bush/Blair wars on Iraq and Afghanistan most obviously come to mind). We believe skin in the game is a heuristic for a safe and just society. By this we mean not only that it is a good rule of thumb, but that it is as close to a justifiable ethical principle as one can convincingly reach, which is not to say that it can be shown to be exceptionless.[2] At the heart of this heuristic lies a simple objection to negative asymmetry (viz. any stance or behaviour in which the agent reaps any benefit while pushing potential costs on to another). This objection is both prudential *and* moral. It is prudential because it warns us of the practical risks associated with tolerating negative asymmetry. It is moral because it denounces as selfish those who are willing to put others at risk for their own benefit.

Proto-versions of symmetrical ethics may be found in some of the oldest and best known moral ideas. All of the following sayings, for examples, advise one to behave in a symmetrical fashion:

> Do not do unto others what you would not have them do unto you (Hillel the Elder).

> Do not do to others that which angers you when they do it to you (Isocrates 3.61).

> An eye for an eye, a tooth for a tooth (Exod. 21.24)

> Love your neighbor as yourself (Lev. 19.18)

> Do unto others as you would have them do unto you (Mt. 7.12)

While these do not quite embody the letter of our heuristic (or focus on leadership in particular), they are all motivated by the same symmetrical spirit.

In the Quran, we also find an instance of what we call *positive* asymmetry, viz. the stance that one should even be willing to lose out on what one is owed for the sake of others:

> Then, whoever proves charitable and gives up on his right for reciprocation, it will be an atonement for him. (Quran, Surat Al-Ma'idat, 45, our translation)

Positive asymmetry is marked by the agent taking a personal hit for the benefit of others, as in all cases of self-sacrifice for the greater good. Those who practice positive asymmetry risk their own skin in other people's games. One of the best examples of a leader practicing this form of risk-related altruism is Ernest Shackleton. Commentators have recently suggested that business leaders in times of financial crisis would do well to follow Shackleton's example of how to lead people in times of deep crisis, when all hope appears to have been lost (Morrell and Capparell 2001; Koehn et al. 2003/2010). What matters here is not the fact that Shackleton's exhibition is seen as a success story of survival: for every Shackleton and Mandela there is Martin Luther King and Gandhi. Indeed, part of Shackleton's leadership success is based on his attitude towards and preparedness[3] for the possibility of total failure (Lansing 1959). Scholars have commented on various positive and negative aspects of leadership (from

hiring an outstanding crew to ignoring whalers' warnings about the pack ice).
Not all of these concern ethical dimensions, and we shall even ignore some
which arguably do.

Koehn writes:

> Shackleton ... faced harsh conditions in a way that speaks more directly to our
> time. The Shackleton expedition, from 1914 to 1916, is a compelling story of
> leadership when disaster strikes again and again .... Consider just a handful
> of recent events: the financial crisis of 2008; the gulf oil spill of 2010; and the
> Japanese nuclear disaster, the debt-ceiling debacle and euro crisis this year.
> Constant turbulence seems to be the new normal, and effective leadership is
> crucial in containing it. (Koehn 2011)

Shackleton wrote that when the party's food supply, health and moral reached
critical levels:

> [t]he conclusion was forced upon me that a boat journey in search of relief was
> necessary and must not be delayed. The nearest port where assistance could
> certainly be secured was Port Stanley, in the Falkland Islands, 540 miles away;
> but we could scarcely hope to beat up against the prevailing north-westerly
> wind in a frail and weakened boat with a small sail area ... South Georgia
> [Island], which was over 800 miles away but lay in the area of west winds [which
> would carry the boat toward the island], must be our objective. (Shackleton
> 1919: Ch. IX)

What matters from the point of view of the symmetrical constraint is that
'Shackleton assumed ultimate responsibility for his team', possessed a 'deep
sense of loyalty and obligation to his fellow crew members' (Koehn 2011) and
led by example (Morrell and Capparell 2001: 107ff.). Morrell and Capparell
have dubbed this a 'people-centred approach to leadership' (ibid.: 1–14) which
cultivates a 'spirit of carmaraderie and fairness' (ibid.: 81–103). These are all
qualities that flourish within a symmetrical framework, or one in which the
leader practices positive asymmetry by putting the well-being of others ahead
of his or her own. Arguably such leadership requires a courageous disposition.[4]

Opposed to both symmetry and positive asymmetry in ethics is the practice
of placing the well-being of others in a negative asymmetry to one's own, for
example by taking all (or much of) the praise and benefits of good fortune
whilst disassociating oneself as much as possible from the results of bad luck
or miscalculation. A classic instance of this kind of negative asymmetry is that
of investing other people's money with little liability for loss. Such agents lack a
symmetrical amount of skin in the game. While we do not expect investment

brokers or insurance companies to make self-sacrifices, we should ask ourselves whether it is prudent to follow the advice of any person who has absolutely nothing to lose by any advice they give, or would not be interested in following their own advice in relevant circumstances.[5] Such behaviour is vicious across the board, but they are particularly dangerous in 'leaders' who are responsible for the well-being of large collectives. We are not in the business of proposing a particular punishment for such leaders (which will in any case vary from case to case). Our symmetrical constraint is ethical, not legal: if one's actions are to be ethically sound one must be prepared to suffer in symmetry.

Of course real-life cases are rarely pure and there will frequently exist *degrees* of symmetry or asymmetry in every particular case. Perhaps agents, corporations and institutions will in principle always stand to lose *something* (popularity, commissions, future investments, and so on) but it remains the case that we can sharply distinguish between the owners, directors or partners of (typically small) companies who put their livelihood on the lines with the decisions they make, from those (such as the bosses of nationalized banks or companies deemed 'too big to fail') who give themselves bonuses while the taxpayer foots the bill.[6]

Arguably, all great leaders are at least prepared to employ positive asymmetry. It might be objected here that Hitler's leadership was to some extent symmetrical. This may be so,[7] but it is important to emphasize that our heuristic presents only a necessary condition for good leadership and not a sufficient one: one cannot be a good leader whilst practicing negative asymmetry but one may adhere to the symmetrical heuristic and remain a terrible leader, be it morally and/or prudentially.[8]

An operator who wants to hide risk from others can exploit skewness by creating a situation which offers a small or bounded harm to him, while exposing others to large harm, thus exposing others to the bad side of this distribution by fooling them with the tail properties. The policy of taking harm when you inflict harm automatically removes many who have a deficit of risk from society (there may be exceptions such as psychopaths who do not feel harm easily, though their concern with their own skin is high). The incompetent captain who goes down with the ship cannot steer any further ships into disaster. This reduces the potential harm to others by reducing incompetence from society (it is better for bad leaders to die in battle than to lead new armies into bloodshed). By contrast the incompetent captain who abandons his sinking ship remains a danger to society if not properly trialled. A case in point is Captain Francesco Schettino, who at his hearing claimed to have tripped and fallen into a lifeboat as the Costa

Concordia, which he crashed into the rocks, began to sink, causing the death of 32 people.[9] Our heuristic separates the Schettinos of this world from the Shackletons.

The economic literature focuses on incentives as encouragement or deterrent, but not on disincentives as potent evolutionary filters that remove incompetent and nefarious risk-takers from the system. Consider that the symmetry of risks incurred on the road increases the likelihood of the bad driver eventually exiting the system. An unskilled forecaster with skin in the game would eventually go bankrupt or out of business. Shielded from potentially (financially) harmful exposure, he would continue contributing to the build-up of risks in the system. Those who repeatedly and unremorsefully practice positive asymmetry would voluntarily remove themselves from the social pool (e.g. through suicide or self-imposed exile) rather than harm it.[10]

We should distinguish the crooks who abuse randomness from those who are themselves fooled by it. Our skin in the game heuristic not only eliminates the first of these in the short term (this is the standard agency problem), it also removes a second one in the long term by forcing a certain class of undesirable risk-takers to exit from the game (which is not to say that they may have other desirable leadership qualities). It thereby moves way beyond that of the agent problem best associated with Nobel-prize winning economist Joseph Stiglitz. When Stiglitz's own Fannie-Mae predictions went horribly wrong, not only did he not remove himself from the pool, he himself refused to even hold himself accountable for his misprediction, cherry-picking his prior statements so as to make them appear to have been predicting something quite different. Standard economic theory makes an allowance for the agency problem, but not the compounding of moral hazards in the presence of informational opacity (see Taleb and Sandis 2014: 117).

In what follows we argue that the lack of negative asymmetry in one's relations with others is a minimal condition of leadership of any kind. We shall focus on the application of the skin in the game heuristic to leadership across all spheres including business and finance, politics, the military, education, medicine. As we are said to be living in financially precarious times we shall pay particular attention to identifying leadership in times of austerity.

Skin in the leadership game

Skin in the game is a useful sports metaphor but we must not be misled by it. *Pace* Berne (1964), leadership – even within sports games – is itself no more a game than marriage is. If people are to take their responsibilities as leaders seriously, they must share an equal part of the cost risks they are putting others in. Consider, for example, the case of higher management in many universities.[11] This managerial body frequently makes important decisions which can seriously affect the daily life of members of the academic body, with any 'consultation' process typically occurring after the proposed policies have been drafted and in many cases all but ratified. The policies in question relate directly to questions concerning teaching and research and yet the policy-makers do neither of these things. This is not a point about experience. It is true that some managers have no experience in the field but that it is a different (albeit equally important) worry. What we are concerned with in this essay is whether one's policy making affects one in a personal way.

The manager who neither teaches nor researches has little skin in the teaching/research game. She or he may receive great praise for successful decisions and might even pay *some* price for any bad effects bad decision making may have, but the potential benefits always outweigh these (see p. 241 for a study case relating to remuneration in Higher Education). We appreciate that skin in the game is a matter of degree, not kind. We sometimes use the 'no skin in the game' rhetoric to describe people whose real-life investment in their decisions is negligible.[12] Such is the case with many senior managers in Higher Education: their potential gains are far higher than any potential loss because the real hit is taken by those on the ground. In this respect the situation mirrors that of the banks in crisis and other 'too big to fail' organizations whose bailout packages offer them selfish incentives to bet against odds that are considerably worse than those of even the most criminal of casinos.[13]

One might object here that this is simply what rational choice theory dictates. If so then those who criticize the theory for promoting selfishness are obviously in the right. However, this is not due to a conflict between rationality and ethics, but one between individual-based and social-based rationalities. It may be instrumentally rational for a person to act selfishly in order to fulfill their preferences, but it is irrational for societies to allow – let alone enable or foster – such practices. This is the symmetrical motivation behind social contract theories such as that of Hobbes. In what follows we present three indicative ongoing problems and proposed solutions relating to what happens when the relation between a so-called 'leader' and those being 'lead' is asymmetrical in the sense in which the 'leader' in question hasn't got enough to lose for us to be able to trust them in their decision making.

First, people frequently misunderstand the incentive structure of corporate managers, executives, directors and other so-called 'leaders'.[14] Between 2000 and 2010, in the US, the stock market lost (depending how one measures it) up to $2 trillion for investors, compared to leaving their funds in cash or treasury bills. It is tempting to think that at least those managers paid on incentive would be incurring losses. On the contrary: there is an irrational and unethical asymmetry. Due to the embedded option in their profession, corporate managers statistically received more than $400 billion dollars in compensation. The manager who loses money does not generally return his bonus or incur a negative one. As we write this, for example, the Lloyds Banking Group chief executive António Horta-Osório protests that it was right to accept a £1.7 million bonus because one 'should link compensation to performance'. Yet on the very same day, the bank's finance director 'admitted that Lloyds would not recover the £1.6 billion it cost to strip out TSB branches after the bungled sale to the Co-op bank was aborted',[15] not to mention the £10.3 billion in provisions for PPI misspending. The built-in optionality in the compensation of corporate managers is best removed by forcing them to absorb some of the relevant (e.g. financial) losses. Any leader worthy of the name would do this voluntarily (compare Horta-Osório to 'the world's poorest president', Jose Mujiga, who donates 90 per cent of his salary to charity[16]).

Second, there is the case of those so-called 'leaders' who make decisions about whether or not a nation is to send soldiers to war without there being a question of them going themselves. To deal with such cases, Ralph Nader has rightly proposed that those who vote in favor of war should subject themselves (or their own kin) to the draft. This is just an illustration of the *sort* of shape that a symmetrical constraint might take. Our heuristic is not intended as an algorithm for setting policies but as a *constraint* upon them which may legitimately take a variety of forms. Symmetry can be achieved in a plurality of ways. Winston Churchill may have not fought on the front lines, but he risked his entire political career and arguably his life (if one considers potential assassination attempts) by leading Britain into World War II.[17]

Third, consider leaders in policy making and politics at large. In a decentralized system, say municipalities, these people may be kept in check by feelings of shame upon harming others with their mistakes or via local laws.[18] In a large centralized system, the sources of error are easier to hide within incomprehensible spreadsheets which might cause private shame but are harder to monitor publicly. The penalty of shame offers a *pro tanto* reason in favour of governments (and businesses) that are small, local, personal, transparent and decentralized versus ones that are large, national or multi-national, anonymous and centralized. When the latter fail, it is harder to make the culprit pay for the whole cost. It is much easier to introduce 'austerity' measures. The symmetrical constraint is not against austerity per se, but if we are liable to share the costs we should also be entitled to our symmetrical share of the rewards.[19]

In relation to all of the above, it is worth considering the following facts in relation to Higher Education in the UK. In the 2011–12 academic year the remuneration of University vice-chancellors in the UK for the most part[20] did not rise too significantly, especially when compared with the private sector (Grove 2013). In more recent years of 'austerity', however, the pay increases of University vice-chancellors' salaries have been disproportionately related to budget cuts affecting teaching and administrative staff as well as students. In 2013, for example, vice-chancellors at Russell Group Universities received pay rises averaging 8.1 per cent (approx. £22,000) compared to an average 1 per cent rise for regular staff, during a period in which tuition fees for undergraduate students nearly tripled.[21] Some cases were particularly extreme, for example the vice-chancellor of Sheffield University took a pay rise of £105,000 while refusing to raise employees, salaries to the living wage (Garner 2014b). Such 'leaders' are not even nominally sharing in austerity by accepting the same percentages as their followers.

These asymmetrical tactics are economically, socially and ethically problematic. We believe that the only viable solution is to build symmetrical behaviour into the very job descriptions of all 'leadership' roles. It is not enough to suppose that if a vice-chancellor consistently keeps messing up badly enough they will be let go. For one, vice-chancellors frequently have the power of rhetoric over what counts as success (consider the Lloyds cases noted above). It takes a true catastrophe for them to disappear, and even then it is the rest of us that are left with the debris. What we need is regulation which enforces fired vice-chancellors to clean up their mess before they leave.

Symmetry and the concept of leadership

In this final section we put forward a *prima facie* case for the more radical view that argues that *all* leadership (and not just good leadership) is in actual fact incompatible with asymmetrical stances.

The asymmetries described in the previous sections have hardly gone unnoticed. For example, the above-mentioned vice-chancellors have been accused of being 'hypocritical leaders' (see Garner 2014a; Malnick 2014) and have been condemned by teachers unions which issued strikes.[22] Interestingly, even the harshest of critics frequently continue to use the term 'leader' to characterize those whom they are arguing against. The objection seems only to be that asymmetrical behaviour is a mark of unethical or hypocritical leadership (Machiavellians might even argue that not only does this *not* amount to bad leadership but that such features are a requirement for any leadership to be effective). We have tried to show that asymmetrical behaviour is bad for society at large. In this section we wish to go further, arguing that 'leadership' that is bad in this way is, in a very important sense, not leadership at all.

The concept of leadership within corporate speech has broadened significantly in recent years. So while the verb 'to lead' is sometimes still used as a success verb, this is not always the case. There is a world of difference, then, between someone who leads one down the garden path and she who leads her people out of slavery. Both notions are legitimate, but it is crucial to not conflate them. Our suggestion is that the notion of leadership has taken on the form of doublespeak. This does not entail that all leaders need to be great leaders or even successful in leading people in some common aim. Excellent leadership is an ideal to be approximated and too many variables determine whether one's leadership (be it poor, average, good or great) succeeds in its further aims. But even leadership which fails in this instrumental sense may be successful *qua* leadership viz. *qua* the norms for the correct application of the disambiguated concept.

How many leaders succeed in this popular sense is an empirical question which we do not propose to settle here. It seems obvious to us that some of our most 'famous' leaders fail to live up to the constraint, but it may be overly pessimistic to generalize from such examples. We do not deny that should the two concepts of leadership continue to be conflated in thought, speech and print they might eventually be reduced to one. Perhaps we are already on our way to such a sorry state of affairs in which the criteria for leadership are minimal. If so then we will soon yearn for the days when 'leaders were *leaders*', to adapt a common turn of phrase. Either way, we propose that leadership that is successful in the sense described above is subject to symmetrical constraint.

In *Zettel*, Wittgenstein contrasts the rules of chess and grammar with those of cooking and washing to emphasize that a person who breaks the former set of rules is not making bad chess moves or uttering falsehoods, but altogether failing to play chess or speak the language in question:

> Why don't I call cookery rules arbitrary, and why am I tempted to call the rules of grammar arbitrary? Because 'cooking' is defined by its end, whereas

'speaking' is not. That is why the use of language is in a certain sense autonomous, as cooking and washing are not. You cook badly if you are guided in
your cooking by rules other than the right ones; but if you follow other rules
than those of chess you are *playing another game*; and if you follow grammatical
rules other than such-and-such ones, that does not mean you say something
wrong, no, you are speaking of something else. (§ 320)

Similarly, we maintain that a person with no skin in the game cannot qualify
as a leader in the popular sense defined above. A bad leader, in this sense, may
make mistakes, both trivial and significant ones, but lacking any skin in the
game is not a mistake of leadership. Rather, it is failing to be a leader *tout court*,
for one cannot lead the way if one doesn't take it. In sum, there is no such thing
as asymmetrical leadership. By this we mean that it is a necessary condition of
being a leader that one is at all times prepared to have skin in the game. Those
who delegate without any skin in the game are only leaders in the sense in
which a total failure may still qualify as one. So not only is it both irrational and
unethical to reward people for taking risks in games they have no skin in, it is
also misleading to dub them 'leaders'.[23]

Notes

1   For this and other forms of fragility (and how to combat them), see Taleb 2013.
2   We remain neutral here on whether or not moral particularism is true.
3   Needless to say, being prepared to sacrifice oneself does not entail that
    self-sacrifice is always the best way to lead in times of crisis or failure.
4   For real-life examples of the relationship between leadership and courage, see
    Browne 2007.
5   One may of course (as is all too frequently the case) offer good personal advice to
    others that one is too weak-willed to follow oneself but this is not the sort of case
    we are envisaging. What we have in mind is the person who predicts that a certain
    horse will win the race and urges you to place good money on it while refraining
    from doing so themselves.
6   This is not a point about abilities but about character traits or dispositions.
7   But see Note 7 below.
8   What the precise metric should be here is a further question. We are not
    endorsing an 'eye for an eye' morality of revenge but a 'skin for skin' morality of
    personal investment.
9   http://www.theguardian.com/world/2012/jan/18/costa-concordia-captain-tripped-
    lifeboat

10   Whether or not the failed leader who takes cyanide is noble or cowardly
     ultimately depends on his or her motive.

11   In the UK what follows is particularly true of 'new' universities but increasingly
     also the case with many older ones.

12   This should be distinguished from non-measurable personal investments (such as
     one's conscience), the rhetoric of which it is all too easy to hide behind.

13   See Taleb 2012.

14   We explore changing notions of leadership below.

15   Ebrahimi 2014.

16   http://www.huffingtonpost.com/2012/11/16/jose-mujica-charity_n_2145089.html

17   Biographers may dispute the factual accuracy of precise examples. We are not here
     interested in defending or attacking particular people: fictionalized accounts may
     serve equally well.

18   Famously, in ancient Greece, the law was tied to attributions of shame and
     pollution.

19   See also McQuillan 2013 and Orr 2013; cf. the 'many hands' problem discussed
     by Thompson 1987. These points against 'big government' models should not
     be confused with the standard libertarian argument against states securing the
     welfare of their citizens, but only against doing so in a centralized fashion that
     enables people to hide behind bureaucratic anonymity. It is preferable to have a
     communitarian municipal approach: in situations in which we cannot enforce skin
     in the game we should change the system to lower the consequences of errors.

20   The largest exceptions were vice-chancellors at the 'new universities' of Bolton (25
     per cent increase), Northampton (21 per cent) and Bedfordshire (13 per cent).

21   For a full table of vice-chancellors' pay in 2011–13, see http://www.ucu.org.uk/
     index.cfm?articleid=6886&from=1676

22   See, for example, http://www.unison.org.uk/news/unison-condemns-outrageous-
     pay-rises-for-vice-chancellors

23   Many thanks to Jacqueline Boaks, Michael Levine and Candida Lord for their
     constructive criticism and suggestions.

Bibliography

Berne, E. (1964), *Games People Play: The Psychology of Human Relationships*. New
     York: Ballantine Books.

Browne, G. (2007), *Courage: Eight Portraits*. London: Bloomsbury.

Ebrahimi, H. (2014), 'Lloyds returns to profit, bonus pool $655 million', *CNBC*, 13
     February 2014, available at http://www.cnbc.com/id/101408455

Garner, R. (2014a), 'The academic fat cats: Vice-chancellors at Britain's top universities
     get £22,000 pay rises – as lecturers are stuck on 1 per cent', *The Independent*, 2

January 2014, available at http://www.independent.co.uk/student/news/university-chiefs-under-fire-for-huge-pay-rises-after-tuition-fee-hikes-9034893.html

—(2014b), 'Fury at £105,000 pay rise for Sheffield University boss Sir Keith Burnett after he refused to raise employees' salaries to the living wage', *The Independent*, 24 January 2014, available at http://www.independent.co.uk/student/news/fury-at-105000-pay-rise-for-sheffield-university-boss-sir-keith-burnett-after-he-refused-to-raise-employees-salaries-to-the-living-wage-9084027.html

Grove, J. (2013), 'Higher education pay survey', *Times Higher Education*, 28 March 2013, available at http://www.timeshighereducation.co.uk/story.aspx?storyCode=2002791 Dec 24

Koehn, N. F., Helms, E. and Mead, P. (2011), 'Leadership lessons from the Shackleton expedition', *New York Times*, available at http://www.nytimes.com/2011/12/25/business/leadership-lessons-from-the-shackleton-expedition.html?pagewanted=all&_r=0

—(2003/2010), 'Leadership in crisis: Ernest Shackleton and the epic voyage of the *Endurance*', *Harvard Business School Case* (April 2003, rev. December 2010): 803–27.

Lansing, A. (1959), *Endurance: Shackleton's Incredible Voyage*. London: Hodder & Stoughton.

Malnick, E. (2014), 'Russell Group universities boost pay for vice-chancellors', *The Telegraph*, 2 January 2014, available at http://www.telegraph.co.uk/education/universityeducation/10547834/Russell-Group-universities-boost-pay-for-vice-chancellors.html

McQuillan, M. (2013), 'The severity of austerity', *Times Higher Education*, 3–9 January 2013: 30–5.

Morrell, M. and Capparell, S. (2001), *Shackleton's Way: Leadership Lessons from the Great Antarctic Explorer*. London: Penguin.

Orr, D. (2013), 'It wasn't Labour who spent too much, it was the banks. How did we forget this?', *The Guardian*, 5 January 2013 39.

Shackleton, E. H. (1919), *South!: The Endurance Expedition*. London: Penguin.

Taleb, N. N. (2001), *Fooled by Randomness: The Hidden Role of Chance in Life and in the Markets*. New York: Random House.

—(2004), 'Bleed or blowup? Why do we prefer asymmetric payoffs?' *Journal of Behavioral Finance*, 5 (1): 2–7.

Taleb, N. N. and Sandis, C. (2014), 'The skin in the game heuristic for protection against tail events'. *Review of Behavioral Economics*, 1: 1–21, available at http://www.nowpublishers.com/articles/review-of-behavioral-economics/RBE-0006

Thompson, D. F. (1983), 'Ascribing responsibility to advisers in government'. *Ethics*, 93 (3), 546–60.

Wittgenstein, L. (1967), *Zettel* (ed. G. E. M. Anscombe and G. H. von Wright, trans. G. E. M. Anscombe). Oxford: Blackwell.

Index

power and influence xi, 3, 82–3, 87, 91, 114, 175–6
Prabhakar, R. 204
practical wisdom 37, 14, 138
pre-socratic 137
Profit-Only view 201–2, 206
Price, T. L. xviii nn. 7, 12, 151, 154, 162, 164–5
Prince, The xi, 39
principled 74, 78, 81, 87–8, 92, 119, 207, 209 n. 6
privacy 160–1
private lives of 7, 165–6, 168
Psychologie des foules 12
psychology
  industrial xiv
  organizational xiv, 50–1, 65
  philosophical 11
psychoanalysis 11
psychoanalytic theory 11–15
Public and Private Morality 38, 165–6
public life 206
public service 175

qualification 186–7
Quran 235

Ramsay, M. 19 n. 11
Rawls, John. 1, 219, 228
Raz, J. 120, 126 n. 88
Read, J. H. 213, 229
Reagan, Ronald 105
Reed, J. 159
relational nature 27
religious beliefs 57
Republic xvi, 1, 19 n. 4, 25, 28–31, 35, 37–8, 42 nn. 7, 8, 13, 64, 131, 139, 142
Republicanism 206–7, 211–12
Riggio, R. E. 153
rights 62, 67, 113, 136, 155, 161–3, 177, 79–80, 86–7, 203, 220, 222–3, 225, 227
  women's 177, 187
Roman xvi
Romney, Mitt 152–3
Ross, W. D. 43 n. 19
Rost, Joseph xiv, xvii n. 2, 51, 69 n. 8
Rousseau, J. J. 184
Rudd, Kevin 81, 90, 194 n. 14

rule of law 49
rulers (reluctant and willing) 129–30
Rumsfeld, Donald 148
Ruskin, J., evil 140
Russell Group Universities 241
Russell, R. F. 213

Sandis, Constantine 19, 234, 238
Sartre, J. P. 43 n. 17
Sealy, Ruth 187–8, 194 n. 15
Scanlon, Thomas 228
Schettino, Captain Francesco 237–8
schools 38–9
Schumpeter, J. 106–7
self-interest 53, 61–2
Shackleton, Ernest 235–6, 238
Sheffield University 241
Simola, S. (et. al) 70 n. 36
'skin in the game' 19, 233–4
social Contract theory 239
social co-ordination 73, 77–8, 92 n. 1
social ontology 47–8
social science (scientists) xvii, 82, 151
Socrates 28–9 42 n. 13, 43 n. 15, 134–5
Sophocles 133–4
Sorial, Sarah 16–17, 85
Southern Christian Leadership Conference 88
Speech acts 85
Spicker, P. 77–8, 84
Spinoza, B. 1
stakeholding 18, 199–200
Steidlmeier, P. 80–1, 213
Stiglitz, Joseph 238
Stocker, Michael 38
Stone, A. G. 213
strong leaders xi
Sun Tzu 41 n. 1
symmetrical constraints 19, 233–4
symmetrical ethics 235
  positive symmetry 235

Takala, T. 105, 125 n. 35
Taleb, Nassim 19, 234, 238, 243 n. 1, 244 n. 13
Taylor, C. C. W. 64, 70 n. 43
Taylor, Paul 98, 123 n. 2
Teaching 3
Tebartz-van Elst, Franz-Peter 153

Printed in Poland
by Amazon Fulfillment
Poland Sp. z o.o., Wrocław

54921891R00159